Bilingual Children's Books in English and Spanish

Los libros bilingües para niños en inglés y en español

# Bilingual Children's Books in English and Spanish

*An Annotated Bibliography, 1942 through 2001*

DORIS CRUGER DALE

McFarland & Company, Inc., Publishers
*Jefferson, North Carolina, and London*

# Los libros bilingües para los niños en inglés y en español

*Una bibliografía con anotaciones, 1942 a 2001*

DORIS CRUGER DALE

McFarland & Company, Inc., Publishers

*Jefferson, North Carolina, and London*

**Library of Congress Cataloguing-in-Publication Data**

Dale, Doris Cruger
    Bilingual children's books in English and Spanish : an annotated
bibliography, 1942 through 2001 / Doris Cruger Dale = Los libros
bilingües para los niños en inglés y en español : una bibliografía
con anotaciones, 1942 a 2001 / Doris Cruger Dale.
      p.    cm.
    Includes indexes.

    ISBN 0-7864-1316-6 (softcover : 50# alkaline paper)

    1.  Children's literature—Translations into Spanish—Bibliography
2.  Children's literature, American—Bibliography.   3.  Children's
literature, Spanish American—Bibliography.   4.  Bilingual books—
United States—Bibliography.   5.  Children—Books and reading—
United States—Bibliography.   6.  Hispanic American children—
Books and reading—United States—Bibliography.  I.  Title:
Libros bilingües para los niños en inglés y en español.  II.  Title.
Z1037.7.D36   2003
011.62—dc21                                  2002013462

British Library cataloguing data are available

Manufactured in the United States of America

Cover image: Detail from Inocencio Jimenez Chino, "The Watering," 1993,
acrylic on amate, 23½" × 15"

*McFarland & Company, Inc., Publishers*
  *Box 611, Jefferson, North Carolina 28640*
   *www.mcfarlandpub.com*

To my dear parents
Anna and Victor Cruger

A mis queridos padres
Anna y Victor Cruger

# Contents

*Introduction*    1

*Organization of the Bibliography*    29

The Bibliography
(with annotations in English)    33

*Appendix A: Publishers and Numbers of Bilingual Children's Titles*    141

*Appendix B: Review Journals Cited*    145

*Index of Coauthors, Illustrators and Translators*    149

*Index of Titles, Series and Awards*    156

*Index of Subjects*    167

# Contenido

*Introducción*                                                          15

*La organización de la bibliografía*                                    31


## La bibliografía
*(con anotaciones en inglés)*                                           33


*Apéndice A: Editoriales y números de títulos bilingües para los niños*   141

*Apéndice B: Revistas críticas citadas*                                 145

*Índice de co-autores, ilustradores y traductores*                     149

*Índice de títulos, series y premios*                                   156

*Índice de temas*                                                       171

# Introduction

The earliest bilingual Spanish/English book that I was able to identify since I began this research in 1975 was a copy of *McGuffey's First Eclectic Reader*, a revised edition of which was published in 1891 in New York by the American Book Company. The cover title was *McGuffey's First Spanish-English Reader*. This title was located in the foreign language shelf list in the children's room of the Denver Public Library. The book was in storage, and I was unable to see it. When an interlibrary loan request was submitted for the book, the Denver Public Library reported on March 18, 1982, that they did not own the title.

## The 1940s

In 1942 *The Spanish-American Song and Game Book* was published by A. S. Barnes in a bilingual format. This book was compiled by the workers of the Work Projects Administration in New Mexico. The publication was sponsored by the University of New Mexico and the State Superintendent of Public Instruction of New Mexico. Barnes reprinted it in 1973 as *Canciones y Juegos de Nuevo México = Songs and Games of New Mexico*.

Ann Nolan Clark began to write bilingual books for the Tewa Indian children at the Tesuque Pueblo in Santa Fe in the 1940s when she was a teacher for the United States Bureau of Indian Affairs/United States Indian Service. She wrote two books in the 1940s: *Sun Journey = La jornada del sol* and *Young Hunter of Picuris = El cazadorcito de Picuris*. She wrote another title which was published about 1950: *Little Boy With Three Names = El muchachito con tres nombres*. It is part of a series of bilingual books done in English and various Indian languages and Spanish.

Leo Politi's works appeared in the 1940s, and two of his books, *Juanita* and *Song of the Swallows*, contained some Spanish words and phrases. Although in recent years his books have been criticized for being too romantic, they do represent an early attempt to include the Spanish language in children's books in English. In evaluating these books, it is important to read the reviews published at the time the books were written as well as the criticism of today.

## The 1950s

Of the titles published in the 1950s, two are outstanding because of their illustrations. The illustrations in *Los aguinaldos del infante*, a story of the three wise men, are richly colored tipped-in serigraphs. This first edition published in Puerto Rico is in the Kerlan Children's Literature Research Collections at the University of Minnesota and is noted there as "expensive." Westminster Press reprinted this title in 1976 with the same illustrations, but they are not tipped-in serigraphs and are not as vivid as in the original edition of 1954. Woodcuts by Antonio Frasconi illustrate *See and Say*, a picture book in four languages: English, Italian, French, and Spanish. The woodcuts by this outstanding illustrator are bright and very colorful. A copy of this title is in the Rare Book Collection at the Library of Congress.

## The 1960s

The 1960s witnessed a dramatic increase in the publication of bilingual books over the preceding two decades, with over five times as many books listed in this bibliography. The most popular types of books were the Spanish-language readers, both traditional and nontraditional, which presented the language to English-speaking children. These books ranged from Sesyle Joslin's humorous stories about learning the Spanish language (*Señor Baby Elephant the Pirate* and *There is a Bull on My Balcony*) to *Babar's Spanish Lessons*. Readers appeared in various formats. Alex Rider's books present the nouns in both languages in a differently colored typeface, either red, orange, or green. The illustrations are unusual in these books, for a northern environment is illustrated above the English text and a southern environment above the Spanish text. *Our Friends in Spain* uses a great deal of repetition to teach a 300-word Spanish vocabulary to young children. In the 1960s the National Textbook Company in Skokie, Illinois, began to publish its bilingual books with the appearance of *Bedtime Stories in Spanish*, a collection of twelve familiar stories translated and originally published in Spanish in *La Luz*.

Several of the well-known Beginner Books were issued in bilingual formats under the Spanish series title *Yo lo puedo leer solo*. These were translated by Carlos Rivera and included the familiar illustrations used in the original English-language versions. These are typical examples of the bilingual books of the 1960s.

Works of many well-known authors, among them H. A. Rey and Lois Lenski, were translated during this decade and published in bilingual versions. The most interesting titles of the decade were those written by Mariana Prieto. Two of them presented Latin American legends: *Ah Ucu and Itzo*, a story of the Mayan people of Yucatan, and *The Wise Rooster*, a Latin American legend about Christmas Eve. Two other books by this author (*Johnny Lost* and *A Kite for Carlos*) are about Cuban boys in the United States.

Antonio Frasconi illustrated two books in the 1960s which are beautifully designed and showcase his talent: *The Snow and the Sun*, a South American folk rhyme, and *Bestiario* by Pablo Neruda.

One title that should be more widely available is *Our Book*, a photographic story of the first- and second-grade pupils at San Xavier Mission School near Tucson, Arizona, with text in Papago, Spanish, and English. This was printed in a paper-covered edition by the Carmel Print Shop in Salpointe High School in Tucson. My attempts to purchase a personal copy failed. Publishers would do well to look for original titles such as this one rather than to continue the reprinting of *Little Red Riding Hood* in Spanish.

Bilingual books of the 1960s were issued in a variety of formats. Sometimes the two languages appeared on opposite pages or in opposite columns; sometimes the languages alternated word by word or phrase by phrase; and sometimes the complete story was told in one language, followed by the story told in the other. *El gato travieso* by Denise and Alain Trez appeared in a back-to-back format, with one language from the front of the book to the middle and the other language from the back of the book to the middle. Later the flip-flop books would appear, with one language upside down. This was done so that the reader would always read the book from the front to the middle.

## The 1970s

The number of bilingual titles published in the 1970s almost doubled the number published in the 1960s. The origins of this trend can be traced in part to the passage of the Bilingual Education Act of 1974 and the Lau v. Nichols Supreme Court decision, which was handed down on January 21, 1974.

Two excellent series, specifically designed as bilingual editions, were published in the second half of the decade by Children's Book Press in San Francisco. Both series were titled *Fifth World Tales*. One series carried the subtitle *Legends in Spanish and English for All the Children of North America* and included nine titles. Eight of them presented legends from Latin American countries; one presented a creation myth from the Philippines. The second series carried the subtitle *Stories for All Children from the Many Peoples of America*. Two titles in that series were contemporary stories in Spanish and English.

Small presses continued to publish bilingual books in the 1970s: All of Us Inc., Amigos del Museo del Barrio, Eakin Press, Feminist Press, Four Winds Press, Kids Can Press, New Seed Press, Oasis Press, Quinto Sol Publications, Totinem Publications, Tundra Books, and Twin Palms Editorial. Some of these publishers issued only one or two titles; some of them are no longer in existence. Few titles from small presses are reviewed, and it is difficult to locate them in libraries and bookstores.

Universities and school districts also published bilingual books in this decade, sometimes as the result of a bilingual/bicultural education program such as the one at California State University in Fullerton, or for use in bilingual programs in the public schools, such as those titles published by the Intercultural Development Research Association in San Antonio, Texas. The Montebello Unified School District in California published two books—folk tales translated and adapted by Olga Arciniega Gross and illustrated by the children of the Montebello Gardens School. Most of the publications of these agencies were designed as curriculum materials, but those included in this bibliography are suitable for libraries.

Many of the Prism Press books published by Blaine Ethridge Books are marred by typographical errors, lack of illustrations or the use of stereotypical illustrations, poor design, unattractive format, mistakes in translation, and in most cases, insipid stories. Although the books are sturdily bound, the covers would not lure children to read these titles.

The National Textbook Company continued to issue many titles during this period. In the series *Fables in Spanish and English* the Spanish version is told first, and the English version is presented second in separately numbered pages. This results in the repetition of the illustrations, as they appear with each version of the story. The titles are designed for use in schools, but they would also be useful in libraries. The company's series *¡Hola, Amigos!: The Bilingual Series* includes two excellent titles, one a photographic story of a little girl who lives in Acopilco, a small town in Mexico, and the other a photographic essay about a little girl who lives in Mexico City.

Margaret K. McElderry edited two notable titles for Atheneum during the 1970s: *Crickets and Frogs* and *The Elephant and His Secret*, fables by Gabriela Mistral, translated and adapted by Doris Dana, with illustrations by Antonio Frasconi. Both of these titles received ten or more reviews.

The Anaya Bilingual Classics published by Anaya in Madrid are distributed in the United States through the L.A. Publishing Company. The three *La Ranita* books make effective use of repetition and have amusing, colorful illustrations, but the bindings are quite fragile.

Many outstanding titles were published in the 1970s. For the first time more attention was devoted to the design of bilingual texts, instead of just adding the second language as an afterthought. A good example of excellent design is shown by *My Mother the Mail Carrier* as well as by the *Fifth World Tales* published by Children's Book Press.

Many titles from the small presses need to be revised and redesigned and distributed more widely as they would be useful in libraries in addition to being culturally relevant. Examples include: *El gran César, Una luminaria para mis palomitas, Un nombre chistoso, Oferta de una familia*, and *Stories That Must Not Die*.

## The 1980s

The increase in the number of bilingual books did not continue in the 1980s. There are only 74 titles included in this bibliography for the 1980s as opposed to

113 included from the 1970s. The publications of this period include dictionaries and alphabet books; collections of poetry, nursery rhymes, songs, and games; and stories and legends. Culturally significant stories include: *Canciones de mi isla, A Chicano Christmas Story, The Cricket Sings, Kikiriki, The Legend of Food Mountain, The Legend of the Bellringer of San Agustín, Piñatas and Paper Flowers, The Tamarindo Puppy, Tortillitas para mamá,* and *Viaje a las pirámides mexicanas.*

The most unusual title of this period was *Trictionary = Triccionario,* a dictionary in three languages: English, Spanish, and Chinese. The trictionary was written by a group of adults and young people and represents the languages as spoken on the lower east side of Manhattan in New York City. The National Endowment for the Humanities funded this project.

Lulu Delacre began collecting traditional songs and rhymes during the 1980s, and *Arroz con leche: Popular Songs and Rhymes from Latin America* was published by Scholastic in 1989. Scholastic published her collection *Las Navidades: Popular Christmas Songs from Latin America* in 1990. Her award-winning book *Vejigante = Masquerader* was published by the same press in 1993.

## The 1990s and 2000s

Publication of bilingual books increased in the 1990s, more than doubling the previous decade. Up to the present date (December 31, 2001) only fifteen titles have been identified which have been published in 2000 and 2001.

In the 1990s many Latino authors began writing bilingual children's books. Alma Flor Ada wrote five books. She has also translated many books for publishers. In *The Christmas Tree = El árbol de Navidad: A Christmas Rhyme in English and Spanish* she adds a note about how her family celebrated Christmas in Cuba and in the United States, both on December 25 and on January 6. In her alphabet book *Gathering the Sun* she adds a note: "By the year 2000, to make it easier for computers to alphabetize text, Ch and Ll will no longer be considered separate letters in the Spanish alphabet. They have been retained here as unripe fruit, not yet ready to be taken from the tree, since all of us who love our language and the traditions it keeps alive will need some time to grow accustomed to this change." Three of her books have won awards.

Francisco X. Alarcón began writing his seasonal poems in the 1990s. Spring poems are included in *Laughing Tomatoes and Other Spring Poems = Jitomates risueños y otros poemas de primavera.* Summer poems are included in *From the Bellybutton of the Moon and Other Summer Poems = Del ombligo de la luna y otros poemas de verano.* Fall poems can be found in *Angels Ride Bikes and Other Fall Poems = Los ángeles andan en bicicleta, y otros poemas de otoño.* The book of winter poems has just been published in 2001: *Iguanas in the Snow y otros poemas de invierno = Iguanas en la nieve and Other Winter Poems.* It is interesting to note that the titles of this last book are in both English and Spanish. Children's Book Press published all four titles.

Other Latino authors writing in the 1990s and 2000s are George Ancona, Gloria Anzaldúa (who wrote a reinterpretation of the famous Mexican legend about La Llorona), Diane Gonzales Bertrand, Juan Felipe Herrera, Carmen Lomas Garza (with three award-winning books), and José-Luis Orozco. The art of Lomas Garza has been exhibited at the Laguna Gloria Art Museum in Austin, Texas. A catalog of her paintings was published as *A Piece of My Heart = Pedacito de mi corazón: The Art of Carmen Lomas Garza*. This catalog of her paintings includes a critical essay by Amalia Mesa-Bains entitled *Chicano Chronicle and Cosmology: The Works of Carmen Lomas Garza*.

Lori Marie Carlson edited three collections suitable for teenagers. *Cool Salsa* is a collection of bilingual poems on growing up Latino in the United States. *Sol a sol* is another collection of bilingual poems. *You're On!* is a collection of seven plays in English and Spanish. In this book she includes notes about the playwrights.

Northland Publishing and its Rising Moon Books for Young Readers issued four books by Jan Romero Stevens. A young boy Carlos is the central figure in these stories: *Carlos and the Carnival = Carlos y la feria, Carlos and the Cornfield = Carlos y la milpa de maíz, Carlos and the Skunk = Carlos y el zorrillo*, and *Carlos and the Squash Plant = Carlos y la planta de calabaza*. Ofelia Dumas Lachtman has written one book about a little girl named Lupita: *Big Enough = Bastante grande;* and three books about Pepita: *Pepita Takes Time = Pepita, siempre tarde, Pepita Talks Twice = Pepita habla dos veces*, and *Pepita Thinks Pink = Pepita y el color rosado*. Piñata Books published all of these titles.

Trails West Publishing and more recently Cinco Puntos Press has published the works of the well-known storyteller Joe Hayes. Trails West Publishing published his first four books, none of which was ever reviewed. Cinco Puntos Press has published his recent books. *Tell Me a Cuento = Cuéntame un story* includes the four stories previously published as individual books by Trails West Publishing. Two of the most recent books by Joe Hayes, also published by Cinco Puntos Press, are *¡El cucuy!: A Bogeyman Cuento in English and Spanish* (published in 2001) and *Estrellita de oro = Little Gold Star: A Cinderella cuento* (published in 2000). In a note for readers and storytellers, the author tells us that this Cinderella story was very popular in the mountain communities of New Mexico. In this version Cinderella is named Arcía. Joe Hayes edited and translated J. Manuel Espinosa's collection of Spanish folk tales from New Mexico which were originally published by the American Folklore Society in their *Memoirs*. The adaptation of the Spanish by Hayes mainly involved changes in spelling and some verb forms to make the stories more readable.

One of the most interesting books published in the 1990s is *The Story of Colors = La historia de los colores*. This is a folk tale from the jungles of Chiapas. The Mexican government claims Marcos is Rafael Sebastián Guillén Vicente. Elena Abós has written an essay on the publication of this book. See the annotation in the bibliography for the exact reference.

The themes of the 1990s and 2000s were similar to those of previous decades: folk tales, collections of songs and games, poetry, and stories about little boys and girls. Three books dealt specifically with emotions expressed by children. Charles Avery wrote about the feelings of children in *Everybody Has Feelings: The Moods of Children = Todos tenemos sentimientos.* Ellen Bass wrote *I Like You to Make Jokes with Me, But I Don't Want You to Touch Me = Me gusta que bromees conmigo, pero no quiero que me toques.* And Sharon Landeen wrote *When You Get Really Mad! = ¡Cuando estás muy enojado!*

Of the fifteen books which have been published in the 2000s, Children's Book Press published four; Cinco Puntos Press, three; and Piñata Books, three. These publishers are continuing their fine record of issuing well-designed bilingual children's books.

## The Bibliography

In *Bilingual Books in Spanish and English for Children* (Littleton, Colo.: Libraries Unlimited, 1985) I listed and annotated 254 bilingual titles: 8 from the 1940s, 12 from the 1950s, 68 from the 1960s, 142 from the 1970s, and 24 from the 1980s. These titles have been incorporated into this volume with the exception of forty-five titles which I did not recommend and two out-of-date dictionaries, leaving a total of 207 titles. The new titles annotated for this edition numbered 226; therefore the total number of titles in this volume is 433. Some additional titles are listed in the annotations. The cut-off date for inclusion of titles was December 31, 2001. The breakdown by decade is as follows: 1940—7, 1950—4, 1960—58, 1970—113, 1980—74, 1990—162, and 2000—15. (See Appendix A, "Publishers and Numbers of Bilingual Children's Titles.")

Bilingual books have been identified in several ways: from book reviews, from publishers' catalogs both in print form and on line, from visits to publishers' exhibits at professional conferences, from bibliographies of multicultural titles, from visits to library collections and bookstores, and from personal friends and professional colleagues. These books remain difficult to locate, and although I have been collecting them for many years, I still cannot say that this list is complete. I have examined all of the titles in the bibliography. They are either in my collection or in public libraries in the Phoenix area.

For the purpose of this bibliography, bilingual books are books with both Spanish and English in the same volume. In Great Britain, these books are called dual language books. The majority of titles in this bibliography are truly bilingual, but the two languages may appear in a variety of formats. The languages may be in alternate paragraphs or on opposite pages. Sometimes the text may be in one language with the second language at the back of the book; for example, *El alfabeto.* The text may be in one language from the beginning of the book to the middle. When you flip the book over, the other version is also from the beginning of the book to the middle. Gary Paulsen's *Sisters = Hermanas* is published this way.

I have included a few titles in which the text is in English with many Spanish words used throughout the stories. Often in these books a glossary of Spanish terms is appended. More titles in this format are appearing. Examples include: *T Is for Tortilla* by Jody Alpers, *Pablo Remembers* by George Ancona, *Abuela* and *Isla* by Arthur Dorros, *Gracias, Rosa* by Michelle Markel, *The Little Seven-Colored Horse: A Spanish American Folktale* by Robert D. San Souci, *Grandmother's Adobe Dollhouse* by MaryLou M. Smith, *Chato's Kitchen* by Gary Soto, and *La Boda: A Mexican Wedding Celebration* by Nancy VanLaan. Highsmith Press has published three titles by Francisco X. Mora in this format: *La gran fiesta, Juan Tuza and the Magic Pouch,* and *The Legend of the Two Moons.*

Several titles include three or more languages: *I Love the World and Other Voices from the Chorus* by Alma Flor Ada and others, *From Albatross to Zoo* by Patricia Borlenghi, *Alphabet Times Four* by Ruth Brown, *First Words* by Ivan and Jane Clark Chermayeff, *Pie-Biter* by Ruthanne Lum McCunn, *Sleep Rhymes Around the World* and *Street Rhymes Around the World* by Jane Yolen. In each of Yolen's books poems are presented in sixteen different languages.

The majority of books in this bibliography are picture books. The book by Gary Paulsen entitled *Sisters = Hermanas* is one young adult title I have included. *¡Aplauso!* edited by Joe Rosenberg is a collection of plays presented by the first university bilingual theater company founded in Kingsville, Texas, in 1972. Lori Marie Carlson has collected seven plays in English and Spanish in a volume called *You're On! The Emerald Lizard* is a collection of fifteen stories from various Latin American countries and cultures which have been retold by Pleasant DeSpain. Books that are clearly for an adult audience have not been included. Only a few dictionaries are listed and no workbooks or coloring books. Alphabet books and counting books are included.

Major authors are now writing or have written bilingual books: Alma Flor Ada, Sandra Cisneros, Lulu Delacre, Arthur Dorros, Lois Ehlert, Joe Hayes, Myra Cohn Livingston, Francisco X. Mora, Pat Mora, Robert D. San Souci, Gary Soto, and Jane Yolen. Other names frequently seen as illustrators or translators are Lucy Jelinek and Beatriz Zeller.

One unusual development is the publication of bilingual Spanish/English books with a Chinese theme or a classical folk tale theme by Yuan-Liou Publishing Company in Taipei, Taiwan, distributed by Pan Asian Publications of Union City, California. Monica Chang and Kuang-ts'ai Hao are two authors represented. In 1996 Pan Asian Publications issued *Simon and His Boxes = Simón y las cajas* by Gilles Tibo.

## Awards

Four awards have been established for books by Latino authors or on Latino themes. Hispanic Books Distributors of Tucson, Arizona, established the Arroz con Leche award. The first award was given in 1993 to a bilingual book *Green*

*Corn Tamales = Tamales de elote* by Gina Macaluso Rodríguez. The purpose of this award is to encourage more Hispanic authors to write for children. Authors must be of Latino heritage born, raised, or residing permanently in the United States. The 1997 award went to *The Cactus Wren and the Cholla = El Reyezuelo y La Cholla* by Valerie Chellew García. (www.hispanicbooks.com/)

The Américas Award and Commended List was also established in 1993. This award recognizes a work (picture book, poetry, fiction, folklore, and selected non-fiction) published in the United States in the previous year in English or Spanish that authentically presents the experience of individuals in Latin America or the Caribbean, or of Latinos in the United States. The award focuses on cultural heritages within the hemisphere. The Consortium of Latin American Studies Programs (CLASP), Committee on Teaching and Outreach, at the University of Connecticut, within the Latin American and Caribbean Studies Program, originally administered this program. The Center for Latin American Studies at the University of Wisconsin in Milwaukee is the current administrator. The first award was given in 1993 to Lulu Delacre for *Vejigante = Masquerader*, a bilingual book published by Scholastic. In 1996 the award was given to Carmen Lomas Garza for *In My Family = En mi familia*. Beginning with the 1995 awards, a new category of honorable mentions was added. Honorable mentions are given to books which contended as finalists for the award. *Chato's Kitchen* by Gary Soto was one of three honorable mentions in 1995. *Magic Windows = Ventanas mágicas* by Carmen Lomas Garza received an honorable mention in 1999. Thirty-five books in this bibliography have received Américas awards. (www.uwm.edu/Dept/CLACS/outreach_americas.html)

The Pura Belpré Award was established in 1996. It is given to a Latino/Latina writer and illustrator whose work portrays and celebrates the Latino cultural experience in books for children and young people. The Association for Library Service to Children, a division of the American Library Association, and the National Association to Promote Library Services to the Spanish Speaking (REFORMA), an ALA Affiliate, co-sponsor this award. The award is named after Pura Belpré who was the first Latina librarian in the New York Public Library. She enriched the lives of Puerto Rican children in the United States through her work in preserving and disseminating Puerto Rican folklore. The awards are given biennially. Ten books in this bibliography have received Pura Belpré awards. Susan Guevara received the first award, the 1996 medal, for her illustrations for *Chato's Kitchen,* written by Gary Soto. Carmen Lomas Garza received the 2000 medal for her illustrations for *Magic Windows = Ventanas mágicos,* a book which she also wrote. (www.ala.org/alsc/belpre.html)

A new award was announced in the Spring 2001 *Newsletter of the United States Board on Books for Young People.* Piñata Books, an imprint of Arte Público Press, and El Paso Energy Corporation have joined forces to establish the "Reading with Energy" Hispanic Children's Book Award. The "Reading with Energy" award will be given on an annual basis to one manuscript for a children's picture book reflecting culturally relevant, bilingual (Spanish/English) reading materials. (www.arte.uh.edu)

## Publishers

One hundred seventy-six publishers have produced the books listed in this bibliography. Many bilingual books continue to be published by small presses, such as Beautiful America Publishing, Cinco Puntos Press, La Estancia Press, High Desert Productions, Northland Publishing & Rising Moon, Ol' Stone Press, Old Hogan Publishing, Passport Books, Red Crane Books, Trails West Publishing, and Wordsong. However, trade publishers have also entered the market: Dutton Children's Books/Windmill Books, HarperCollins and Harper Trophy, Highsmith Press, Holt, Knopf, Little Brown, Putnam, and Scholastic, to name only a few. Children's Book Press of San Francisco, California, continues to publish many fine bilingual titles. The following 18 publishers each with five or more titles account for 182 titles or 42.03 percent of the titles included in this bibliography:

| Name of Publisher | Number of Books |
| --- | --- |
| Alegría Hispana Publications | 6 |
| Blaine Ethridge Books | 7 |
| Children's Book Press | 40 |
| Cinco Puntos Press | 9 |
| Doubleday/Doubleday Books for Young Readers | 5 |
| Dutton Children's Books/Windmill Books | 7 |
| Editorial Patria | 7 |
| Harcourt Brace and Harcourt Brace Jovanovich | 14 |
| Little Brown | 8 |
| National Textbook Company | 19 |
| Northland Publishing and Rising Moon | 9 |
| Pan Asian Publications | 5 |
| Piñata Books | 18 |
| Putnam | 5 |
| Random House | 6 |
| Scholastic | 5 |
| Trails West Publishing | 5 |
| Whitman | 7 |

Clearly the leaders in the field of bilingual book publishing since 1990 are Children's Book Press and Piñata Books. Children's Book Press (www.cbookpress.org) is a nonprofit publisher of multicultural and bilingual literature for children. It is supported in part by grants from the California Arts Council. Piñata Books is an imprint of Arte Público Press (www.arte.uh.edu). This press was founded in 1979 and is at the University of Houston.

## Reviews

Reviews have been selected from *Children's Book Review Index: Master*

*Cumulation 1985-1994* published in four volumes in 1996 by Gale Research. The individual volumes for 1995-2001 have also been searched. The citations in CBRI are taken from *Book Review Index*, which indexes more than 500 publications. CBRI includes citations to all books and periodicals appearing in BRI during the past year that at least one reviewer recommended for children ages ten and younger. Entries are arranged by author's name. In most instances, only the first page of the review is indicated in CBRI; and I have followed that practice in citing page numbers. The fine periodical *Book Links* is not indexed in this reference work, nor is the *EMIE Bulletin*. Discussions by Barbara Elleman and others in *Book Links* have been included. Many reviews are taken from journals devoted to children's literature, such as *Horn Book* and *School Library Journal*. Review articles are also indexed. Three examples follow:

Melissa Ann Renck, "Many People, Many Places, Other Times: An Annotated Bibliography of Multicultural Books for 3- to 8-Year-Olds," *Early Childhood Education Journal*, volume 25, number 1 (Fall 1997), pages 45-50. This is a list of 100 titles, only a few of which are Spanish and English bilingual works. The annotations are descriptive rather than critical. The author, a children's librarian, states: "Each book includes a positive and accurate portrayal of various ethnic or religious groups."

"Bilingual Books for Children," prepared by the 1998-99 and 1999-2000 International Relations Committees, *Journal of Youth Services in Libraries*, volume 14, number 2 (Winter 2001), pages 32-37. Books chosen for this list had to meet three criteria: suitability for children up to age fourteen, representation of a complete translation, and high literary quality in each language.

Judith Márquez, "Bilingual Books," *Newsletter of the United States Board on Books for Young People*, volume 26, number 1 (Spring 2001), pages [13-14]. The titles in this list are all Spanish/English bilingual books.

Reviews listed in the composite bibliography appeared in 95 different journals. Only 46 journals reviewed bilingual books in the 1985 bibliography of bilingual books. In this bibliography twenty-seven journals included ten or more reviews:

| *Title of Journal* | *Number of Reviews* |
| --- | --- |
| *Book Links* | 22 |
| *Booklist* | 177 |
| *Cartel* | 32 |
| *Center for Children's Books Bulletin* | 60 |
| *Childhood Education* | 16 |
| *Children's Book Review Service* | 40 |
| *Children's Bookwatch* | 36 |
| *Christian Science Monitor* | 14 |
| *Five Owls* | 11 |
| *Horn Book* | 84 |
| *Horn Book Guide* | 76 |
| *Hungry Mind Review* | 13 |
| *Instructor* | 14 |

| Title of Journal | Number of Reviews |
|---|---|
| Interracial Books for Children | 13 |
| Journal of Youth Services in Libraries | 32 |
| Kirkus Reviews | 82 |
| Language Arts | 15 |
| Lector | 11 |
| Library Journal | 51 |
| Library Talk | 13 |
| New York Times Book Review | 19 |
| Proyecto Leer Bulletin | 25 |
| Publishers Weekly | 71 |
| Reading Teacher | 54 |
| Saturday Review/Saturday Review of Literature | 10 |
| School Library Journal | 149 |
| Social Education | 19 |

Several of these reviewing journals are no longer published, including *Cartel, Interracial Books for Children, Lector, Proyecto Leer Bulletin,* and *Saturday Review/Saturday Review of Literature.* There were 1370 reviews of the 433 books listed in this volume, for an average of 3.16 reviews per title. (See Appendix B, "Review Journals Cited.") *Booklist* and *School Library Journal* each reviewed over 100 titles. Thirty-seven titles received ten or more reviews.

| Entry Number | Title of Book | Number of Reviews |
|---|---|---|
| 10 | From the Bellybutton of the Moon and Other Summer Poems | 10 |
| 23 | The Piñata Maker | 10 |
| 43 | Juan Bobo | 13 |
| 75 | Cool Salsa | 21 |
| 82 | Hairs | 12 |
| 90 | Fun With Spanish | 10 |
| 96 | The Woman Who Outshone the Sun | 13 |
| 97 | The Elephant and His Secret | 13 |
| 105 | Arroz con leche | 15 |
| 106 | Las Navidades | 11 |
| 119 | Abuela | 27 |
| 120 | Isla | 13 |
| 127 | Cucú | 12 |
| 128 | Moon Rope | 16 |
| 143 | See and Say | 10 |
| 144 | The Snow and the Sun | 14 |
| 161 | The Bossy Gallito | 12 |
| 196 | Calling the Doves | 13 |
| 216 | There Is a Bull on My Balcony | 10 |
| 218 | My Dog Is Lost | 10 |
| 220 | Fernando's Gift | 10 |
| 238 | Family Pictures | 17 |
| 239 | In My Family | 11 |
| 250 | Yagua Days | 13 |
| 267 | Crickets and Frogs | 10 |
| 282 | The Tree is Older Than You Are | 15 |
| 291 | Ten Little Fingers | 12 |

| *Entry Number* | *Title of Book* | *Number of Reviews* |
|---|---|---|
| 298 | Have You Seen a Comet? | 10 |
| 304 | Juanita | 13 |
| 305 | Song of the Swallows | 16 |
| 306 | The Tamarindo Puppy | 12 |
| 316 | Tortillas and Lullabies | 12 |
| 342 | The Invisible Hunters | 13 |
| 352 | Uncle Nacho's Hat | 15 |
| 389 | Chato's Kitchen | 15 |
| 428 | Diego | 13 |
| 432 | Street Rhymes Around the World | 11 |

In the 1985 bibliography only twelve titles received ten or more reviews. In the 1985 bibliography 107 out of 254 titles were not reviewed (42.12 percent). In the current combined compilation 127 titles were not reviewed (29.33 percent). Coverage of bilingual books in review journals has doubled since 1985. However, books published by small presses are still not well reviewed.

"The Hispanic market is here for good," Linda Goodman said at a REFORMA meeting in Los Angeles in 1983 (*American Libraries*, vol. 14, no. 8, September 1983, p. 528). It is very encouraging that so many fine picture books for children in Spanish and English are being published today. Only when good titles are demanded and purchased will publishers increase their output. Librarians and teachers must search out the publications of the small presses even though it means additional work, because their publications are some of the best. Selection from catalogs of publishers and distributors should be done with great caution. There are some good reviewing journals available now to help in the selection of good bilingual and Spanish-language materials. It is important to: (1) select wisely on the basis of established criteria, (2) identify quality materials not only from reviews but also by examination if possible, and (3) purchase good materials in large quantities.

# Introducción

En 1975 comencé esta investigación. El primer libro bilingüe en español e inglés que encontré fue *McGuffey's First Eclectic Reader,* una edición revisada y publicada en 1891 en Nueva York por el American Book Company. El título en la cubierta fue *McGuffey's First Spanish-English Reader.* Encontré este libro en una lista de la sala para los jóvenes del Denver Public Library. El libro estaba en el almacenaje, y no pude verlo. Más tarde cuando lo pedí como un préstamo, la biblioteca me informó que no tenía el libro.

## Los años cuarenta

En 1942, A. S. Barnes publicó *The Spanish-American Song and Game Book* en inglés y en español. Los trabajadores del Work Projects Administration en Nuevo Mexico escribieron este libro. La Universidad de Nuevo Mexico y el State Superintendent of Public Instruction del Nuevo Mexico fueron los patrocinadores del proyecto. Barnes reimprimió el libro en 1973 con el título *Canciones y Juegos de Nuevo México.*

Ann Nolan Clark escribió libros bilingües para los Tewa indios en el Tesuque Pueblo en Santa Fe en los años cuarenta cuando era una maestra para United States Bureau of Indian Affairs/United States Indian Service. Escribió dos libros: *La jornada del sol* y *El cazadorcito de Picuris.* Escribió otro libro cerca de 1950: *El muchachito con tres nombres.* Este libro es parte de una serie de libros bilingües en inglés, los idiomas indios y español.

Los libros de Leo Politi se publicaron en los años cuarenta. Dos libros, *Juanita* y *Song of the Swallows,* contuvieron algunas palabras y frases españolas. Recientemente los libros se criticaron porque estaban demasiado románticos. Sin embargo, representaron un intento temprano para incluir algunas palabras españolas en los libros en inglés para los jóvenes. En evaluar los libros por Politi, es importante leer las críticas publicadas en los años cuarenta y también las críticas de hoy.

## Los años cincuenta

Dos libros publicados en los años cincuenta tienen ilustraciones destacadas. Las ilustraciones en *Los aguinaldos del infante*, un cuento de los Reyes

Magos, tienen una riqueza de colores. La primera edición publicada en Puerto Rico está en la University of Minnesota en las Kerlan Children's Literature Research Collections. Una nota en el catálogo lo describe como "caro." Westminster reimprimió este libro en 1976 con las mismas ilustraciones, pero no tuvieron la riqueza de la edición original de 1954. Los grabados de Antonio Frasconi ilustran *Mira y habla*, un libro en cuatro lenguajes: inglés, italiano, francés, y español. Los grabados son llenos de color y luz. Este libro está en la Rare Book Collection en la Library of Congress.

## Los años sesenta

Hubo un gran aumento en la publicación de los libros bilingües en los años sesenta comparado con las dos décadas pasadas. Cinco veces el número de libros en esta década están mencionados en esta bibliografía. Los libros más populares fueron los libros de lectura, ambos tradicionales y modernos, que se presentaron en español a los jóvenes de habla inglesa. Estos libros van desde los cuentos graciosos de Sesyle Joslin (*Señor Baby Elephant the Pirate* y *Hay un toro en mi balcón*) hasta *Babar's Spanish Lessons*. Los libros de lectura estaban en varios formatos. Los libros de Alex Rider presentan los nombres en colores diferentes, rojo, naranja, o verde. Las ilustraciones son raras, porque arriba del texto inglés son de alrededores del norte y arriba del texto español son de alrededores del sur. *Our Friends in Spain* se usa mucha repetición para enseñar 300 palabras en español. En los años sesenta el National Textbook Company en Skokie, Illinois, comenzó a publicar libros bilingües con *Bedtime Stories in Spanish*, una colección de doce cuentos familiares, traducidos y publicados en español en la revista *La Luz*.

En esta década, los *Beginner Books* se publicaron en inglés y en español con el título *Yo lo puedo leer solo*. Carlos Rivera tradujo esta serie. Las ilustraciones fueron familiares porque se usan en las versiones originales en inglés. Estos libros son ejemplos típicos de los libros bilingües en los años sesenta.

Los libros de muchos autores bien conocidos, incluyendo H. A. Rey y Lois Lenski, se tradujeron durante esta década y se publicaron en versiones bilingües. Mariana Prieto escribió cuatro libros interesantes durante esta época. *Ah Ucu and Itzo* es un cuento de los Mayas de Yucatan, y *The Wise Rooster* es una leyenda latina-americana de la Nochebuena. También Prieto escribió *Johnny Lost* y *A Kite for Carlos* acerca de muchachos cubanos en los Estados Unidos.

Antonio Frasconi ilustró dos libros en los años sesenta que son de dibujo muy creativo y muestra su talento: *La nieve y el sol*, una rima de Sud América, y *Bestiario* por Pablo Neruda.

Un libro que tendría que ser más disponible es *Nuestro libro*, un cuento con fotografías de los estudiantes en el primer y segundo grado en San Xavier Mission School, cerca de Tucson, Arizona. El texto es en un idioma indio, español, y inglés. Se imprima en una edición con cubiertas de papél por Carmel Print

Shop en Salpointe High School en Tucson. No pude encontrar una copia para comprarlo. Las editoriales deben buscar los títulos originales como este libro en vez de continuar publicando las hadas como *La caperucita* en español.

Los libros bilingües de los años sesenta se imprimieron en varios formatos. A veces los dos idiomas están en las páginas opuestas o en las columnas opuestas. A veces los idiomas se alternan palabra por palabra o frase por frase. A veces el cuento completo se contó en un idioma, y entonces en otro idioma. *El gato travieso* por Denise y Alain Trez está en otro formato. El libro empieza con un idioma del principio al centro del libro y el otro es al revés: del final al centro. Más tarde los libros "flip-flop" se publicaron, con un idioma al revés. Se hacen para que los niños pueden leer cada cuento del frente al centro.

## Los años setenta

El número de los libros bilingües publicados en los años setenta casi dobló el número de publicados en los años sesenta. Los orígenes de esta tendencia pueden ser atribuidos al ley, el Bilingual Education Act de 1974, y la decisión Lau v. Nichols, del U. S. Supreme Court, el 21 de enero 1974.

Dos ciclos excelentes, creados específicamente como ediciones bilingües, se publicaron en la segunda mitad de la década por Children's Book Press en San Francisco. Ambos ciclos se llaman *Cuentos del quinto mundo*. Una serie tuvo el sub-título *Leyendas en español e inglés para todos los niños de Norteamérica*. Eran nueve libros en esta serie. En ocho se presentan las leyendas de Latinoamérica, en uno se presenta un mito de creación de las Filipinas. La segunda serie tuvo el sub-título *Cuentos de los muchos pueblos de América para todos los niños*. Dos libros en esta serie fueron cuentos contemporáneos en español y en inglés.

Las editoriales pequeñas seguían publicando libros bilingües en los años setenta: All of Us Inc., Amigos del Museo del Barrio, Eakin Press, Feminist Press, Four Winds Press, Kids Can Press, New Seed Press, Oasis Press, Quinto Sol Publications, Totinem Publications, Tundra Books, y Twin Palms Editorial. Algunas de estas editoriales publicaron solamente uno o dos libros. Algunas de estas ya no existen. No hay muchas críticas en las revistas acerca de los libros de las editoriales pequeñas. También es muy difícil encontrarlos en las bibliotecas o en las librerías.

Universidades y distritos escolares publicaron algunos libros bilingües en esta década, a veces el resultado de un programa educacional como el programa de California State University en Fullerton, o para usar en programas bilingües en las escuelas públicas, como los títulos publicados por la Intercultural Development Research Association en San Antonio, Texas. El Montebello Unified School District en California publicó dos libros—leyendas traducidas y adaptadas por Olga Arciniega Gross y ilustradas por los niños de la escuela de Montebello Gardens. Muchas de las publicaciones de estas organizaciones se diseñaron como materias para las escuelas, pero sin embargo son útiles para las bibliotecas.

Muchos de los libros publicados por Prism Press de Blaine Ethridge Books tienen errores. Los libros no tienen ilustraciones, son diseñados sin creatividad, y tienen formatos feos. Las cubiertas de estos libros no podrían atraer a los jóvenes a leer los libros.

El National Textbook Company continuaba publicando muchos libros durante esta década. En la serie *Fábulas bilingües* la versión en español se cuenta primero, y la versión en inglés segundo. Resulta en la repetición de las ilustraciones. Los libros se podrían utilizar en las escuelas y en las bibliotecas. La serie de esta editorial que se llama *¡Hola, Amigos!* incluye dos cuentos excelentes. Uno es un cuento con fotografías de una niña que vive en Acopilco, un pueblo en Mexico. Otro es un cuento, también con fotografías, de una niña que vive en la ciudad de Mexico.

Margaret K. McElderry preparó para la imprenta dos libros por Atheneum en los años setenta. *Grillos y ranas* y *El elefante y su secreto* son fábulas por Gabriela Mistral, traducidas y adaptadas por Doris Dana, con ilustraciones por Antonio Frasconi. Ambos libros recibieron más de diez críticas.

Anaya Bilingual Classics publicados por Anaya en Madrid son distribuidos en los Estados Unidos por L.A. Publishing Company. Los tres *La ranita* libros usan repeticiones efectivamente y tienen ilustracions con muchos colores.

En los años setenta, por primera vez, se dió más atención a los diseños de textos bilingües, en vez de añadir otro idioma como una consideración segunda. Algunos buenos ejemplos de dibujo excelente son el libro *Mi mamá la cartera* y también la serie *Cuentos del quinto mundo* publicados por Children's Book Press.

Muchos libros de las editoriales pequeñas tienen que ser revisados con dibujos nuevos y entonces distribuidos a las bibliotecas y las librerías. Los ejemplos incluyen: *El gran César, Una luminaria para mis palomitas, Un nombre chistoso,* y *Stories That Must Not Die.*

## Los años ochenta

El aumento de los números de los libros bilingües publicados en los años ochenta no continuó. Hay solamente 74 libros incluidos en esta bibliografía de los años ochenta comparado a 113 incluidos de los años setenta. Los libros en esta época incluyeron diccionarios, abecedarios, colecciones de poesía, cuentos de cuna, canciones, juegos, cuentos y leyendas. Muchos libros tienen importancia como libros culturales: *Canciones de mi isla, A Chicano Christmas Story, The Cricket Sings, Kikiriki, The Legend of Food Mountain, The Legend of the Bellringer of San Agustín, Piñatas and Paper Flowers, The Tamarindo Puppy, Tortillitas para mamá,* y *Viaje a las pirámides mexicanas.*

El libro más raro fue *Triccionario,* un diccionario en tres idiomas: inglés, español, y chino. El libro fue escrito por un grupo de adultos y adolescentes y representa los idiomas como se hablan en el este de Manhattan en Nueva York. El National Endowment for the Humanities dió la moneda por este proyecto.

Lulu Delacre empezó la colección de las canciones y rimas tradicionales en los años ochenta. Scholastic publicó *Arroz con leche: Popular Songs and Rhymes from Latin America* en 1989. Scholastic también publicó la colección *Las Navidades: Popular Christmas Songs from Latin America* en 1990. *Vejigante*, un libro que ganó un premio, se publicó por la misma editorial en 1993.

## Los años noventa y dos mil

La publicación de los libros bilingües aumentó en los años noventa, con dos veces los libros de los años ochenta. Hasta la fecha en curso, 31 de diciembre 2001, solamente quince libros se identificaron en 2000 y 2001.

En los años noventa muchos autores latinos empezaron escribiendo libros bilingües para los jóvenes. Alma Flor Ada escribió cinco libros. Y también ha traducido muchos libros para las editoriales. En *El árbol de Navidad: A Christmas Rhyme in English and Spanish* añade una nota acerca de su familia y las celebraciones de la Navidad en Cuba y en los Estados Unidos, el 25 de diciembre y el 6 de enero. En el abecedario *Gathering the Sun*, ella añade otra nota: "By the year 2000, to make it easier for computers to alphabetize text, Ch and LL will no longer be considered separate letters in the Spanish alphabet. They have been retained here as unripe fruit, not yet ready to be taken from the tree, since all of us who love our language and the traditions it keeps alive will need some time to grow accustomed to this change." Tres libros que escribió han ganado premios.

Francisco X. Alarcón empezó escribiendo los poemas de las estaciones en los años noventa. Los poemas de la primavera se incluyen en *Jitomates risueños y otros poemas de primavera*. Los poemas del verano se incluyen en *Del ombligo de la luna y otros poemas de verano*. Los poemas del otoño se incluyen en *Los ángeles andan en bicicleta, y otros poemas de otoño*. El libro de los poemas del invierno acaba de ser publicado en 2001: *Iguanas in the Snow y otros poemas de invierno = Iguanas en la nieve and other Winter Poems*. Es muy interesante ver que los títulos de este libro son ambos en inglés y español. Children's Book Press publicó todos los cuatro libros.

Otros escritores hispanos escribiendo en estas décadas son George Ancona, Gloria Anzaldúa (esbribió una interpretación nueva de la famosa leyenda mexicana de La Llorona), Diane Gonzales Bertrand, Juan Felipe Herrera, Carmen Lomas Garza (con tres libros que han ganado premios), y José-Luis Orozco. El arte de Lomas Garza tuvo una exposición crítica en la Laguna Gloria Art Museum en Austin, Texas. Un catálogo de sus pinturas se publicó como *Pedacito de mi corazón: The Art of Carmen Lomas Garza*. El catálogo incluyó un ensayo de Amalia Mesa-Bains que se llama *Chicano Chronicle and Cosmology: The Works of Carmen Lomas Garza*.

Lori Marie Carlson preparó para la imprenta tres colecciones aptas para los adolescentes. *Cool Salsa* es una colección de los poemas bilingües de crecer como latinos en los Estados Unidos. *Sol a sol* es otra colección de los poemas bilingües.

*You're On!* es una colección de siete obras para el teatro en inglés y español. En este libro incluye notas de los autores.

Northland Publishing y Rising Moon Books for Young Readers publicó cuatro libros de Jan Romero Stevens. Un chico Carlos es el protagonista en estos cuentos: *Carlos y la feria, Carlos y la milpa de maíz, Carlos y el zorrillo,* y *Carlos y la planta de calabaza.*

Ofelia Dumas Lachtmas escribió un libro sobre una niña que se llama Lupita: *Bastante grande;* y tres libros de Pepita: *Pepita, siempre tarde, Pepita habla dos veces,* y *Pepita y el color rosado.* Piñata Books publicó estos libros.

Trails West Publishing y recientemente Cinco Puntos Press ha publicado las obras del autor bien conocido, Joe Hayes. Trails West Publishing publicó sus primeros cuatro libros. Ninguno de estos libros recibieron críticas. Cinco Puntos Press ha publicado sus libros recientes. *Tell Me a Cuento = Cuéntame un story* incluye los cuatro cuentos publicados originalmente por Trails West Publishing. Dos libros nuevos por Joe Hayes, también publicados de Cinco Puntos Press, son *¡El cucuy!: A Bogeyman Cuento in English and Spanish* (2001) y *Estrellita de oro = Little Gold Star: A Cinderella cuento* (2000). En una nota el autor nos dice que este cuento de Cenicienta fue muy popular en los pueblos montañosos de Nuevo Mexico. En esta versión Cenicienta se llama Arcía. Joe Hayes preparó para la imprenta la colección de J. Manuel Espinosa. El libro contiene leyendas españolas de Nuevo Mexico que fueron publicadas originalmente por la American Folklore Society en sus *Memoirs.* En la adaptación del español por Hayes, solamente cambió la ortografía y los verbos para hacer los cuentos mas fácil de leer.

Un libro que es muy interesante y muy raro es *La historia de los colores.* Es una leyenda de las selvas de Chiapas. El gobierno de Mexico dice que el autor Marcos es en realidad Rafael Sebastián Guillén Vicente. Elena Abós ha escrito un ensayo acerca de la publicación de este libro. Véanse las notas en la bibliografía para ver el título exacto de este ensayo.

Los temas de los años noventa y dos mil fueron similares a los temas de las décadas pasadas: leyendas, colecciones de canciones y juegos, poesía, y cuentos de niños y niñas. Se publicaron tres libros acerca de las emociones de las jovenes. Charles Avery escribió de los sentimientos de los niños en *Todos tenemos sentimientos.* Ellen Bass escribió *Me gusta que bromees conmigo, pero no quiero que me toques.* Y Sharon Landeen escribió *¡Cuando estás muy enojado!*

Quince libros han sido publicados en los años dos mil. Children's Book Press publicó cuatro; Cinco Puntos Press, tres; and Piñata Books, tres. Estas editoriales siguen publicando libros para jóvenes en inglés y español que están muy bien diseñados.

## La bibliografía

En el libro *Bilingual Books in Spanish and English for Children* (Littleton,

Colo.: Libraries Unlimited, 1985) creé una lista de 254 libros bilingües: 8 de los
años cuarenta, 12 de los años cincuenta, 68 de los años sesenta, 142 de los años
setenta, y 24 de los años ochenta. Estos libros se incluyen en este volumen con
la excepción de 45 títulos que no recomendé y dos diccionarios anticuados, por
un total de 207 libros. Los libros nuevos en esta versión son 226. Por lo tanto,
el total número de libros en esta bibliografía es 433. Algunos títulos se incluyen
en las descripciones. Ningunos títulos se añadieron después de 31 de diciembre
2001. Por década, estos libros son: 1940—7, 1950—4, 1960—58, 1970—113,
1980—74, 1990—162, and 2000—15. (Véase Apéndice A, "Editoriales y números
de títulos bilingües para los niños."

Para encontrar los libros bilingües, he buscado las críticas en las revistas,
los catálogos de las editoriales, exposiciones a los congresos profesionales, las
bibliografías de títulos multilingües, y colecciones de libros en bibliotecas y librerías. Amigas y colegas han recomendado algunos libros. Estos libros son muy
difíciles de encontrar, y aunque los he coleccionado hace muchos años, no puedo
decir que esta lista es completa. He mirado a todos los libros en la bibliografía.
Hay en mi colección o en las bibliotecas en Phoenix.

Por el propósito de esta bibliografía, los libros bilingües son libros en español
y en inglés en el mismo volumen. En Inglaterra, estos libros se llaman "dual-
language" libros. La mayoría de los libros en esta bibliografía son bilingües, en
realidad. Los dos idiomas pueden estar en una variedad de formatos. Los idiomas
pueden estar en párrafos alternativos o en páginas opuestas. A veces el texto
puede estar en un idioma con el segundo idioma al final del libro, por ejemplo
*El alfabeto*. El texto puede estar en un idioma del principio del libro al centro.
Cuando se da vuelta al libro, otra versión es también del principio al centro. El
libro *Hermanas* por Gary Paulsen se publicó en esta manera.

He incluido algunos títulos en que el texto es en inglés con muchas palabras españolas en los cuentos. Frecuentemente en estos libros hay un glosario
de las palabras españolas al final del libro. Ejemplos incluyen: *T is for Tortilla*
por Jody Alpers, *Pablo Remembers* por George Ancona, *Abuela* e *Isla* por Arthur
Dorros, *Gracias, Rosa* por Michelle Markel, *The Little Seven-Colored Horse: A
Spanish American Folktale* por Robert D. San Souci, *Grandmother's Adobe Dollhouse* by MaryLou M. Smith, *Chato's Kitchen* por Gary Soto, y *La Boda: A Mexican Wedding Celebration* by Nancy VanLaan. Highsmith Press ha publicado tres
libros por Francisco X. Mora en este formato: *La gran fiesta, Juan Tuza and the
Magic Pouch*, y *The Legend of the Two Moons*.

Algunos libros incluyen tres o más idiomas: *I Love the World and Other
Voices from the Chorus* por Alma Flor Ada y otros autores, *From Albatross to Zoo*
por Patricia Borlenghi, *Alphabet Times Four* por Ruth Brown, *Primeras palabras*
por Ivan y Jane Clark Chermayeff, *Comepasteles* por Ruthanne Lum McCunn,
*Sleep Rhymes Around the World* y *Street Rhymes Around the World* por Jane Yolen.
En cada de los libros por Yolen, los poemas están en 16 idiomas.

La mayoría de los libros en esta bibliografía son libros para mirar. El libro por Gary Paulsen, *Hermanas*, es un libro para los adolescentes. *¡Aplauso!* por Joe Rosenberg es una colección de obras para el teatro que se fueron presentadas por el primer teatro bilingüe en una universidad de Kingsville, Texas, en 1972. Lori Marie Carlson ha escrito una colección de siete obras para el teatro en inglés y en español en un libro con el título *You're On! La lagartija esmeralda* es una colección de quince cuentos de varios paises y culturas en Latinoamérica. El autor es Pleasant DeSpain. Los libros para adultos no se incluyen. Algunos diccionarios se incluyen, pero no libros escolares o para colorear. Los abecedarios y libros de contar también se incluyen.

Actuales autores bien conocidos de libros bilingües son Alma Flor Ada, Sandra Cisneros, Lulu Delacre, Arthur Dorros, Lois Ehlert, Joe Hayes, Myra Cohn Livingston, Francisco X. Mora, Pat Mora, Robert D. San Souci, Gary Soto, y Jane Yolen. Otros como Lucy Jelinek y Beatriz Zeller son traductores y pintores.

Algunos libros muy raros son los libros bilingües con un tema chino o una leyenda clásica publicados por Yuan-Liou Publishing Company en Taipei, Taiwan, distribuidos por Pan Asian Publications de Union City, California. Monica Chang y Kuang-ts'ai Hao son dos autores de esta editorial. En 1996 Pan Asian Publications publicó *Simón y las cajas* por Gilles Tibo.

## Los premios

Existen cuatro premios para los libros por escritores latinos o con temas latinos. Hispanic Books Distributors de Tucson, Arizona, estableció el premio Arroz con Leche. El primer premio se dió en 1993 a un libro bilingüe *Tamales de elote* por Gina Macaluso Rodríguez. El propósito de este premio es para fomentar más autores latinos a escribir para jóvenes. Los autores tienen que ser de la herencia latina nacidos, crecidos, o que han vivido permanentemente en los Estados Unidos. El premio de 1997 se dió a *El Reyezuelo y La Cholla* por Valerie Chellew García. (El sitio-web es www.hispanicbooks.com)

El premio Américas también se estableció en 1993. Este premio se da en reconocimiento a un libro (libro para mirar, poesía, cuento, leyenda, y algunos de información) publicado en los Estados Unidos en el año pasado en inglés o español que cuenta de las experiencías de las personas en Latinoamérica o el Caribe, o de latinos en los Estados Unidos. El premio enfoca las herencias culturales en el hemisferio. El Consortium of Latin American Studies Programs (CLASP), Committee on Teaching and Outreach, en la University of Connecticut, en el programa de Latinoamérica y el Caribe, originalmente administró el programa. El Center for Latin American Studies a la University of Wisconsin en Milwaukee es el administrador ahora. El primer premio se dió en 1993 a Lulu Delacre por el libro *Vejigante*, un libro bilingüe publicado por Scholastic. En 1996 el premio se dió a Carmen Lomas Garza por el libro *En mi familia*. Empezando en 1995, una categoría nueva se añadió: mención de honor. Una mención de honor en 1995 fue *Chato's Kitchen* por Gary Soto. *Ventanas mágicas* por Carmen Lomas Garza recibió una mención de honor en 1999. Treinta y cinco libros en esta bibliografía han recibido los premios Américas. (El sitio-web es www.uwm.edu/Dept/CLACS/outreach_americas.html)

El premio Pura Belpré fue establecido en 1996. Se da a un autor o pintor latino/latina que escribe o pinta acerca de la experiencia latina en libros para jóvenes y adolescentes. The Association for Library Service to Children, una división de la American Library Association, y la National Association to Promote Library Services to the Spanish Speaking (REFORMA), afiliado con ALA, son los patrocinadores de este premio. Pura Belpré fue la primera bibliotecaria latina en el New York Public Library. En la biblioteca enriqueció las vidas de los niños puertorriqueños en los Estados Unidos por la preservación y diseminación de las leyendas puertorriqueñas. Los premios se dan cada dos años. Diez libros en esta bibliografía han recibido los premios Pura Belpré. Susan Guevara recibió el primer premio en 1996 por las ilustraciones en *Chato's Kitchen*, escrito por Gary Soto. Carmen Lomas Garza recibió el premio en 2000 por las ilustraciones en *Ventanas mágicas*, un libro que también escribió. (El sitio-web es www.ala.org/alsc/belpre.html)

Un nuevo premio fue anunciado en la primavera de 2001 *Newsletter of the United States Board on Books for Young People*. Piñata Books afiliado con Arte Público Press y El Paso Energy Corporation son los patrocinadores de este premio: el "Reading with Energy" Hispanic Children's Book Award. El premio será dado cada año al manuscrito de un libro para mirar para los jóvenes que tiene la cultura pertinente y es bilingüe en inglés y en español. (El sitio-web es www.arte.uh.edu)

## Las editoriales

Los libros en esta bibliografía han sido publicados por 176 editoriales. Muchos libros bilingües continuan siendo publicados por las editoriales pequeñas, como: Beautiful America Publishing, Cinco Puntos Press, La Estancia Press, High Desert Productions, Northland Publishing & Rising Moon, Ol' Stone Press, Old Hogan Publishing, Passport Books, Red Crane Books, Trails West Publishing, y Wordsong. Otras editoriales bien conocidas son Dutton Children's Books/Windmill Books, HarperCollins & Harper Trophy, Highsmith Press, Holt, Knopf, Little Brown, Putnam, y Scholastic, para mencionar solamente unas pocas. Children's Book Press de San Francisco continua publicando muchos títulos excelentes. Cada una de las editoriales en la lista siguiente ha publicado cinco o más libros por un total de 182 títulos o 42.03% de los libros incluidos en esta bibliografía.

| *Nombre de la editorial* | *Número de libros* |
|---|---|
| Alegría Hispana Publications | 6 |
| Blaine Ethridge Books | 7 |
| Children's Book Press | 40 |

| Nombre de la editorial | Número de libros |
|---|---|
| Cinco Puntos Press | 9 |
| Doubleday/Doubleday Books for Young Readers | 5 |
| Dutton Children's Books/Windmill Books | 7 |
| Editorial Patria | 7 |
| Harcourt Brace y Harcourt Brace Jovanovich | 14 |
| Little Brown | 8 |
| National Textbook Company | 19 |
| Northland Publishing y Rising Moon | 9 |
| Pan Asian Publications | 5 |
| Piñata Books | 18 |
| Putnam | 5 |
| Random House | 6 |
| Scholastic | 5 |
| Trails West Publishing | 5 |
| Whitman | 7 |

Las editoriales más importantes desde 1990 son Children's Book Press y Piñata Books. Children's Book Press (el sitio-web es www.cbookpress.org) es una editorial sin provecho monetario. Publica muchos libros multiculturales y bilingües para jóvenes. El California Arts Council es uno de los patrocinadores de esta editorial. Piñata Books es una división de Arte Público Press (el sitio-web es www.arte.uh.edu). Esta editorial fue fundado en 1979 y está en la University of Houston.

## Las críticas

Las críticas se escogieron de *Children's Book Review Index: Master Cumulation 1985-1994* publicado en cuatro volumenes en 1996 por Gale Research. Las volumenes de 1995-2001 se buscaron también. Las referencias en CBRI están en el *Book Review Index*, que incluye más de 500 revistas. CBRI incluye referencias por todos los libros y las revistas de BRI durante el año pasado que se recomiendan para los jóvenes de diez años y menores de diez años. Los libros se arreglan por los apellidos de los autores. En casi todos los casos, solamente la primera página de la crítica se indica. He seguido esta práctica en esta bibliografía. La revista excelente *Book Links* no es incluido en CBRI ni es *EMIE Bulletin*. Ensayos por Barbara Elleman y otras en *Book Links* se incluyen en la bibliografía. Hay muchas críticas de la literatura para los jóvenes en revistas, como *Horn Book* y *School Library Journal*. Los artículos de críticas también se incluyen. Tres ejemplos son:

Melissa Ann Renck, "Many People, Many Places, Other Times: An Annotated Bibliography of Multicultural Books for 3- to 8-Year Olds," *Early Childhood Education Journal*, volumen 25, número 1 (otoño 1997), en las páginas 45-50. Es una lista de 100 libros, pero solamente unos pocos son libros bilingües en inglés y en español. Los apuntos son descriptivos en vez de criticativos. La escritora, una bibliotecaria para los jóvenes, dice: "Each book includes a positive and accurate portrayal of various ethnic or religious groups."

"Bilingual Books for Children" fue preparado por 1998-99 y 1999-2000 International Relations Committees, *Journal of Youth Services in Libraries*, volumen 14, número 2 (invierno 2001), en las páginas 32-37. Los libros escogidos para esta lista tuvieron que cubrir tres criterios: apto para niños hasta la edad de catorce, representación de una traducción completa, y una calidad literaria de primer orden en cada idioma.

Judith Márquez escribió "Bilingual Books," en *Newsletter of the United State Board on Books for Young People*, volumen 26, número 1 (primavera 2001), en las páginas 13-14. Todos de estos libros son bilingües.

Las críticas en esta bibliografía completa estaban en 95 revistas. En la bibliografía de 1985 solamente 46 revistas incluyeron críticas de libros bilingües. En esta bibliografía 27 revistas incluyeron diez or más críticas. Siguen:

| Las revistas | Número de críticas |
|---|---|
| Book Links | 22 |
| Booklist | 177 |
| Cartel | 32 |
| Center for Children's Books Bulletin | 60 |
| Childhood Education | 16 |
| Children's Book Review Service | 40 |
| Children's Bookwatch | 36 |
| Christian Science Monitor | 14 |
| Five Owls | 11 |
| Horn Book | 84 |
| Horn Book Guide | 76 |
| Hungry Mind Review | 13 |
| Instructor | 14 |
| Interracial Books for Children | 13 |
| Journal of Youth Services in Libraries | 32 |
| Kirkus Reviews | 82 |
| Language Arts | 15 |
| Lector | 11 |
| Library Journal | 51 |
| Library Talk | 13 |
| New York Times Book Review | 19 |
| Proyecto Leer Bulletin | 25 |
| Publishers Weekly | 71 |
| Reading Teacher | 54 |
| Saturday Review/Saturday Review of Literature | 10 |
| School Library Journal | 149 |
| Social Education | 19 |

Varias de estas revistas no son publicadas ahora incluyendo *Cartel, Interracial Books for Children, Lector, Proyecto Leer Bulletin,* y *Saturday Review/Saturday Review of Literature.* Hay 1370 críticas de los 433 libros en este volumen, un promedio de 3.16 críticas por cada título. (Véase Apéndice B, "Revistas críticas citadas.") Treinta y siete libros recibieron diez o más críticas. Siguen:

| Número | Título | Número de críticas |
|---|---|---|
| 10 | Del ombligo de la luna y otros poemas de verano | 10 |
| 23 | El piñatero | 10 |
| 43 | Juan Bobo | 13 |
| 75 | Cool Salsa | 21 |
| 82 | Pelitos | 12 |
| 90 | Fun With Spanish | 10 |
| 96 | La mujer que brillaba aún mas que el sol | 13 |
| 97 | El elefante y su secreto | 13 |
| 105 | Arroz con leche | 15 |
| 106 | Las Navidades | 11 |
| 119 | Abuela | 27 |
| 120 | Isla | 13 |
| 127 | Cucú | 12 |
| 128 | Un lazo a la luna | 16 |
| 143 | Mira y habla | 10 |
| 144 | La nieve y el sol | 14 |
| 161 | El gallo de bodas | 12 |
| 196 | El canto de las palomas | 13 |
| 216 | Hay un toro en mi balcón | 10 |
| 218 | My Dog Is Lost | 10 |
| 220 | El regalo de Fernando | 10 |
| 238 | Cuadros de familia | 17 |
| 239 | En mi familia | 11 |
| 250 | Yagua Days | 13 |
| 267 | Grillos y ranas | 10 |
| 282 | The Tree is Older Than You Are | 15 |
| 291 | Diez deditos | 12 |
| 298 | Have You Seen a Comet? | 10 |
| 304 | Juanita | 13 |
| 305 | Song of the Swallows | 16 |
| 306 | The Tamarindo Puppy | 12 |
| 316 | Tortillas y cancioncitas | 12 |
| 342 | Los cazadores invisibles | 13 |
| 352 | El sombrero de tío Nacho | 15 |
| 389 | Chato's Kitchen | 15 |
| 428 | Diego | 13 |
| 432 | Street Rhymes Around the World | 11 |

En la bibliografía de 1985, solamente doce libros recibieron diez o más críticas. En la bibliografía de 1985, 107 de 254 títulos no recibieron críticas (42.12 por ciento). En esta bibliografía 127 títulos no recibieron críticas (29.33 por ciento). Las críticas de los libros bilingües en las revistas se han doblado desde 1985. Sin embargo, los libros publicados por las editoriales pequeñas no recibieron muchas críticas.

"The Hispanic market is here for good," dijo Linda Goodman a una reunión de REFORMA en Los Angeles en 1983 (*American Libraries*, volumen 14, número 8, septiembre 1983, página 528). Muchos libros excelentes para mirar en inglés y en español se publican hoy. Cuando los buenos títulos se solicitan y se compran, las editoriales aumentarán la publicación de los libros bilingües. Las bibliotecarias y las maestras tienen que buscar las publicaciones de las editoriales pequeñas aunque requiera mucho trabajo, porque dichos libros son muy buenos. La selección de los catálogos de las editoriales y distributores tienen que hacerse con gran cuidado. Hay algunas revistas de críticas disponibles ahora para ayudar en la selección de buenos libros bilingües. Es importante: (1) escoger con inteligencia en la base de criterios establecidos, (2) identificar libros de buena calidad no solo de las críticas pero también examinando los libros si es posible, y (3) comprar libros buenos en cantidades grandes.

# Organization of the Bibliography

The bibliography is arranged in alphabetical order by the first author's last name and then by book title; names of coauthors, illustrators and translators are not considered in the alphabetization. Spellings and accent marks in author names are reproduced as they appear on the title pages of the books, even though they may be incorrect. Spanish last names often contain more than one element. In alphabetizing these names, an attempt was made to use the form of the name as the author wished. The Library of Congress follows this practice, and I have tried to do the same.

An index to coauthors, illustrators, and translators is provided. The index of titles includes references to series and to awards. There is an index to subjects in both English and Spanish. The Spanish subject headings have been selected from *Bilindex: A Bilingual Spanish-English Subject Heading List: Spanish Equivalents to Library of Congress Subject Headings.* The California Spanish Language Data Base in Oakland, California published this reference resource in 1984. It has not been updated.

Prices were not included because they are subject to change, and many of the older titles are out of print. ISBNs were included when they were available.

Errors in translation in the texts have been noted in several books. Publishers need to be careful in selecting qualified translators, and reviewers need to point out errors.

# La organización
# de la bibliografía

La bibliografía se arregla en un orden alfabético por el apellido del primer autor, y entonces por el título del libro; los co-autores, los ilustradores y los traductores no se consideran en la organización alfabética. Se ofrece un índice de los coautores, ilustradores, y traductores. La ortografía y los acentos en los nombres de los autores se reproducen como aparecen en las páginas de los títulos en los libros, aunque sean errados. Los apellidos de los nombres españoles frecuentemente contienen más de uno elemento. En poniendo estos nombres en orden alfabético, traté de usar la forma del nombre de preferencia de cada autor. Esta práctica se sigue en el Library of Congress, y he tratado de hacer el mismo.

El índice de títulos incluye referencias a los ciclos y a los premios. Hay un índice de los temas en inglés y en español. Los temas españoles se escogieron de *Bilindex: Una lista bilingüe en español e inglés de encabezamientos de materia (Equivalentes en español de los encabezamientos de la Biblioteca del Congreso de Estados Unidos de Norteamérica)*. California Spanish Language Data Base en Oakland, California, publicó este recurso en 1984. No hay una edición reciente.

Los precios no se incluyen porque cambian frecuentemente, y muchos de los libros están agotados. Los números de ISBN se incluyen cuando disponibles.

Los errores en traducción en los textos se notan en varios libros. Las editoriales tienen que tener cuidado escogiendo traductores, y las críticas tienen que mencionar los errores.

# The Bibliography
*(with annotations in English)*

# La bibliografía
*(con anotaciones en inglés)*

1. **500 palabras nuevas para tí = 500 Words to Grow On.** New York: Random House, 1982. unp. Illustrated by Harry McNaught. Translated into Spanish by Pilar de Cuenca and Inés Alvarez.

Each of the words in this book is given first in Spanish and then in English. The words are grouped in the following categories: colors, people, clothing, toys, kitchen, food, vehicles, the country, the house, air and sea, animals, buildings, birds, insects, tools, and the seasons. Each word is illustrated by a colorful and realistic drawing.

2. Ada, Alma Flor. **The Christmas Tree = El árbol de Navidad: A Christmas Rhyme in English and Spanish.** New York: Hyperion Books for Children, 1997. ISBN: 0-7868-0151-4. unp. Illustrated by Terry Ybáñez.

A cumulative rhyme telling how one family decorated the Christmas tree with a candle, a candy cane, a sleigh, a carved deer, and a star on the top. The illustrator uses very dark colors, often making it difficult to see the pictures very clearly. The author adds a note about how her family celebrated Christmas in Cuba and the United States, both on December 25 and on January 6.

REVIEWS: *Kirkus Reviews*, December 15, 1997, p. 1832; *Publishers Weekly*, October 6, 1997, p. 54.

3. Ada, Alma Flor. **Gathering the Sun: An Alphabet in Spanish and English.** New York: Lothrop, Lee & Shepard, 1st edition, 1997. ISBN: 0-688-13903-5. unp. English translation by Rosa Zubizarreta. Illustrated by Simón Silva.

These poems are about working in the fields and the harvest. There is one poem for each letter of the Spanish alphabet. The author adds a note on the verso: "By the year 2000, to make it easier for computers to alphabetize text, Ch and Ll will no longer be considered separate letters in the Spanish alphabet. They have been retained here as unripe fruit, not yet ready to be taken from the tree, since all of us who love our language and the traditions it keeps alive will need some time to grow accustomed to this change." Pura Belpré honor book 1998 for illustrations. Américas Commended List 1997.

REVIEWS: *American Book Review*, November 1997, p. 12; *Center for Children's Books Bulletin*, June 1997, p. 348; *Children's Book Review Service*, Spring 1997, p. 138; *Children's Bookwatch*, May 1997, p. 2; *Horn Book Guide*, Spring 1998, p. 116; *Journal of Youth Services in Libraries*, Winter 2001, p. 34; *Publishers Weekly*, March 31, 1997, p. 76; *School Library Journal*, March 1997, p. 169; *Social Education*, April 1998, p. 3

**4.** Ada, Alma Flor; Harris, Violet J.; and Hopkins, Lee Bennett. **I Love the World and Other Voices from the Chorus**. Carmel, Calif.: Hampton-Brown Books, 1993. ISBN: 1-56334-327-4. 40 p.

Thirty-six poems dealing with a diversity of cultures are included in this brief collection. Often the culture can only be identified by the illustration, because the poems cover universal themes. Cultures included are: African American, Native American, Hispanic American, Asian American, and European American. Only two bilingual (Spanish and English) poems are included: *Orgullo = Pride* by Alma Flor Ada and *El año nuevo = The New Year* by Margot Pepp.

**5.** Ada, Alma Flor. **The Lizard and the Sun = La lagartija y el sol: A Folktale in English and Spanish**. New York: Doubleday Books for Young Readers, 1997. ISBN: 0-385-32121-X. unp. Illustrated by Felipe Dávalos. Translated by Rosa Zubizarreta.

A folktale of long ago about the disappearance of the sun. The animals set out to find the sun, but they all give up the search except for the lizard. He finally finds the sun asleep inside a rock. It takes all the emperor's musicians and dancers to wake up the sun so that sunlight is back in the world. Illustrations are dark and gloomy and are reminiscent of an Aztec community. The last pages are bright and sunny. Américas Commended List 1997.

REVIEWS: *Booklist*, December 15, 1997, p. 698; *Center for Children's Books Bulletin*, October 1997, p. 40; *Horn Book Guide*, Spring 1998, p. 116; *Journal of Youth Services in Libraries*, Winter 2001, p. 34; *Kirkus Reviews*, July 1, 1997, p. 1026; *Publishers Weekly*, April 16, 1999, p. 85; *Reading Teacher*, September 1998, p. 61; *School Library Journal*, August 1997, p. 180; *Social Education*, April 1998, p. 7.

**6.** Ada, Alma Flor. **Mediopollito = Half-chicken**. New York: Delacorte Press, 1995. ISBN: 0-385-32044-2. unp. Illustrated by Kim Howard. Translated by Rosalma Zubizarreta. (A Doubleday Book for Young Readers)

In this tale set in colonial Mexico, a mother hen hatches her thirteenth egg which turns out to be half a chicken. Half-chicken becomes so vain with all the attention he gets that he decides to travel to Mexico City to see the viceroy. On the way he helps a stream, a fire, and the wind. When he ends up in the soup pot in the kitchen of the viceroy. the stream, the fire, and the wind help him out. He ends up as a weather vane looking out over the world. Américas Commended List 1995.

REVIEWS: *Booklist*, September 15, 1995, p. 165; *Horn Book*, November 1995, p. 749-750; *Journal of Youth Services in Libraries*, Winter 2001, p. 35; *Reading Teacher*, February 1997, p. 426; *Social Studies*, January 1997, p. 29.

7.   Agnew, Edith J. **Treasures for Tomás.** New York: Friendship Press, 1964. 126 p. Illustrated by Brinton Turkle.

The story of the Aragon family in Colorado and their problems when the father loses his job for an unusual reason. The story is in English, with a few Spanish words. After each of the ten chapters, the Spanish words used are listed with phonetic pronunciations. There are a few black-and-white illustrations.

8.   Ainsworth, Len. **The Turtle and the Rabbit Run a Race = La tortuga y el conejo juegan una carrera.** San Antonio: Naylor, 1971. unp. Illustrations by Margaret Waddell.

The familiar story of the rabbit and the turtle is told in alternating lines of Spanish and English. Simple black-and-white illustrations.

REVIEW: *Library Journal*, October 15, 1971, p. 3456.

9.   Alarcón, Francisco X. **Angels Ride Bikes and Other Fall Poems = Los ángeles andan en bicicleta, y otros poemas de otoño.** San Francisco: Children's Book Press, 1999. ISBN: 0-89239-160. 31 p. Illustrations: Maya Christina Gonzalez.

In an afterword, the author tells the readers that "These poems celebrate Los Angeles as a Promised Land where people from all over the world can make their dreams come true." Most of the poems are about family life and going to school. Américas Commended List 1999.

REVIEWS: *Booklist*, December 1, 1999, p. 707; *Booklist*, August 2000, p. 2154; *Horn Book Guide*, Spring 2000, p. 151; *Journal of Youth Services in Libraries*, Winter 2001, p. 35; *Kirkus Reviews*, July 1, 1999, p. 1050; *Publishers Weekly*, August 30, 1999, p. 86; *School Library Journal*, October 1999, p. 130; *School Library Journal*, August 2000, p. 37.

10.   Alarcón, Francisco X. **From the Bellybutton of the Moon and Other Summer Poems = Del ombligo de la luna y otros poemas de verano.** San Francisco: Children's Book Press, 1998. ISBN: 0-89239-153-7. 31 p. Illustrations: Maya Christina Gonzalez.

These bilingual poems were inspired by the poet's recollections of childhood summers in Atoyac, Mexico, where his mother was raised. Pura Belpré honor book 2000 for narrative. Américas Commended List 1998.

REVIEWS: *Booklist*, October 15, 1998, p. 423; *Booklist*, July 1999, p. 1958; *Booklist*, March 15, 2000, p. 1342; *Children's Bookwatch*, February 1999, p. 2; *Horn*

*Book Guide*, Spring 1999, p. 130; *Journal of Youth Services in Libraries*, Winter 2001, p. 35; *Kirkus Reviews*, July 1, 1998, p. 964; *Publishers Weekly*, July 20, 1998, p. 222; *School Library Journal*, December 1998, p. 98; *School Library Journal*, August 1999, p. 38.

**11.**  Alarcón, Francisco X. **Iguanas in the Snow y otros poemas de invierno = Iguanas en la nieve and Other Winter Poems.** San Francisco: Children's Book Press, 2001. ISBN: 0-89239-168-5. 31 p. Illustrations by Maya Christina Gonzalez.

This is the final collection of seasonal poetry by this poet and illustrator. The poems invite us to celebrate winter as it occurs in San Francisco and northern California. The artist has created a spirited family of children and adults illustrating these wonderful poems. A beautifully designed bilingual book.

**12.**  Alarcón, Francisco X. **Laughing Tomatoes and Other Spring Poems = Jitomates risueños y otros poemas de primavera.** San Francisco: Children's Book Press, 1997. ISBN: 0-89239-139-1. 31 p. Illustrations: Maya Christina Gonzalez.

This collection includes twenty poems in English and Spanish celebrating spring and the wonders of nature. The illustrations are bright and fanciful. The author adds a note saying that he started writing poems by putting down the songs his grandmother sang. Pura Belpré honor book 1998 for narrative. Américas Commended List 1997.

REVIEWS: *Booklist*, June 1, 1997, p. 1707; *Center for Children's Books Bulletin*, June 1997, p. 349; *Horn Book Guide*, Fall 1997, p. 338; *Hungry Mind Review*, Summer 1997, p. 26; *Journal of Youth Services in Libraries*, Winter 2001, p. 35; *Kirkus Reviews*, March 15, 1997, p. 458; *Reading Teacher*, May 1998, p. 686; *School Library Journal*, May 1997, p. 118.

**13.**  Alba, Juanita. **Calor: A Story of Warmth for All Ages.** New York: Lectorum Publications, 1995. ISBN: 1-56796-069-3. 30 p. Illustrations by Amado M. Peña.

The story of warmth, from the heat of the sun to grandmother's warmth and mother's cooking, is simply told. The full page illustrations opposite each page of text show bold angular figures and strong colors.

REVIEWS: *Horn Book Guide*, Spring 1998, p. 117; *School Library Journal*, August 1995, p. 114.

**14.**  Alen, Paule. **The Busy Day = El día atareado.** New York: Derrydale Books, 1988. ISBN: 0-517-65558-6. 29 p. Illustrations by Myriam Deru.

There are two other titles in this series: **A Birthday Surprise = Una sorpresa de cumpleaños** and **First Day of School = El primer día de escuela.** In **The Busy Day**, a story about two mongooses, Maggie hurts her hand helping Mike build a tree house. Then Mike cooks lunch for her, but it is not edible.

They go to a restaurant for lunch. Each double page spread consists of vocabulary words in English and Spanish on the left page (with illustrations) and a picture on the right page with the English and Spanish texts side by side.

REVIEW: *Horn Book*, November 1988, p. 809.

**15.** Alexander, Frances. **Mother Goose on the Rio Grande.** Skokie, Ill.: National Textbook Company, 1973. 89 p. Illustrated by Charlotte Baker. (The Spanish for Young Americans Series)

The original edition of this title was published in 1960 by Banks Upshaw of Dallas. The rhymes are the same, but there have been some minor changes in the section on games. The type has been reset, the size of the book is different, and the illustrations have been rearranged.

REVIEW: *Cartel*, June 1976, p. 178.

**16.** Alexander, Frances. **Mother Goose on the Rio Grande: Rimas sin ton ni son = Mexican Folklore.** Dallas: Banks Upshaw, 1960. 101 p. Collected, translated, and arranged by Frances Alexander. Illustrated by Charlotte Baker.

The author states in her foreword: "The Mexican nursery rhymes in this collection are a part of the rich heritage of the Mexican people. They have been gathered from the memories of the old and the playgrounds of the young in the Texas-Rio Grande region and have been given free translations into English rhymes." Simple black-and-white line drawings with single colors added.

**17.** Alexander, Sue. **America's Own Holidays = Días de fiesta de los Estados Unidos.** New York: Watts, 1988. ISBN: 0-531-10293-9. 47 p. Illustrated by Leslie Morrill. Translated into Spanish by Sandra Martin Arnold.

Each double page is devoted to one of the holidays celebrated in the United States. The English words are on one page, and the Spanish words are on the opposite page. Black and white illustrations portray some of the activities of each day. The holidays start with New Year's Day and end with Christmas. The translator was born in Cuba, but came to the United States as either a twelve-year-old child or a ten-year-old child, depending on whether you read her biographical note in English or Spanish.

REVIEWS: *Booklist*, February 1, 1989, p. 935; *Children's Book Review Service*, December 1988, p. 43; *School Library Journal*, August 1989, p. 158.

**18.** **El alfabeto.** Lincolnwood, Ill.: Passport Books, 1991. ISBN: 0-8442-7564-6. 40 p. Illustrated by Gwen Connelly.

All of the letters of the Spanish alphabet are presented in sentences, often with silly illustrations to help the reader remember them. At the end of the book the translations into English are given, along with some hints on pronouncing Spanish, and a glossary of the Spanish words in the text.

**19.** Alpers, Jody. **T Is for Tortilla: A Southwestern Alphabet Book.** Hurst, Tex.: Fry-Innovations, 1993. 30 p. Illustrated by Celeste Johnson.

An alphabet book from A to Z featuring many Spanish words and other items found in the Southwest. Some examples include adobe, burro, fiesta, hacienda, luminarias, mesa, ollas, piñata, tortilla, uno, vigas, and zia. The text itself is in English.

**20.**   Alvarez, Juan and Kwapil, Marie Jo. **Cinco cuentos escritos en español y inglés = Five Stories Written in Spanish & English.** Dallas: Leslie Press, 1972. 31 p. Illustrated by Anne Marie Kilb.

The stories in this book are intended as supplementary material for children in either English or Spanish. The English version is on green paper, and the Spanish version is on gold paper. Before each story, new words in each language are introduced with small illustrations in black and white.

**21.**   Alvarez Lecuona, Consuelo. **Tan sencillas como tu: canciones infantiles, música y letra = How Sweet You Are: Children's Songs with Music and Words.** San Antonio: Intercultural Development Research Association, 1982. 52 p.

The music for twenty-five songs is included in this book which accompanies an audiocassette. The words are given in both English and Spanish. Six songs have actions to go along with the singing.

REVIEW: *Booklist*, October 1, 1990, p. 348.

**22.**   Ancona, George. **Pablo Remembers: The Fiesta of the Day of the Dead.** New York: Lothrop, Lee & Shepard, 1993. ISBN: 0-688-12894-7. 42 p.

A description of the three days of celebration for their ancestors which the Mexicans hold each year. The first day is October 31—All Hallows Eve. The second day is November 1—All Saints Day, and the third day is November 2—All Souls Day. The preparations, the food, the flowers, and the customs are all given in detail. The author, a photojournalist, uses photographs of one family, a mother, father, and four children in Oaxaca to depict the fiesta. In English with many Spanish words for the items used in the fiesta. A glossary is appended. Pura Belpré honor book 1996 for illustrations.

REVIEWS: *Horn Book*, March 1994, p. 213-214; *Reading Teacher*, November 1994, p. 252; *Reading Teacher*, April 1995, p. 637.

**23.**   Ancona, George. **The Piñata Maker = El piñatero.** San Diego: Harcourt Brace, 1994. ISBN: 0-15-261875-9. unp.

Set in Mexico, this photographic essay tells the story of Don Ricardo, who is the village piñata maker. The text follows the steps needed to make a piñata, and the photographs illustrate the process. Beto and Daniela are the children featured in the story. The story concludes with the breaking of the piñata at Daniela's birthday party.

REVIEWS: *AB Bookman's Weekly*, November 13, 1995, p. 1189; *Book Links*, July 1994, p. 6; *Early Childhood Education Journal*, Fall 1997, p. 45; *Horn Book*, July 1994, p. 469; *Horn Book Guide*, Fall 1994, p. 346; *Kirkus Reviews*, March 1,

1994, p. 297; *New Advocate*, Fall 1994, p. 290; *Reading Teacher*, November 1994, p. 252; *School Library Journal*, April 1994, p. 116; *Social Education*, April 1995, p. 218.

**24.**   Anzaldúa, Gloria. **Friends from the Other Side = Amigos del otro lado.** San Francisco: Children's Book Press, 1993. ISBN: 0-89239-113-8. unp. Pictures by Consuelo Méndez.

Prietita, a Mexican American girl, living on the border in Texas, meets Joaquín, a Mexican who has crossed the river illegally. She befriends him and hides him when the border patrol drives by. There are some problems with the translation, because in one instance the meaning of a phrase in English is different from the meaning of the phrase in Spanish. Both English and Spanish versions seem to be written by the same author.

REVIEWS: *Book Links*, March 1996, p. 25; *Children's Bookwatch*, April 1993, p. 2; *Children's Bookwatch*, April 1998, p. 3; *Instructor*, November 1995, p. 49; *Kirkus Reviews*, May 1, 1993, p. 592; *Learning*, March 1997, p. 54; *School Library Journal*, August 1993, p. 203; *Small Press*, Summer 1993, p. 88.

**25.**   Anzaldúa, Gloria. **Prietita and the Ghost Woman = Prietita y La Llorona.** San Francisco: Children's Book Press, 1995. ISBN: 0-89239-136-7. unp. Pictures by Christina Gonzalez.

The author reinterprets one of the most famous Mexican legends—the story of La Llorona. Prietita is asked by the healer to find rue to mix a remedy for Prietita's mother. As she hunts for the rue, she asks the deer, the salamander, the dove, and the lightning bugs to help her. Finally she sees La Llorona who guides her to the plant and then helps her find the way home. Américas Commended List 1996.

REVIEWS: *Center for Children's Books Bulletin*, April 1996, p. 255; *Children's Bookwatch*, May 1996, p. 4; *Curriculum Review*, May 1996, p. 12; *Horn Book Guide*, Fall 1996, p. 326; *Kirkus Reviews*, March 1, 1996, p. 370; *School Library Journal*, July 1996, p. 82; *Smithsonian*, November 1996, p. 169.

**26.**   Argueta, Jorge. **A Movie in My Pillow: Poems = Una película en mi almohada: Poemas.** San Francisco: Children's Book Press, 2001. ISBN: 0-89239-165-0. 31 p. Illustrations, Elizabeth Gómez.

The poems in this collection are based on the author's life when he first came to the United States from El Salvador. He compares his life in the two countries, and remembers his grandmother's stories. The illustrations are in brilliant colors with many details. The poem about the yo yo goes up and down the page.

**27.**   Argueta, Manlio. **Magic Dogs of the Volcanoes = Los perros mágicos de los volcanes.** San Francisco: Children's Book Press, 1990. ISBN: 0-89239-064-6. 30 p. Pictures by Elly Simmons. English translation by Stacey Ross.

The author, one of El Salvador's foremost writers, has written an original story about the magic dogs called cadejos, folkloric animals that protect people from danger.

REVIEWS: *Bloomsbury Review*, April 1991, p. 8; *Bookwatch*, February 1991, p. 11; *Center for Children's Books Bulletin*, February 1991, p. 135; *Horn Book*, September 1991, p. 629; *Kirkus Reviews*, December 1, 1990, p. 1667; *School Library Journal*, February 1991, p. 66; *Social Studies*, January 1997, p. 29

**28.**   Arnold, Rist. **I Like Birds**. Plattsburgh, N.Y.: Tundra Books,1977. unp.

On each double page the names of the months and the numbers from one to twelve are given on the left side in English, French, Italian, German, and Spanish. On the right side are colorful, whimsical drawings of rain birds, fancy birds, little birds, big birds, etc. with descriptions. These phrases are in English.

**29.**   Atkinson, Mary. **María Teresa.** Chapel Hill, N.C.: Lollipop Power, 1979. 39 p. Pictures by Christina Engla Eber.

This is the story of María Teresa Villaronga, who moves from New Mexico to a new school in a small town in Ohio in which everyone has a hard time pronouncing her name. She finds comfort talking in Spanish to Monteja, her puppet; and when she takes the puppet to "show and tell" at school, the classmates are impressed that she and her puppet can speak Spanish. The Spanish passages included in the story, which is in English, are translated at the end of the book. Sonia Nieto in her *Interracial Books for Children Bulletin* review points out some flaws in the story but concludes: "This book would certainly be a good introduction to the issue of prejudice for children who have never suffered its effects." (p. 21) Pleasant line drawings.

REVIEWS: *Booklist*, September 1, 1981, p. 54; *Interracial Books for Children Bulletin*, 11, no. 3 & 4, 1980, p. 21; *Top of the News*, Summer 1981, p. 342.

**30.**   Avery, Charles E. **Everybody Has Feelings: The Moods of Children = Todos tenemos sentimientos**. Seattle: Open Hand Publishing, 1992. ISBN: 0-940880-34-2. unp. Photographed by Charles E. Avery. Translation, Sandra Marulanda.

In Spanish and English the moods of children are shown in expressive photographs. The children, many of them African American, are happy, sad, lonely, friendly, curious, talkative, playful, excited, proud, hungry, and angry.

REVIEWS: *Publishers Weekly*, March 16, 1992, p. 81; *Reading Teacher*, September 1994, p. 70; *School Library Journal*, August 1992, p. 187; *Small Press*, Summer 1992, p. 62; *Small Press Book Review*, November 1992, p. 19.

**31.**   Baca, Ana. **Benito's Bizcochitos = Los bizcochitos de Benito**. Houston: Arte Público Press, Piñata Books, 1999. ISBN: 1-55885-264-6. unp. Illustrations by Anthony Accardo. Spanish translation by Julia Mercedes Castilla.

Cristina's grandmother tells her the story of the magic butterfly who introduced bizcochitos to her great grandfather in New Mexico. On the day before Christmas, they prepare these Christmas cookies that taste like licorice and are shaped like butterflies. The recipe, in both Spanish and English, is included.

REVIEWS: *Horn Book Guide*, Spring 2000, p. 27; *School Library Journal*, October 1999, p. 102.

**32.**   Ballesteros, Octavio A. **Mexican Proverbs: The Philosophy, Wisdom and Humor of a People.** Burnet, Tex.: Eakin Press, 1979. 66 p. Illustrated by María Del Carmen Ballesteros.

This book contains 367 proverbs that the author collected on both sides of the Rio Grande. Some of them are old and familiar, some are new. They are grouped under five headings: philosophical proverbs, proverbs that advise, humorous proverbs, religious proverbs, and proverbs about animals. The author includes a preface, some suggested ways to use this book, and a list of references. A few black-and-white sketches.

**33.**   Barbe, Walter B. **Reading Adventures in Spanish and English.** Columbus, Ohio: Highlights for Children, 1977. 32 p.

Contains a variety of stories (folktales, biographies, stories of Mexico, and a Christmas story) and activities to foster creative thinking. Magazine format with a variety of illustrations.

**34.**   Barry, Robert. **The Musical Palm Tree: A Story of Puerto Rico.** New York: McGraw-Hill, 1965. 32 p.

In order to earn enough money to buy his mother a mantilla, Pablito serves as a guide for the tourists and sailors from a cruise ship stopping in Puerto Rico. Sensitive illustrations in pink, brown, and green. A list of the Spanish words used in the story precede the text, along with phonetic pronunciations and definitions. The majority of the text is in English.

REVIEWS: *Kirkus Reviews*, July 1, 1965, p. 622; *Library Journal*, September 15, 1965, p. 3776; *New York Herald Tribune Book Week*, September 12, 1965, p. 28; *Young Readers Review*, October 1965, p. 6.

**35.**   Barry, Robert. **Ramón and the Pirate Gull: A Story of Puerto Rico.** New York: McGraw-Hill, 1971. unp.

Ramón finds a red gull along the beach in Ponce, Puerto Rico. When he discovers that it is wanted at the Marine Research Station in San Juan, he and his friends return the gull by taxi. About twenty Spanish words are included in this English story, and their pronunciations are given at the beginning of the book. Pink-and-green illustrations.

REVIEW: *Library Journal*, September 15, 1971, p. 2902.

**36.**   Bass, Ellen. **I Like You to Make Jokes with Me, But I Don't Want You to Touch Me = Me gusta que bromees conmigo, pero no quiero que me toques.**

Durham, N.C.: Lollipop Power/Carolina Wren Press, rev. ed., 1993. ISBN: 0-914996-27-4. 28 p. Illustrated by Margo Lemieux. Translated into Spanish by María A. Salgado.

This book was funded, in part, by the generous support of the Ms. Foundation for Education and Communication. Sara and her mother go to the grocery store, where the little girl becomes frightened of the produce clerk because he is so big, and he comes too close to her. When they get home Sara's mother teaches her how to handle the situation by telling Jack that she likes to make jokes with him, but that she does not want him to touch her. Black and white illustrations.

**37.**   **Bedtime Stories in Spanish** by the editors of *La Luz*. Skokie, Ill.: National Textbook Company, 1969. 163 p. Introduction by Dorothy Sword Bishop. Illustrated by Robert Borja. (Spanish for Young Americans Library)

Twelve familiar stories are included in this anthology: *Little Red Riding Hood, Cinderella, The Pied Piper of Hamelin, The Rooster and the Fox, The Seven Kids, Goldilocks and the Three Bears, The Three Little Pigs, Hansel and Gretel, Jack and the Beanstalk, The Water Sprite and the Woodcutter, The Cat with Boots,* and *The Milkmaid.* The book is designed to provide supplementary reading for beginning Spanish students. The stories are presented first in Spanish (pp. 3-91), with questions to promote conversation at the end of each story. The translations into English (pp. 95-163) appear at the back of the book, also with questions in English to promote conversation. The few black, red, and white illustrations capture the folk- and fairy-tale quality of the stories.

REVIEW: *Cartel*, December 1973, p. 5.

**38.**   Bellber, William; Montañez, Marta; Benitez, Emerito; and Rodriguez, William. **Canciones de mi isla = Songs from My Island.** New York: A.R.T.S., Inc., rev. ed., 1981. 44 p. Illustrated by Armando Soto and Martin Rubio.

The only review listed is a review of the first edition of this book, published in 1975 with a spiral binding. This brief collection includes fourteen Puerto Rican folk and children's songs and five composed adult songs. The notes on the music are in English. The Spanish words for each song are given with the scores. The English translations are at the end of each song. The illustrations are simple sketches. The English title on the verso of the title page is **Songs of My Island.**

REVIEW: *Booklist*, February 1, 1976, p. 793.

**39.**   Benedetto, Armando Sabino de. **Mi libro de valores: una colección de valores patrióticos, sociales, y morales = My Book of Values: A Collection of Patriotic, Social, and Moral Values.** New York: Vantage Press, 1979. 92 p. Illustrated by Richard A. Diez.

A collection of many sayings and proverbs that his Italian parents taught the author when he was a child. The ideas and values have been handed down from generation to generation. The arrangement of the sayings is somewhat confusing. Instead of having the English and Spanish on opposite pages, the Spanish is on one page, and the English is on the next page. The sepia drawings are well done. Includes many of the "golden rules" and the Pledge of Allegiance.

**40.**　Bennett, Archie and Gutiérrez, Marta. **The Beginner's English/Spanish Dictionary = Diccionario español/inglés para principiantes.** New York: Delair Publishing, 1981. 511 p. Illustrated by Nancy Sears.

Over 2,900 words are defined by use of examples in both English and Spanish, and more than 800 words are illustrated in full color. The main part of the dictionary is in English alphabetical order with the English in black typeface and the Spanish in red typeface. There is an index to the Spanish words.

REVIEW: *Lector*, June 1983, p. 16.

**41.**　Berenstain, Stan and Berenstain, Jan. **El bebe de los osos Berenstain = The Berenstain Bears' New Baby.** New York: Random House, 1982. unp. Translated into Spanish by Pilar de Cuenca and Inés Alvarez.

Small Bear has outgrown his little bed just in time to pass it on to a new baby sister. Humorous and colorful illustrations.

REVIEW: *Booklist*, July 1982, p. 1438.

**42.**　**Berlitz Spanish Alphabet and Numbers for Children** by the editorial staff of The Berlitz Schools of America. New York: Grosset & Dunlap, 1963. unp. Illustrations by Art Seiden.

The English alphabet is presented (with the exception of w), then a word beginning with each of the letters is given, then a sentence is given using the word in Spanish (with phonetic pronunciation) and in English. The letters ll and ñ are excluded. The numbers from one to twelve are also presented. Realistic illustrations in color on one double-page spread alternate with black-and-white illustrations on the next double-page spread.

**43.**　Bernier-Grand, Carmen T. **Juan Bobo: Four Folktales from Puerto Rico.** New York: HarperTrophy, 1994. ISBN: 0-06-444185-7. 58 p. Pictures by Ernesto Ramos Nieves. (An I Can Read Book, Level 3.)

The four tales in this collection are: *The Best Way to Carry Water*, *A Pig in Sunday Clothes*, *Do Not Sneeze, Do Not Scratch-Do Not Eat!* and *A Dime a Jug*. The stories are told and illustrated in English. The Spanish versions appear at the end of the book on the last five pages with no illustrations. Américas Commended List 1994.

REVIEWS: *Booklist*, April 1, 1994, p. 1465; *Booklist*, June 1, 1996, p. 1726; *Center for Children's Books Bulletin*, July 1994, p. 350; *Emergency Librarian*, January 1995, p. 18; *Five Owls*, May 1994, p. 104; *Horn Book Guide*, Fall 1994, p. 346; *Kirkus Reviews*, June 15, 1994, p. 840; *Library Talk*, November 1994, p. 39; *Parents' Choice*, Summer 1994, p. 3; *Publishers Weekly*, April 25, 1994, p. 78;

*School Library Journal*, August 1994, p. 149; *School Library Journal*, July 1995, p. 26; *Wilson Library Bulletin*, June 1944, p. 129.

**44.**   Bertrand, Diane Gonzales. **Family = Familia**. Houston: Piñata Books, 1999. ISBN: 1-55885-269-7. unp. Illustrations by Pauline Rodriguez Howard. Spanish translation by Julia Mercedes Castilla.

Daniel reluctantly goes to a family reunion in San Antonio with his parents and two sisters. He meets aunts and uncles and cousins, and discovers that he has a good time eating, listening to music, and playing with Brian, his cousin from Dallas. English and Spanish texts are on the left page with a small illustration separating them. The right pages have full colorful illustrations of activities at the family reunion.

REVIEWS: *Horn Book Guide*, Spring 2000, p. 28; *Journal of Youth Services in Libraries*, Winter 2001, p. 35; *School Library Journal*, September 1999, p. 174.

**45.**   Bertrand, Diane Gonzales. **Sip, Slurp, Soup, Soup = Caldo, caldo, caldo.** Houston: Piñata Books, 1996. ISBN: 1-55885-183-6. unp. Illustrated by Alex Pardo DeLange.

With repetitive phrases the author tells how the children watch Mamá make soup and then go with Papá to get tortillas before they all sit down to eat. The recipe is included.

REVIEWS: *Horn Book Guide*, Spring 1998, p. 117; *Publishers Weekly*, May 12, 1997, p. 75; *School Library Journal*, August 1997, p. 128.

**46.**   Bielawski, Joseph G. **I Didn't Say a Word = No dije una palabra: A Bilingual Picture Book of Nonverbal Communication.** Ridgefield, Conn.: RD Communications, 1976. 95 p. Photographs by Marjorie Pickens. The Spanish translation is by Nilda Rahman.

Photographs of various activities portray language through facial expressions and movements of hands and feet. The text then asks the reader to describe how the person in the picture feels or what the movements mean. Black-and-white photographs are very expressive and thought provoking. The introduction by the author is in English.

**47.**   Bielawski, Joseph G. **Who Are You? = ¿Quién eres tú?: A Bilingual Picture Book.** Bristol, Conn.: JJ Publications, 1977. 61 p. Translation by Brunilda Rahman. Photographs by Marjorie Pickens.

A young teacher tries to find out something about her students, especially two new ones, Rose and Paul. The book concentrates on self-identification and evaluation. The Spanish and English texts alternate on the left page. The photographs of the teacher, the students, and their families are on the right page. The photographs are excellent. The accompanying teacher's manual includes concepts, ideas for vocabulary enrichment, and related activities.

48. Bishop, Dorothy Sword. **Chiquita y Pepita: dos ratoncitas = Chiquita and Pepita: Two Little Mice.** Skokie, Ill.: National Textbook Company, 1972. 33, 33 p. (Fábulas bilingües = Fables in Spanish and English)

A short story about Chiquita, the city mouse, and Pepita, the country mouse. After a visit to the city, Pepita decides she likes the quiet and peace of her poor country home. The amusing illustrations are repeated twice as the story is told first in Spanish and then in English.

REVIEW: *Cartel*, December 1973, p. 43.

49. Bishop, Dorothy Sword. **Leonardo el león y Ramón el ratón = Leonard the Lion and Raymond the Mouse.** Skokie, Ill.: National Textbook Company, 1972. 28, 28 p. (Fábulas bilingües = Fables in Spanish and English)

The mouse saves the lion by gnawing the ropes of the net that he is caught in. With this act, the two become friends for life. The amusing illustrations are repeated twice as the story is told first in Spanish and then in English.

REVIEW: *Cartel*, December 1973, p. 43.

50. Bishop, Dorothy Sword. **Tina la tortuga y Carlos el conejo = Tina the Turtle and Carlos the Rabbit.** Skokie, Ill.: National Textbook Company, 1972. 35, 35 p. (Fábulas bilingües = Fables in Spanish and English)

The familiar story about the famous race between the turtle and the rabbit. The amusing illustrations are repeated twice, as the story is told first in Spanish and then in English.

51. Blanco, Alberto. **Angel's Kite = La estrella de Angel.** Emeryville, Calif.: Children's Book Press, 1994. ISBN: 0-82939-121-9. 32 p. Pictures by Rodolfo Morales. English translation by Dan Bellm.

In a Mexican town, there was a church, but the bell was missing. The people were used to the silence, but Angel, who was a kite maker, missed the bell. One day he makes a huge kite and flies it on a windy day. The wind carries it away, and people follow it very far, until Angel is the only one left still searching. At dawn the kite, which had pictures on it of the town and of the bell, drifts to earth, but the picture of the church bell is missing. Then Angel hears the bell ringing from the church in town, and when he returns a fiesta is being held to celebrate the return of the bell. Américas Commended List 1994.

REVIEWS: *Children's Bookwatch*, May 1994, p. 6; *Children's Bookwatch*, May 1995, p. 7; *Horn Book Guide*, Fall 1994, p. 346; *Kirkus Reviews*, May 15, 1994, p. 696; *School Library Journal*, August 1994, p. 181; *School Library Journal*, July 1995, p. 26.

52. Blanco, Alberto. **The Desert Mermaid = La sirena del desierto**. San Francisco: Children's Book Press, 1992. ISBN: 0-89239-106-5. 32 p. Pictures by Patricia Revah. English translation by Barbara Paschke.

The author, who is a Mexican poet, has written this story in the form of a folktale. A mermaid is stranded in the Sonoran Desert. In order to return to the sea, she must learn some of the old songs. She sets out on a magic horse, Silver Star, to find the melody, the words, the rhythm, and a guitar to play the songs. The illustrations are of tapestry art created by Patricia Revah, the wife of the author.

REVIEWS: *Booklist*, March 1, 1993, p. 1241; *Children's Bookwatch*, July 1992, p. 5; *Christian Science Monitor*, May 1, 1992, p. 10; *Publishers Weekly*, June 22, 1992, p. 61; *School Library Journal*, August 1992, p. 187; *Small Press*, Winter 1993, p. 87.

**53.** Blanco, Tomás. **Los aguinaldos del infante: glosa de epifanía = The Child's Gifts: A Twelfth Night Tale.** San Juan, Puerto Rico: Pan American Book Company, 1954. unp. Translated by Harriet DeOnís. With musical ornaments by Jack Delano and illustrations by Irene Delano.

First edition of a title reprinted by Westminster Press in 1976. Illustrations are tipped-in serigraphs and are much richer than in the reprint.

**54.** Blanco, Tomás. **Los aguinaldos del infante: glosa de epifanía = The Child's Gifts: A Twelfth Night Tale.** Philadelphia: Westminster Press, 1976. 33 p. Translated by Harriet DeOnís. With musical ornaments by Jack Delano and illustrations by Irene Delano. Originally published in 1954 by Pan American Book Company of San Juan.

Describes the journey of the three wise men: Balthasar, the Monarch of the West; Gaspar, the Emperor of the Orient; and Melchior, the King of the South. The people governed by each possess one virtue—faith, hope, or charity—but lack the other two. In their search for peace the three wise men follow the star, taking their treasures to the unknown Lord. On their return home, they discover that each possesses each virtue, to give to all of their people. Illustrations are in perfect harmony with the text. A synopsis of the musical score written for the original radio broadcast of this story in Puerto Rico in 1954 is included.

REVIEWS: *Center for Children's Books Bulletin*, December 1976, p. 53; *Horn Book*, April 1977, p. 190; *Kirkus Reviews*, September 1, 1976, p. 973; *Proyecto Leer Bulletin*, Fall 1980, p. 29; *Publishers Weekly*, October 4, 1976, p. 74; *School Library Journal*, October 1976, p. 87.

**55.** Blue, Rose. **I Am Here = Yo estoy aquí.** New York: Watts, 1971. unp. Pictures by Moneta Barnett.

The story of Luz's first day of kindergarten. Only a few Spanish words are included in the book, but it is a moving story of how a Spanish-speaking teacher makes Luz feel comfortable. Sensitive green-and-black illustrations.

REVIEWS: *Interracial Books for Children*, Spring 1972, p. 8; *Library Journal*, March 15, 1972, p. 1165; *School Library Journal*, January 1981, p. 32.

**56.** Bofill, Francesc. **Jack and the Beanstalk = Juan y los frijoles mágicos.** San Francisco: Chronicle Books, 1998. ISBN: 0-8118-1843-8. unp. Illustrations by Arnal Ballester.

An adaptation of the familiar story of Jack and the magic beanstalk. There are two other titles in this series: **Goldilocks and the Three Bears = Ricitos de oro y los tres osos,** and **Little Red Riding Hood = Caperucita roja.**

REVIEWS: *Booklist*, November 15, 1998, p. 598; *School Library Journal*, August 1998, p. 148.

**57.** Borlenghi, Patricia. **From Albatross to Zoo: An Alphabet Book in Five Languages.** New York: Scholastic, 1992. ISBN: 0-590-45483-8. unp. Pictures by Piers Harper.

Each animal in this ABC book represents one letter of the English alphabet. All of the names of the animals begin with the same letters in German, French, Spanish, and Italian. Each language has its own distinctive lettering so you can always tell which language is which. The words are printed up and down and all around the pictures of the animals. Sometimes this makes it difficult to read the words.

REVIEWS: *Booklist*, October 1, 1992, p. 334; *Childhood Education*, Spring 1993, p. 172; *Children's Book Review Service*, December 1992, p. 38; *Children's Bookwatch*, September 1992, p. 3; *Library Talk*, May 1993, p. 35; *Publishers Weekly*, September 28, 1992, p. 78; *School Library Journal*, September 1992, p. 214.

**58.** Brown, Richard. **Muchas palabras sobre animales = 100 Words about Animals.** San Diego: Harcourt Brace Jovanovich, 1989. ISBN: 0-15-200531-5. 32 p. Illustrated by Richard Brown.

Pets at home, animals on the farm, in the sea and on the shore, in the mountains, in ice and snow, in the jungle, on the grasslands, and in the past are presented in large, bright illustrations. The names in Spanish are in large type, and the English words are given in smaller type.

REVIEW: *Horn Book*, July 1989, p. 521.

**59.** Brown, Richard. **Muchas palabras sobre mi casa = 100 Words about My House.** San Diego: Harcourt Brace Jovanovich, 1989. ISBN: 0-15-200532-3. 32 p. Illustrated by Richard Brown.

Illustrations in bright colors show items found around the house, from the front of the house, through all of the rooms, to the backyard. Words in Spanish are in large type. The English words are given below in smaller type.

REVIEW: *Horn Book*, July 1989, p. 521.

**60.** Brown, Ruth. **Alphabet Times Four: An International ABC: English, Spanish, French, German.** New York: Dutton Children's Books, 1991. ISBN: 0-525-44831-4. unp.

An ABC book with a word for every letter of the alphabet in four languages: English, Spanish, French, German. Many of the words illustrated have common roots, showing the similarities among the four languages. The following words are identical in all four languages: hamster, jaguar, kiwi (a Maori word), and yeti (a Tibetan word). Two Spanish letters have not been illustrated: ll and ñ.

REVIEWS: *Center for Children's Books Bulletin*, November 1991, p. 57; *Kirkus Reviews*, September 15, 1991, p. 1230; *School Library Journal*, October 1991, p. 107.

61.   Brunhoff, Laurent de. **Babar's Spanish Lessons = Las lecciones españoles de Babar.** New York: Random House, 1965. unp. Spanish words by Roberto Eyzaguirre.

Babar gives children fourteen brief Spanish lessons. The Spanish words are printed in red, and the English translations of those words are in bold-faced type. This is not completely bilingual, as the story is in English with only selected words and phrases translated into Spanish, for example: "I wear a nice tie—una bonita corbata—with a pink shirt, una camisa rosada." The colorful illustrations are the familiar ones by Brunhoff.

REVIEW: *Library Journal*, December 15, 1965, p. 5498.

62.   Brusca, María Cristina and Wilson, Tona. **Three Friends: A Counting Book = Tres amigos: un cuento para contar.** New York: Holt, 1995. ISBN: 0-8050-3707-1. unp. Illustrated by María Cristina Brusca.

Count your way from one to ten and back again with words and illustrations of the Southwest. Includes such words as armadillos, roadrunners, and tumbleweeds.

REVIEWS: *Booklist*, November 15, 1995, p. 561; *Horn Book Guide*, Spring 1996, p. 98; *Journal of Youth Services in Libraries*, Winter 2001, p. 35; *School Library Journal*, December 1995, p. 95.

63.   Buchanan, Ken. **This House Is Made of Mud = Esta casa está hecha de lodo.** Flagstaff, Ariz.: Northland Publishing, 1994. ISBN: 0-87358-580-1. unp. Illustrated by Libba Tracy. Translated by Patricia Hinton Davison.

This is a gentle story of a house made of mud. It is also a house made of love, for the people in it share their home with the plants and creatures of the desert.

REVIEWS: *Bloomsbury Review*, October 1991, p. 22; *Booklist*, September 15, 1991, p. 172; *Children's Bookwatch*, September 1991, p. 6; *Instructor*, September 1993, p. 61; *Publishers Weekly*, June 7, 1991, p. 64.

64.   Burningham, John. **La alacena = The Cupboard.** Mexico City: Editorial Patria, 1984. ISBN: 968-39-0050-X. unp. (Colección pre-escolar bilingüe)

A little boy plays with pots and pans from the kitchen cupboard, then must put them all back. Simple pastel illustrations appear in all of the books in this series.

REVIEW: *Hispania*, September 1986, p. 702.

65.   Burningham, John. **El amigo = The Friend.** Mexico City: Editorial Patria, 1984. ISBN: 968-39-0049-6. unp. (Colección pre-escolar bilingüe)

A curious little boy tells about his friend Arthur.

REVIEWS: *Hispania*, September 1986, p. 702; *School Library Journal*, February 1989, p. 108.

**66.** Burningham, John. **El bebé = The Baby**. Mexico City: Editorial Patria, 1984. ISBN: 968-39-0051-8. unp. (Colección pre-escolar bilingüe)

There is a new baby in the house. Sometimes the little boy likes the baby, at other times he does not.

REVIEW: *Hispania*, September 1986, p. 702.

**67.** Burningham, John. **La cobija = The Blanket**. Mexico City: Editorial Patria, 1984. ISBN: 968-39-0048-8. unp. (Colección pre-escolar bilingüe)

A little boy, before going to bed, can't find his blanket. He and mother and father look all over for it, then the little boy finds it under his pillow.

REVIEWS: *Hispania*, September 1986, p. 702; *School Library Journal*, February 1989, p. 108.

**68.** Burningham, John. **El conejo = The Rabbit**. Mexico City: Editorial Patria, 1984. ISBN: 968-39-0046-1. unp. (Colección pre-escolar bilingüe)

The little boy has a rabbit who sometimes gets away from him. The boy searches for and finds the rabbit and puts it back in the hutch. British spelling is used.

REVIEW: *Hispania*, September 1986, p. 702.

**69.** Burningham, John. **La escuela = The School**. Mexico City: Editorial Patria, 1984. ISBN: 968-39-0047-X. unp. (Colección pre-escolar bilingüe)

Describes a little boy's day in school.

REVIEWS: *Hispania*, September 1986, p. 702; *School Library Journal*, February 1989, p. 108.

**70.** Burningham, John. **El perro = The Dog**. Mexico City: Editorial Patria, 1984. ISBN: 968-39-0045-3. unp. (Colección pre-escolar bilingüe)

A little boy takes care of the neighbor's dog, but the dog gets into all sorts of trouble. British spelling is used.

REVIEW: *Hispania*, September 1986, p. 702.

**71.** Burstein, Fred. **The Dancer = La bailarina**. New York: Bradbury Press, 1993. ISBN: 0-02-715625-7. unp. Illustrated by Joan Auclair.

Father takes his little girl to ballet class, and as they walk through the city they see a horse, flowers, a boat, and fish. When they arrive at school, father leaves, and the ballet class begins. Twenty-two words are given in English, Spanish, and Japanese. Translations are spelled phonetically.

REVIEWS: *Book Links*, July 1994, p. 6; *Booklist*, March 15, 1993, p. 1354; *Children's Book Review Service*, Spring 1993, p. 133; *Library Talk*, May 1993, p. 36; *Publishers Weekly*, February 8, 1993, p. 84; *School Library Journal*, June 1993, p. 96.

72.   **Caballos y ponies: un libro informativo sobre los animales = Horses & Ponies: An Animal Information Book**. Baltimore: Ottenheimer, 1994. ISBN: 0-8241-0022-0, 0023-9, and 0024-7. unp.

Brief factual information about horses and ponies is accompanied by color photographs. There are two other titles in this series: **Gatos y gatitos = Kittens & Cats** and **Perros y perritos = Puppies & Dogs.**

73.   Campbell, Celina Andrade. **Zenaida: A Bilingual Story.** Boulder, Colo.: All of Us, Inc., 1974. 18 p. Illustrated by Cheri Lynn Jefferson.

Zenaida goes on a picnic to a secret island with Loli and Sara and cuts her foot on a piece of glass. When she arrives home her daddy bandages her foot, and her two brothers wait on her, for a change. Hand lettered on orange paper with simple black illustrations.

74.   Canepari, Nelly. **Mochito: The History of an Ordinary Dog = Mochito: historia de un perrito ordinario.** Detroit: Blaine Ethridge Books, 1975. unp. Photographs, Jorge Schneider. Translation, Edith Rusconi Kaltovich. (A Prism Press Book)

Rejected by visitors because of his white paws, an ordinary puppy runs away from his mother to find a home with a little boy who accepts him and calls him Mochito. This story was originally published in Spanish in Argentina. Black-and-white photographs are appealing.

REVIEWS: *Booklist*, May 15, 1976, p. 1343; *Cartel*, June 1976, p. 177; *Proyecto Leer Bulletin*, Spring 1976, p. 12; *School Library Journal*, May 1976, p. 48.

75.   Carlson, Lori M. **Cool Salsa: Bilingual Poems on Growing Up Latino in the United States**. New York: Holt, 1994. ISBN: 0-8050-3135-9. 123 p. Introduction by Oscar Hijuelos.

Growing up Latino in America means speaking two languages and learning about two cultures. The poets represented in this collection came to the continental United States from Cuba, Mexico, Nicaragua, Puerto Rico, Argentina, Guatemala, El Salvador, Bolivia, Venezuela, and Colombia. Others were born in the United States. Poems selected are about the experiences of teenagers, and they are presented in their original language and in translation. Américas Commended List 1994.

REVIEWS: *Book Links*, March 1996, p. 29; *Book Report*, November 1994, p. 49; *Booklist*, November 1, 1994, p. 489; *Booklist*, April 1, 1995, p. 1399; *Booklist*, April 1, 1995, p. 1412; *Center for Children's Books Bulletin*, September 1994, p. 8; *Childhood Education*, Winter 1994, p. 111; *Horn Book*, November 1994, p. 741; *Horn Book*, May 1995, p. 316; *Horn Book Guide*, Spring 1995, p. 143; *Hungry Mind Review*, Summer 1995, p. 49; *Journal of Reading*, February 1995, p. 409; *Kirkus Reviews*, July 15, 1994, p. 979; *Publishers Weekly*, June 13, 1994, p. 64; *Reading Teacher*, April 1995, p. 606; *School Library Journal*, August 1994, p. 171; *School Library Journal*, December 1994, p. 22; *School Library Journal*, April 1995, p. 44;

*School Library Journal*, July 1995, p. 26; *Social Education*, April 1995, p. 221; *Voice of Youth Advocates*, February 1995, p. 355.

76.   Carlson, Lori Marie. **Sol a sol: Bilingual Poems**, written and selected by Lori Marie Carlson. New York: Holt, 1998. ISBN: 0-8050-4373-X. unp. Translated by Lyda Aponte de Zacklin and Lori Marie Carlson. Illustrated by Emily Lisker.

A collection of poems in celebration of family life from the first one about *Mama=Mami* to the last one about *Stars=Estrellas*. Bold primary colors are used for the illustrations.

REVIEWS: *Booklist*, April 1, 1998, p. 1328; *Booklist*, January 1, 2000, p. 929; *Center for Children's Books Bulletin*, May 1998, p. 316; *Horn Book*, May 1998, p. 351; *Horn Book Guide*, Fall 1998, p. 369; *Publishers Weekly*, March 23, 1998, p. 98; *School Library Journal*, March 1998, p. 194; *Social Education*, May 1999, p. 11.

77.   Carlson, Lori Marie. **You're On! Seven Plays in English and Spanish.** New York: Morrow Junior Books, 1999. ISBN: 0-688-16237-1. 139 p.

The plays included in this collection are from Spain, Latin America, and the United States. Seven plays, each one in both English and Spanish, are presented: *These Shoes of Mine = Estos zapatos míos* by Gary Soto; *Tropical Memories = Remembranzas tropicales* by Pura Belpré; *Jump In = Ven a saltar* by Denise Ruiz; *The Girl Who Waters Basil and the Very Inquisitive Prince = La niña que riega la albahaca y el príncipe preguntón* by Federico García Lorca; *Luck = La buena suerte* by Elena Castedo; *A Dream in the Road = Un sueño en el camino* by Alfonsina Storni; and *Christmas Fantasy = Fantasía de Navidad* by Oscar Hijuelos. Notes on the playwrights are appended.

REVIEWS: *Booklist*, October 1, 1999, p. 353; *Booklist*, January 1, 2000, p. 928; *Center for Children's Books Bulletin*, September 1999, p. 8; *Horn Book Guide*, Spring 2000, p. 148; *Publishers Weekly*, July 19, 1999, p. 197; *School Library Journal*, October 1999, p. 165.

78.   Chang, Monica. **The Mouse Bride: A Chinese Folktale = La novia ratón: cuento popular chino.** Taipei, Taiwan: Yuan-Liou Publishing, 1994. Distributed by Pan Asian Publications, Union City, Calif. ISBN: 957-32-2150-0. unp. Illustrated by Lesley Liu. Spanish translation by Beatriz Zeller.

The head mouse wants to marry off his daughter to the strongest husband in the world to protect her from the cat. He asks the Sun, then the Cloud, then the Wind to marry his daughter; then he asks the Wall. The Wall fears only the mouse Ah-Lang. So the daughter is married to Ah-Lang, and there is a great feast.

REVIEW: *Reading Teacher*, February 1998, p. 424.

79.   Chang, Monica. **Story of the Chinese Zodiac = El zodíaco chino.** Taipei, Taiwan: Yuan-Liou Publishing, 1994. Distributed by Pan Asian Publications,

Union City Calif. ISBN: 957-32-2143-8. unp. Illustrated by Arthur Lee. Spanish translation by Beatriz Zeller.

In order to keep track of the years, the Chinese Zodiac system was developed using twelve animals as the twelve signs. The twelve animals were chosen based on a race. The rat outwits the cat to win the race.

**80.**   Chavarría-Cháirez, Becky. **Magda's Tortillas = Las tortillas de Magda**. New York: Piñata Books, 2000. ISBN: 1-55885-286-7. unp. Illustrations by Anne Vega. Spanish translation by Julia Mercedes Castilla.

Magda is seven years old, and her grandmother is going to teach her how to make tortillas. Magda wants to make them perfectly round, but instead she makes a heart, a football, a star, and many other shapes. She is ashamed of them, but her family loves them; and the tortillas are quickly eaten. The Spanish and English texts are on the left pages, with a small illustration of each fanciful tortilla separating them. The right pages contain full-page illustrations showing the tortilla-making activities. The illustration of Magda with flour all over her face is delightful.

REVIEW: *Newsletter of the United States Board on Books for Young People*, Spring 2001, p. [13].

**81.**   Chermayeff, Ivan and Chermayeff, Jane Clark. **First Words = Premiers mots = Primeras palabras = Erste Worte = Prime parole**. New York: Abrams, 1990. ISBN: 0-8109-3300-4. 27 p.

Thirteen words are given in English, French, Spanish, German, and Italian. They are illustrated with reproductions of famous art and paintings from five museums in Paris. Sometimes only a section of the painting is reproduced, such as Mona Lisa's eyes. The art is identified, and museum locations are given in an appendix.

REVIEWS: *Booklist*, October 1, 1990, p. 348; *Business Week*, September 16, 1991, p. 124; *Horn Book*, September 1990, p. 617; *Kirkus Reviews*, May 1, 1990, p. 646; *Reading Teacher*, March 1993, p. 511; *School Library Journal*, July 1990, p. 68.

**82.**   Cisneros, Sandra. **Hairs = Pelitos**. New York: Knopf, 1994. ISBN: 0-679-86171-8. unp. Illustrated by Terry Ybáñez. Translated by Liliana Valenzuela.

A vignette from the author's **The House on Mango Street**. It describes her family members and all the different types of hair they have. She especially likes Mama's hair that is so soft and sweet to smell. Each member of the family is illustrated in a different color, from purple to blue to green.

REVIEWS: *Belles Lettres*, Spring 1995, p. 62; *Booklist*, September 15, 1994, p. 143; *Center for Children's Books Bulletin*, November 1994, p. 83; *Children's Book Review Service*, January 1995, p. 49; *Day Care & Early Education*, Summer 1995, p. 42; *Horn Book*, November 1994, p. 716; *Horn Book Guide*, Spring 1995, p. 113; *Instructor*, November 1995, p. 49; *Kirkus Reviews*, October 15, 1994, p. 1406;

*Language Arts*, March 1996, p. 207; *Publishers Weekly*, October 31, 1994, p. 61; *School Library Journal*, August 1994, p. 181.

83.    Clark, Ann. **Little Boy with Three Names: Stories of Taos Pueblo = El muchachito con tres nombres.** [Washington]: U.S. Indian Service, [1950?]. 76 p. Spanish translation by Christina [sic] M. Jenkins. Illustrations by Tonita Lujan.

A gentle, well-told story of a young Taos Indian boy who returns home from boarding school for the summer, leaving his school name, Little Joe, behind and becoming again Tso'u. His third name, his church name, is José La Cruz. The author writes sympathetically of the summer activities, of a trip to Blue Lake, and of the long trip to Gallup for the ceremonial dances. Black-and-tan sketches are a perfect complement to the story.

REVIEW: *Elementary English*, May 1972, p. 658.

84.    Clark, Ann. **Sun Journey: A Story of Zuni Pueblo = La jornada del sol.** [Washington]: United States Indian Service, [194–?]. 122 p. Spanish version by Cristina M. Jenkins. Illustrated by Percy Tsisete Sandy.

Ze-do, a Zuni Indian boy, has a year off from the Government School to learn the ways of his people. From one winter solstice to the next, Grandfather Hotima, the Sun Priest, teaches him the Zuni ways. At the end of the year, he returns to school. Twenty-one stories by a master storyteller tell of planting, games, races, and harvest. The tan-and-black illustrations by a Zuni artist capture the moods of the stories. The half title page gives the author's name as Ann Nolan Clark.

REVIEW: *Elementary English*, May 1972, p. 658.

85.    Clark, Ann. **Young Hunter of Picuris = El cazadorcito de Picuris.** [Washington]: Bureau of Indian Affairs, Branch of Education, [1943?]. 56 p. Illustrated by Velino Herrera (Ma-Pi-Wi). Spanish version by Cristina M. Jenkins.

Young Hunter, in his sixth winter in Picuris, wants to go deer hunting with his father, but is told he is too young. His grandfather then takes him turkey hunting, but the boy misses his shot. When his father returns with the deer, Young Hunter realizes that hunting is a serious business, and he agrees that it is better for him to wait a few more years before hunting the deer. The black-and-white sketches are by a Pueblo Indian artist. This is the first Spanish/English reader in this excellent pioneering series, a series that deserves to be reprinted today.

REVIEW: *Elementary English*, May 1972, p. 658.

86.    Codye, Corinn. **Queen Isabella I**. Milwaukee: Raintree Publishers, 1990. ISBN: 0-8172-3380-6. 32 p. Illustrated by Rick Whipple.

A short biography of Isabella of Castile, born in 1451, who became Queen of Spain, by defeating the Portuguese, marrying Ferdinand of Aragon, and driving the Moors and the Jews out of the country. Her greatest achievement was to sponsor Christopher Columbus's trip to the New World. The English and Spanish are in alternate paragraphs. Illustrations are large and realistic. Other biographies in this series include those about Bernardo de Galvez, Pedro Menendez de Aviles, and Hernando de Soto.

REVIEWS: *Booklist*, February 1, 1990, p. 1086; *School Library Journal*, August 1990, p. 173.

**87.** Codye, Corinn. **Vilma Martinez**. Milwaukee: Raintree Publishers, 1990. ISBN: 0-8172-3382-2. 32 p. Illustrated by Susi Kilgore.

Vilma Martinez was born in 1943, her mother was from Texas and her father was from Mexico. She suffered discrimination as a young student because of her background; but she persisted until she finished college at the University of Texas. She earned her law degree in 1967 from Columbia Law School and became involved in civil rights legal work for Mexican Americans. Other biographies in this series include those about Luis W. Alvarez, scientist; and Carlos Finlay, physician.

REVIEWS: *Book Report*, January 1995, p. 29; *Booklist*, February 1, 1990, p. 1086; *Library Talk*, November 1990, p. 43; *School Library Journal*, August 1990, p. 173; *Social Education*, September 1991, p. 332.

**88.** Colón-Vilá, Lillian. **Salsa**. Houston, Piñata Books, 1998. ISBN: 1-55885-220-4. unp. Illustrated by Roberta Collier-Morales.

In New York City Rita dreams of being a salsa orchestra director. She is following in her family's footsteps, as they have been playing and dancing salsa music for generations. Musical notes separate the English and Spanish on each page. Each page also has a border of various designs.

REVIEWS: *Children's Book Review Service*, July 1998, p. 152; *Horn Book Guide*, Fall 1998, p. 370; *Publishers Weekly*, July 20, 1998, p. 222.

**89.** Colyer, Penrose. **I Can Read Spanish: My First English-Spanish Word Book**. New York: Watts, 1976. 116 p. Spanish by María Dolores García Moliner. Illustrated by Colin Mier and Wendy Lewis.

After an introduction in English on "Reading Spanish" and "Talking Spanish," a variety of words and phrases are presented through the eyes of Miguel and his friends. Phrases are given in English and in Spanish with simple pictures.

REVIEWS: *Booklist*, November 1, 1976, p. 406; *Junior Bookshelf*, August 1977, p. 216; *Publishers Weekly*, August 16, 1976, p. 123; *School Library Journal*, October 1976, p. 96.

**90.** Cooper, Lee. **Fun with Spanish**. Boston: Little, Brown, 1960. 118 p. Illustrated by Ann Atene.

The stories in this book introduce Spanish pronunciation and grammar in simple steps, making it easy for children to learn and understand Spanish. Over five hundred Spanish words are introduced. It is not a strictly bilingual book, but it is a well-done introduction to the Spanish language. Black-and-red illustrations. A glossary of terms is included.

REVIEWS: *Booklist*, May 1, 1960, p. 547; *Christian Science Monitor*, May 12, 1960, p. 1B; *Horn Book*, June 1960, p. 230; *Kirkus Reviews*, February 1, 1960, p. 91; *Library Journal*, March 15, 1960, p. 1301; *New York Herald Tribune Book Review*, March 27, 1960, p. 10; *New York Times Book Review*, July 17, 1960, p. 24; *San Francisco Chronicle*, May 8, 1960, p. 38; *Saturday Review*, May 7, 1960, p. 45; *Wisconsin Library Bulletin*, November 1960, p. 352.

**91.**   Corey, Dorothy. **No Company Was Coming to Samuel's House = No llegaban invitados a la casa de Samuel.** Detroit: Blaine Ethridge Books, 1976. unp. Translated by Marguerite Arguedas Baker. Illustrated by Donald Baker. (A Prism Press Book)

Samuel is unhappy because no company is coming for Thanksgiving day, and there will be no special dinner. When the day arrives, however, his cat Gatita has three kittens, making the day special anyway. Black-and-white drawings.

REVIEW: *School Library Journal*, April 1977, p. 53.

**92.**   Corpi, Lucha. **Where Fireflies Dance = Ahi, donde bailan las luciérnagas.** San Francisco: Children's Book Press, 1997. ISBN: 0-89239-145-6. unp. Pictures by Mira Reisberg.

Lucha and Victor visit a haunted house where Juan Sebastián, a revolutionary with General Zapata, used to live. But they only see fireflies dancing in the moonlight. They follow the sound of music to a bar where a jukebox is playing, and they save their coins to play it. Grandmother, who knew Juan Sebastián, tells them many stories; and their father sings them many songs. After the children have grown up, Lucha leaves Jáltipan, Vera Cruz, to go to the United States to seek her destiny as Juan Sebastián sought his; but Victor stays. The story is based on the author's memories. The illustrations are bold and dramatic, and each picture is set in a frame.

REVIEWS: *Booklist*, January 1, 1998, p. 822; *Center for Children's Books Bulletin*, October 1997, p. 47; *Children's Bookwatch*, October 1997, p. 6; *Horn Book Guide*, Spring 1998, p. 117; *Kirkus Reviews*, July 15, 1997, p. 1109; *School Library Journal*, December 1997, p. 87.

**93.**   Covault, Ruth M. **Pablo and Pimienta = Pablo y Pimienta**. Flagstaff, Ariz.: Northland Publishing, 1994. ISBN: 0-87358-588-7. unp. Illustrated by Francisco Mora. Translated by Patricia Hinton Davison.

Pablo, his uncle and his father are traveling from Mexico to the melon fields near Phoenix, Arizona. Suddenly the truck hits a big bump, and Pablo falls off the back end where he is sleeping. A coyote puppy adopts him, and he finally makes his way across the border and is reunited with his father.

REVIEWS: *Bloomsbury Review*, March 1995, p. 27; *Booklist*, January 1, 1995,

p. 824; *Early Childhood Education Journal*, Fall 1997, p. 46; *Horn Book Guide*, Spring 1995, p. 113.

**94.**   Crump, Fred. **Missy and the Duke = Missy y el duque.** Detroit: Blaine Ethridge Books, 1977. 67 p. Translated by Horst Woyde.

Missy and her two kittens are abandoned on the beach by their owner. After several seaside adventures, they are rescued by Duke and taken home to lunch, and perhaps to stay. Several mistakes in the Spanish version. Black-and-white sketches are well done.

REVIEWS: *Cartel*, November 1978, p. 28; *Horn Book*, December 1977, p. 686.

**95.**   Cruz, Manuel and Cruz, Ruth. **A Chicano Christmas Story = Un cuento navideño chicano.** South Pasadena, Calif.: Bilingual Educational Services, 1980. 48 p. Art by Manuel Cruz.

The father of a Chicano family first loses his job at a ranch and then his job at the shoe store in the city. The family has a happy Christmas because everyone helps each other. Sympathetic illustrations.

REVIEWS: *Booklist*, April 1, 1982, p. 1015; *School Library Journal*, October 1981, p. 156.

**96.**   Cruz Martinez, Alejandro. **The Woman Who Outshone the Sun: The Legend of Lucía Zenteno = La mujer que brillaba aún más que el sol: la leyenda de Lucía Zenteno.** San Francisco: Children's Book Press, 1991. ISBN: 0-89239-101-4. 30 p. From a poem by Alejandro Cruz Martínez. Story by Rosalma Zubizarreta, Harriet Rohmer, David Schecter. Pictures by Fernando Olivera.

Lucía Zenteno arrived one day at a small village in Mexico, but she was different from the villagers. The villagers were afraid of her powers and drove her from town. She took the river, the fish, and other animals with her. Then the country suffered a drought. The villagers searched for and found her to ask her forgiveness. She remained in the village to guard and protect them.

REVIEWS: *Book Links*, March 1996, p. 28–29; *Booklist*, March 15, 1992, p. 1373; *Center for Children's Books Bulletin*, February 1992, p. 151; *Children's Bookwatch*, April 1993, p. 3; *Five Owls*, January 1993, p. 53; *Kirkus Reviews*, December 1, 1991, p. 1531; *Language Arts*, March 1993, p. 222; *Library Talk*, November 1992, p. 33; *MultiCultural Review*, October 1992, p. 78; *Publishers Weekly*, January 6, 1992, p. 65; *School Library Journal*, March 1992, p. 226; *Social Studies*, January 1997, p. 29; *Wilson Library Bulletin*, June 1992, p. 119.

**97.**   Dana, Doris. **The Elephant and His Secret: Based on a Fable by Gabriela Mistral in Spanish and English = El elefante y su secreto: basado en una fábula de Gabriela Mistral en español e inglés.** New York: Atheneum, 1974. unp. Illustrated by Antonio Frasconi. (A Margaret K. McElderry Book)

A fable of the elephant, how he got his size and shape and weight, and the secret he learned from the mountain. Large, bold illustrations on double pages separate from the text are in purple, red, and black.

REVIEWS: *America*, December 7, 1974, p. 371; *Booklist*, April 15, 1974, p. 938; *Booklist*, March 15, 1975, p. 765; *Booklist*, May 15, 1976, p. 1342; *Cartel*, December 1974, p. 59; *Center for Children's Books Bulletin*, November 1974, p. 41; *Horn Book*, August 1974, p. 371; *Kirkus Reviews*, April 15, 1974, p. 418; *New York Times Book Review*, May 5, 1974, p. 47; *Parents Magazine*, August 1974, p. 57; *Proyecto Leer Bulletin*, Spring 1976, p. 11; *Publishers Weekly*, March 18, 1974, p. 52; *School Library Journal*, March 1975, p. 88.

98. Daroqui, Julia and Oliden, Agustina. **Mi primer diccionario = My First Dictionary**. Buenos Aires: Editorial Sigmar, 1989. ISBN: 950-11-0757-4. 60 p. Illustrated by Luis Retta.

The 630 nouns in this dictionary were carefully selected to introduce young children to both Spanish and English. After each noun is listed and illustrated, sentences in both languages are given. The flags of the Americas are pictured on the last page.

REVIEW: *Booklist*, February 1, 1991, p. 1135.

99. Dawson, E. Yale. **A Brief Natural History of the Galapagos Islands for Young People = Historia natural de las Islas Galápagos, breve relato para jóvenes**. Washington: General Secretariat of the Organization of American States and Smithsonian Institution, 1971. 55 p. Translation by Eva V. Chesneau. Cover and book design by C. A. Toledo.

This book was written for the young people of the Galapagos Islands. They are asked by the author to take care of all the wonderful wild things on their islands. In the first part of the book there is a brief history of the Islands; in the second part animals and birds are pictured and described in detail. Illustrated by photographs, drawings, and maps.

REVIEW: *Cartel*, June 1976, p. 36.

100. DeCesare, Ruth. **Latin-American Game Songs.** New York: Mills Music, 1949. 17 p. Edited, compiled and arranged by Ruth DeCesare.

Sixteen game songs from the Americas (Mexico, Honduras, Chile, Trinidad, Martinique, New Mexico, Dominican Republic, Jamaica, Spain, Puerto Rico, Brazil, Haiti, and the Eastern Caribbean) are presented, one to a page, with music and English words. The stanzas in Spanish are given at the top of each page, while the directions for the games are in English at the bottom of each page. Black-and-white sketches are included with each song.

101. De Gerez, Toni. **Mi canción es un pedazo de jade: poemas del México antiguo en inglés y español = My Song Is a Piece of Jade: Poems of Ancient Mexico in English and Spanish**. Boston: Little Brown, 1984. ISBN: 0-316-81088-6. 45 p. Illustrated by William Stark.

A collection of Nahuatl poetry from the Toltec people who once lived in the high central plain of Mexico, north of Mexico City. The poems are in English and Spanish and are lavishly illustrated.

REVIEWS: *Booklist*, October 1, 1990, p. 348; *Children's Book Review Service*, September 1984, p. 5; *Journal of Reading*, December 1985, p. 245; *Reading Teacher*, October 1986, p. 306; *Scientific American*, December 1984, p. 38; *Times Educational Supplement*, September 6, 1985, p. 27.

**102.**   DeHoogh, Eugenia. **La lechera y su cubeta = The Milkmaid and Her Pail.** Skokie, Ill.: National Textbook Company, 1977. 29 p. (Fábulas bilingües = Fables in Spanish and English)

A fable about a milkmaid who dreams of selling her milk to become rich and buy a fancy blue dress. While daydreaming, she spills her pail of milk, and her plan is ruined. The amusing illustrations are repeated twice, as the story is told first in Spanish and then in English.

**103.**   DeHoogh, Eugenia. **El muchacho que gritó ¡el lobo! = The Boy Who Cried Wolf.** Skokie, Ill.: National Textbook Company, 1977. 29 p. (Fábulas bilingües = Fables in Spanish and English)

The familiar tale of the boy who cried wolf as a practical joke, and then when he really needs help, no one answers his call. In this retelling Pablo is a shepherd, and the wolf eats his sheep. The amusing illustrations are repeated twice as the story is told first in Spanish and then in English.

**104.**   DeHoogh, Eugenia. **Poniendo la campana al gato—Belling the Cat.** Skokie, Ill.: National Textbook Company, 1977. 30, 30 p. (Fábulas bilingües = Fables in Spanish and English)

The mouse family holds a meeting to try to solve the problem of the cat that wants to eat them. The best solution seems to be to tie a bell around the neck of the cat. It is a good idea, but no one wants to do it. The amusing illustrations are repeated twice, as the story is told first in Spanish and then in English.

**105.**   Delacre, Lulu. **Arroz con leche: Popular Songs and Rhymes from Latin America.** New York: Scholastic, 1989. ISBN: 0-590-41887-4. 32 p. Selected and illustrated by the author. English lyrics by Elena Paz. Musical arrangements by Ana-María Rosado.

A collection of traditional songs and rhymes, some from Puerto Rico, some from Mexico, and some from Argentina. Musical arrangements are included for most of the songs. Spanish and English words are given.

REVIEWS: *Booklist*, April 1, 1989, p. 1378; *Bookwatch*, August 1989, p. 2; *Center for Children's Books Bulletin*, February 1989, p. 146; *Childhood Education*, Winter 1989, p. 122; *Children's Book Review Service*, April 1989, p. 94; *Five Owls*, November 1995, p. 28; *Horn Book*, July 1989, p. 520; *Instructor*, February 1991, p. 44; *Kirkus Reviews*, April 1, 1989, p. 544; *Language Arts*, September 1989, p. 564; *Music Educators Journal*, May 1992, p. 40; *Publishers Weekly*, January 13, 1989, p. 89; *Reading Teacher*, April 1990, p. 588; *School Library Journal*, March 1989, p. 173; *Social Studies*, January 1992, p. 39.

**106.** Delacre, Lulu. **Las Navidades: Popular Christmas Songs from Latin America**. New York: Scholastic, 1990. ISBN: 0-590-43548-5. 32 p. Selected and illustrated by the author. English lyrics by Elena Paz. Musical arrangements by Ana-María Rosado.

Thirteen Christmas songs from Puerto Rico, Santo Domingo, and Mexico are included in this collection with musical arrangements and the words in both Spanish and English. Often accompanying each song is a description of the Christmas customs surrounding the song.

REVIEWS: *Booklist*, November 15, 1990, p. 662; *Children's Book Review Service*, December 1990, p. 42; *Five Owls*, November 1990, p. 39; *Kirkus Reviews*, October 15, 1990, p. 1462; *Library Talk*, November 1990, p. 19; *Music Educators Journal*, May 1992, p. 40; *New Advocate*, Winter 1991, p. 57; *New York Times Book Review*, December 16, 1990, p. 27; *Reading Teacher*, April 1991, p. 586; *School Library Journal*, October 1990, p. 35; *Wilson Library Bulletin*, June 1992, p. 118.

**107.** Delacre, Lulu. **Vejigante = Masquerader**. New York: Scholastic, 1993. ISBN: 0-590-45777-2. unp.

A touching story about Ramón, a little boy in Ponce, Puerto Rico who wants to be one of the masqueraders during February, the month of carnival. Text is in both Spanish and English. Also included are brief descriptions of masquerades in Spain, Venezuela, and Mexico; information on how to make a mask; chants sung during the parades; and a glossary. Américas Award for 1993.

REVIEWS: *Book Links*, July 1994, p. 6; *Booklist*, May 15, 1993, p. 1359; *Children's Book Review Service*, April 1993, p. 99; *Horn Book*, January 1994, p. 105–106; *Language Arts*, October 1994, p. 463; *Publishers Weekly*, January 11, 1993, p. 63; *Reading Teacher*, November 1994, p. 251; *School Library Journal*, February 1993, p. 71.

**108.** Delgadillo, Teresa. **Sé quién soy.** Glenview, Ill.: Scott, Foresman, 1972. 39 p. Teacher's guidebook.

David, alternating between English and Spanish, tells the story of his neighborhood, his family, and the wedding of his aunt. Relatives come from many parts of the United States, and his great-grandmother comes from Mexico. Later in the summer the family goes to Texas to visit Uncle Manuel's ranch. Excellent black-and-white photographs. The teacher's guidebook includes suggestions for activities and a bibliography of books for pupils and for teachers. The translations of the English and Spanish in the text are included on the last two pages of the book.

REVIEW: *Cartel*, December 1973, p. 109.

**109.** Delgado, María Isabel. **Chave's Memories = Los recuerdos de Chave**. Houston: Piñata Books, 1996. ISNB: 1-55885-084-8. unp. Illustrated by Yvonne Symank.

Chave recalls her visits to her grandparents' ranch La Burrita in Mexico, a short ride from her home in Brownsville, Texas. Farming activities are described with realistic and vivid illustrations. Américas Commended List 1996.

REVIEW: *Journal of Youth Services in Libraries,* Winter 2001, p. 35.

**110.**   DePoix, Carol. **Jo, Flo and Yolanda.** Chapel Hill, N.C.: Lollipop Power, 1973. 35 p. Illustrated by Stephanie Sove Ney. Spanish translation by Martha P. Cotera (1979).

Three girls, six-year-old triplets, are very much alike but like to do different things and have different dreams. The illustrations sympathetically portray life in an apartment in the city. Their older brother George fixes supper at night, and they help. Father works the night shift and starts the breakfast when he comes home. Mother takes the subway to work every day. The Spanish translation is on three pages that fold out at the end of the book. It seems to have been an afterthought to include it.

**111.**   DeSauza, James. **El hermano Anansi y el rancho de ganado = Brother Anansi and the Cattle Ranch.** San Francisco: Children's Book Press, 1989. ISBN: 0-89239-044-1. 32 p. Illustrated by Stephen Von Mason.

Based on a Nicaraguan folk tale, Anansi, the spider man, tricks the tiger and becomes rich when he takes all the cattle except one from their joint cattle raising business. Spanish and English are in alternate paragraphs.

REVIEWS: *Booklist,* November 15, 1989, p. 662; *Bookwatch,* September 1989, p. 4; *Horn Book,* May 1990, p. 363; *Hungry Mind Review,* November 1989, p. 28; *Publishers Weekly,* August 11, 1989, p. 458; *Reading Teacher,* April 1990, p. 588; *Reading Teacher,* March 1995, p. 494; *School Library Journal,* February 1990, p. 118.

**112.**   DeSpain, Pleasant. **The Emerald Lizard: Fifteen Latin American Tales to Tell in English and Spanish = La lagartija esmeralda: quince cuentos tradicionales latinoamericanos.** Little Rock: August House, 1999. ISBN: 0-87483-551-8. 183 p.

The fifteen stories in this book come from various Latin American countries and cultures. They are the author's retellings of traditional folktales, myths, and legends. The stories are: *The Emerald Lizard = La lagartija esmeralda, Renting a Horse = Un caballo para alquilar, The Lake of the Moon = La laguna de la luna, Five Eggs = Cinco huevos, The Flood = La inundación, Why Beetle Is Beautiful = Porqué es hermoso el escarabajo, The Crocodile Man = El hombre caimán, The Magic Lake = El lago mágico, The Proud Horseman = El jinete orgulloso, Juan Bobo, The Señorita and the Puma = La señorita y la puma, Tossing Eyes = El arroja ojos, Too Clever = Demasiado listo, The Turquoise Ring = El anillo turquesa,* and *Ashes for Sale = Cenizas a la venta.* For each story the English version is first, followed by the Spanish version. Notes indicate the origins of the stories. A few black and white illustrations are included.

REVIEWS: *Bookwatch*, August 1999, p. 12; *Center for Children's Books Bulletin*, July 1999, p. 385; *Horn Book Guide*, Spring 2000, p. 111; *Social Education*, May 2000, p. 7; *School Library Journal*, March 2000, p. 268.

**113.** Diaz Valcárcel, Emilio. **Borinquen, y después Colón = Borinquen, and Then Columbus.** New York: Los Amigos del Barrio, 1972. unp. Illustrations, Tomás Vega.

The author relates the history of the Taino people and their culture and the colonization of Puerto Rico by the Spaniards. Black-and-white drawings.

REVIEW: *Booklist*, February 1, 1976, p. 793.

**114.** **Diccionario bilingüe ilustrado.** Austin, Tex.: Voluntad Publishers, 1978–1980. 3 volumes.

The first volume includes words in common use in the first grade, organized by topic. In volume two, the words are arranged in alphabetical order by their Spanish names. This volume includes words commonly used in games, classes, and general conversations. Volume three includes words for eight-to-twelve-year-olds in Spanish alphabetical order. Some words are illustrated.

**115.** Dickson, Ardie. **Come to the Pond = Vengan al estanque.** Boulder, Colo.: Mediaworks, 1976. 53 p. Translation consultant Tom Trujillo.

A photographic story of a trip to a pond by a group of children. Full-page black-and-white photographs.

**116.** Dinhofer, Elisa and Dinhofer, Al. **Chicos en la cocina = Kids in the Kitchen.** Santurce, Puerto Rico: Caribbean World Communications, 1971. 34 p. Designed and illustrated by José Villavicencio.

This cookbook, designed for girls and boys between six and sixteen, is divided into three sections from the simplest recipe for snow cones to the most difficult recipe for paella Valenciana. Some of the recipes in the first section utilize numbered instructions. Parents are encouraged to help the children in the kitchen. The recipes are easy to follow. The first edition was made possible by a grant from the First Federal Savings and Loan Association of Puerto Rico.

REVIEWS: *Booklist*, February 1, 1976, p. 739; *Cartel*, December 1974, p. 40.

**117.** Dixson, Robert James and Fox, Herbert. **Mi primer diccionario ilustrado de inglés.** New York: Regents Publishing, rev. ed., 1974. 67 p.

The first edition was published in 1960. A basic vocabulary of 348 words is presented in an alphabetical format based on the English alphabet. The English word is given, then the Spanish word. These are followed by a sentence using the words in both English and Spanish. Each word is accompanied by a small color illustration. A Spanish-English vocabulary of 800 words is appended.

**118.** Dominguez, Emilio "Zapata"; Dominguez, Juanita; Dominguez, Roberto; Dominguez, "J.A."; and Dominguez, Zarife. **Oferta de una familia.** Denver: Totinem Publications, 1970. 32 p.

Includes poems and songs, some traditional and some written for La Raza, in English or in Spanish. Some of the songs were written by the whole family, some by J.A. (at age eight) or Roberto (at age ten). Only a few drawings are included.

**119.** Dorros, Arthur. **Abuela**. New York: Dutton Children's Books, 1991. ISBN: 0-525-44750-4. unp. Illustrated by Elisa Kleven.

Rosalba and her grandmother take a bus to the park. There Rosalba imagines that she and abuela can fly. They fly over Manhattan and visit the Statue of Liberty and other sights before returning to the park. The text is in English with a sprinkling of Spanish words. A glossary is included at the end of the book.

REVIEWS: *Booklist*, October 15, 1991, p. 436; *Center for Children's Books Bulletin*, January 1992, p. 123; *Childhood Education*, Spring 1992, p. 175; *Children's Book Review Service* , December 1991, p. 38; *Early Childhood Education Journal*, Fall 1997, p. 46; *Five Owls*, November 1991, p. 34; *Five Owls*, September 1995, p. 21; *Horn Book*, November 1991, p. 726; *Horn Book*, May 1992, p. 321; *Horn Book Guide*, Spring 1996, p. 99; *Hungry Mind Review*, Spring 1992, p. C12; *Instructor*, September 1999, p. 26; *Kirkus Reviews*, September 1, 1991, p. 1167; *Los Angeles Times Book Review*, September 29, 1991, p. 12; *New York Times Book Review*, December 8, 1991, p. 26; *Newsweek*, December 16, 1991, p. 69; *Parents Magazine*, April 1995, p. 90; *Publishers Weekly*, May 10, 1991, p. 261; *Publishers Weekly*, May 5, 1997, p. 211; *Reading Teacher*, May 1992, p. 708; *Reading Teacher*, April 1995, p. 636; *School Library Journal*, October 1991, p. 90; *School Library Journal*, August 1995, p. 166; *Smithsonian*, November 1991, p. 191; *Social Education*, April 1992, p. 161; *Social Education*, November 1998, p. 416; *Village Voice Literary Supplement*, February 1992, p. 19.

**120.** Dorros, Arthur. **Isla**. New York: Dutton Children's Books, 1995. ISBN: 0-525-45149-8. unp. Illustrated by Elisa Kleven.

In this sequel to **Abuela**, Rosalba and her grandmother fly to Puerto Rico, where grandmother shows her granddaughter the places of the island that she loves. Américas Commended List 1995.

REVIEWS: *Booklist*, November 1, 1995, p. 476; *Horn Book*, March 1996, p. 230; *Horn Book Guide*, Spring 1996, p. 25; *Horn Book Guide*, Fall 1996, p. 327; *Kirkus Reviews*, October 1, 1995, p. 1426; *Language Arts*, October 1996, p. 431; *Los Angeles Times Book Review*, December 3, 1995, p. 27; *Los Angeles Times Book Review*, February 25, 1996, p. 11; *New Yorker*, November 27, 1995, p. 99; *Publishers Weekly*, October 9, 1995, p. 84; *Publishers Weekly*, April 5, 1999. p. 243; *Reading Teacher*, February 1997, p. 426; *Social Education*, November 1998, p. 416.

**121.** Dorros, Arthur. **Radio Man: A Story in English and Spanish = Don Radio: un cuento en inglés y español**. New York: HarperCollins, 1993. ISBN: 0-06-021547-X. unp. Spanish translation by Sandra Marulanda Dorros.

Diego is the son of migrant workers who move from the cabbage fields in

Texas, to the melon fields in Arizona, to the cherry orchards in California, to the apple orchards in Washington. As the family travels, Diego always listens to the radio, sometimes in Spanish and sometimes in English. At each migrant camp, Diego meets relatives and friends. The radio helps to keep them in touch. Américas Commended List 1993.

REVIEWS: *Book Links*, March 1996, p. 26; *Center for Children's Books Bulletin*, January 1994, p. 151; *Kirkus Reviews*, September 1, 1993, p. 1142; *Language Arts*, March 1996, p. 208; *Library Talk*, March 1994, p. 33.

**122.**   Drexel Elementary School, Tucson, Arizona. Third-grade Art Students. **How the Sun Was Born = Como el sol nació.** St. Petersburg, Fla.: Willowisp Press, 1993. ISBN: 0-87406-649-2. unp. Art teacher, Nancy Murray.

A dinosaur lays five eggs, but only four of them hatch. The fifth one stays in the warm sand. A volcano erupts, and the earth becomes too hot. The dinosaurs become extinct, and the buried dinosaur egg becomes the sun. A photograph of the students who wrote this book appears on the back cover. This book received the 1992 Kids Are Authors Award.

**123.**   DuBois, William Pène and Po, Lee. **The Hare and the Tortoise & The Tortoise and the Hare = La liebre y la tortuga & La tortuga y la liebre.** New York: Doubleday, 1972. 48 p. Illustrated by William Pène DuBois.

Consists of two tales: the first, the familiar story of how the tortoise outwits the hare; and the second, by Lee Po, a story in which the hare outwits the tortoise. Humorous and colorful illustrations.

REVIEWS: *Book World*, November 5, 1972, p. 3; *Booklist*, February 1, 1973, p. 527; *Cartel*, December 1974, p. 72; *Horn Book*, October 1972, p. 460; *Kirkus Reviews*, July 1, 1972, p. 720; *Kirkus Reviews*, December 1, 1972, p. 1408; *Library Journal*, November 15, 1972, p. 3799; *New York Times Book Review*, September 17, 1972, p. 8; *Publishers Weekly*, January 8, 1973, p. 65.

**124.**   Eastman, P. D. **¿Eres tu mi mamá?** New York: Beginner Books, 1967. 63 p. Illustrated by P. D. Eastman. Translated from the English by Carlos Rivera. (Yo lo puedo leer solo = Beginner Books)

The familiar story of the baby bird that leaves his nest to look for his mother. He is finally rescued by a "Snort"—a big steam shovel. Amusing illustrations. Cover title: **Are You My Mother?**

REVIEW: *Booklist*, July 15, 1968, p. 1275.

**125.**   Eastman, P. D. **Perro grande, perro pequeño: un cuento de las buenas noches = Big Dog, Little Dog: A Bedtime Story.** New York: Random House, 1982. unp. Translated into Spanish by Pilar de Cuenca and Inés Alvarez.

A humorous tale about a big dog and a little dog who like opposite things but who get along well together. Colorful and humorous illustrations.

REVIEW: *Booklist*, July 1982, p. 1438.

**126.**   Edwards, Arthur C. **Feliz Navidad: Spanish Christmas Carols, with Spanish Text, for Treble Voices.** Melville, N.Y.: Belwin Mills Publishing, 1962. 23 p. Edited and arranged by Arthur C. Edwards.

Includes music and Spanish words for eleven carols from various regions of Spain. The English translations follow the music.

**127.**   Ehlert, Lois. **Cucú: un cuento folklórico mexicano = Cuckoo: A Mexican Folktale.** San Diego: Harcourt Brace, 1st ed., 1997. ISBN: 0-15-200274-X. unp. Translated into Spanish by Gloria de Aragón Andújar.

Cuckoo is beautiful but lazy. The other birds get tired of her singing. When they go to sleep, Cuckoo smells fire, gathers all the seeds by herself, and drops them in Mole's cool tunnel. Wonderful vibrant colors in Ehlert's collage style. This story is an adaptation of a Mayan Indian tale from Mexico. Américas Commended List 1997.

REVIEWS: *Booklist,* April 1, 1997, p. 1330; *Booklist,* January 1, 1998, p. 735; *Center for Children's Books Bulletin,* June 1997, p. 356; *Horn Book Guide,* Spring 1998, p. 117; *Instructor,* March 1998, p. 22; *Journal of Youth Services in Libraries,* Winter 2001, p. 35; *Kirkus Reviews,* April 1, 1997, p. 553; *Publishers Weekly,* January 20, 1997, p. 401; *Reading Teacher,* September 1998, p. 64; *School Library Journal,* March 1997, p. 174; *Social Education,* April 1998, p. 7; *Tribune Books (Chicago),* March 9, 1997, p. 7.

**128.**   Ehlert, Lois. **Moon Rope: A Peruvian Folktale = Un lazo a la luna: una leyenda peruviana.** San Diego: Harcourt Brace Jovanovich, 1992. ISBN: 0-15-255343-6. unp. Translated into Spanish by Amy Prince.

A fox wants to go to the moon on a rope of grass. The mole reluctantly accompanies him. The mole slips and returns to earth. Ever after he only goes out after dark. Did the fox reach the moon? Some say yes, but the mole has never seen him. Illustrated in collage with the use of a great deal of silver. Based on a Peruvian folktale.

REVIEWS: *Book Links,* July 1994, p. 6; *Booklist,* October 15, 1992, p. 423; *Center for Children's Books Bulletin,* December 1992, p. 110; *Children's Book Review Service,* November 1992, p. 27; *Early Childhood Education Journal,* Fall 1997, p. 46; *Emergency Librarian,* May 1993, p. 50; *Five Owls,* September 1992, p. 14; *Horn Book,* November 1992, p. 732–733; *Instructor,* March 1995, p. 71; *Kirkus Reviews,* September 1, 1992, p. 1128; *Language Arts,* September 1993, p. 418; *Library Talk,* May 1993, p. 23; *New Directions for Women,* May 1993, p. 38; *Publishers Weekly,* August 17, 1992, p. 499; *School Library Journal,* October 1992, p. 102; *Social Studies,* January 1997, p. 29.

**129.**   Elya, Susan Middleton. **Say Hola to Spanish.** New York: Lee & Low Books, 1996. ISBN: 1-880000-64-4. unp. Illustrated by Loretta Lopez.

Spanish words are introduced to young readers in a verse format using

English phrases. An example is: "A dog is a perro, a cat is a gato." Many topics are covered. Illustrations are humorous.

REVIEWS: *Booklist*, May 1, 1996, p. 1509; *Children's Book Review Service*, June 1996, p. 121; *Children's Bookwatch*, July 1996, p. 5; *Horn Book Guide*, Spring 1997, p. 107; *Instructor*, August 1996, p. 45; *Instructor*, May 1998, p. 64; *Kirkus Reviews*, March 1, 1996, p. 373; *School Library Journal*, June 1996, p. 100.

**130.** Elya, Susan Middleton. **Say Hola to Spanish, Otra Vez (Again!).** New York: Lee & Low Books, 1997. ISBN: 1-880000-59-8. unp. Illustrated by Loretta Lopez.

Again, Spanish words are presented to young readers in a verse format with amusing illustrations. A new title in this series was listed in the *Newsletter of the United States Board on Books for Young People*, Spring 2001, p. [11]. The title is **Say Hola to Spanish at the Circus**, illustrated by Loretta Lopez (New York: Lee & Low Books, 2000).

REVIEWS: *Children's Bookwatch*, February 1998, p. 6; *Horn Book Guide*, Spring 1998, p. 117; *Kirkus Reviews*, November 1, 1997, p. 1643; *Publishers Weekly*, October 27, 1997, p. 75; *School Library Journal*, January 1998, p. 98.

**131.** Emberley, Rebecca. **Let's Go, A Book in Two Languages = Vamos, un libro en dos lenguas.** Boston: Little, Brown, 1993. ISBN: 0-316-2345-0. unp.

**Let's Go** takes the reader to the zoo, the aquarium, camping, to the beach, the circus, the museum, skiing, to the fair, to the airport, on a picnic, and to a parade. All the items identified with each activity are illustrated, and the words are given in English and Spanish. Colorful collages are used for the illustrations.

REVIEWS: *Booklist*, June 1, 1994, p. 1848; *Reading Teacher*, September 1994, p. 69.

**132.** Emberley, Rebecca. **My Day: A Book in Two Languages = Mi día: un libro en dos lenguas.** Boston: Little Brown, 1993. ISBN: 0-316-23450-8. unp.

A typical day in the life of a child from getting up to going to bed is protrayed in colorful collages. The book begins with the times of the day.

REVIEWS: *Booklist*, June 1, 1994, p. 1848; *Reading Teacher*, September 1994, p. 69.

**133.** Emberley, Rebecca. **My House: A Book in Two Languages = Mi casa: un libro en dos lenguas.** Boston: Little Brown, 1990. ISBN: 0-316-23637-3. unp.

Simple pictures illustrate a house, the family who lives there, each of the rooms, the garden, and the yard.

REVIEWS: *Hispania*, May 1992, p. 414; *Horn Book*, September 1990, p. 629; *Kirkus Reviews*, June 1, 1990, p. 805; *New York Times Book Review*, October 14, 1990, p. 33; *School Library Journal*, August 1990, p. 141.

**134.** Emberley, Rebecca. **Taking a Walk: A Book in Two Languages = Caminando: un libro en dos lenguas.** Boston: Little Brown, 1990. ISBN: 0-316-23640-3. unp.

Simple illustrations depict a child going on a walk. The school, post office, shops, library, and park are some of the places visited. Four new titles by Rebecca Emberley have just been listed in the *Newsletter of the United States Board on Books for Young People*, Spring 2001, p. [13]. These titles are: **My Colors = Mis colores, My Numbers = Mis números, My Opposites = Mis opuestos,** and **My Shapes = Mis formas** (Boston: Little Brown, 2000).

REVIEWS: *Booklist*, June 15, 1990, p. 1978; *Horn Book*, September 1990, p. 629; *Kirkus Reviews*, June 1, 1990, p. 805; *School Library Journal*, August 1990, p. 141.

**135.** Espinosa, J. Manuel. **Cuentos de cuanto hay = Tales from Spanish New Mexico.** Albuquerque: University of New Mexico Press, 1998. ISBN: 0-8263-1927-0. 225 p. Collected from the oral tradition by J. Manuel Espinosa. Edited and translated by Joe Hayes. Illustrated by William Rotsaert.

Adapted and translated from **Spanish Folk-Tales from New Mexico** which was published in the *Memoirs of the American Folklore Society*, volume 30, 1937. Reprinted with permission from The American Folklore Society. These folk-tales were collected by Espinosa in the 1930s directly from Spanish-speaking residents in northern New Mexico and southern Colorado. The adaptation of the Spanish by Hayes mainly involved changes in spelling and some verb forms to make the stories more readable. There are 56 folktales in the collection printed in Spanish and English in parallel columns on each page. The source of each folktale is listed with the name of the teller, the age of the teller, and the location. Illustrations consist of small black and white sketches before each story.

**136.** Everett, Louise. **Amigo Means Friend.** Mahway, N.J.: Troll Associates, 1988. ISBN: 0-8167-1001-7. unp. Illustrated by Sandy Rabinowitz.

This is an easy reader which contains only 51 different words in English and 15 different words in Spanish. José and George live next to each other and become acquainted using simple words of greeting in both English and Spanish.

**137.** Eversole, Robyn. **The Flute Player = La flautista.** New York: Orchard Books, 1995. ISBN: 0-531-09469-3. unp. Pictures by G. Brian Karas. (A Richard Jackson Book)

The flute player, who lives on the fifth floor, discovers one day that her flute will not play. On her way to have it fixed she meets the girl who lives on the first floor. Something wonderful happens, and the lives of the people who live on the second, third, and fourth floors are changed happily.

REVIEWS: *Booklist*, October 1, 1995, p. 322; *Catholic Library World*, March 1996, p. 49; *Horn Book*, January 1996, p. 62; *Horn Book Guide*, Spring 1996, p. 99; *Journal of Youth Services in Libraries*, Winter 2001, p. 35; *Kirkus Reviews*, August 1, 1995, p. 1108.

**138.** Figueira, Julia and Hampares, Katherine. **La ranita en la ciudad = The Little Frog in the City.** Madrid: Anaya, 1973. 83 p. (Anaya Bilingual Classics)

The little frog travels to the city and gets into a lot of trouble until Bob rescues her. Bob takes her home, hoping Mom will let her live in the bathtub. Effective use of repetition in both languages. Amusing, colorful illustrations. Published in the United States by L.A. Publishing Co., Long Island City, New York.

**139.** Figueira, Julia and Hampares, Katherine. **La ranita encuentra el arco iris = The Little Frog Finds the Rainbow.** Madrid: Anaya, 1973. 53 p. (Anaya Bilingual Classics)

The little frog and her friends travel along the rainbow to find the clear water in the mountain, but only the frog stays to enjoy it. The rest return to their own little corners of the world. There is a nice use of repetition in both languages. Soft colors are used for the illustrations. Published in the United States by L.A. Publishing Co., Long Island City, New York.

**140.** Figueira, Julia and Hampares, Katherine. **La ranita sale de su charco = The Little Frog Leaves Her Pond.** Madrid: Anaya, 1973. 49 p. (Anaya Bilingual Classics)

The frog leaves her muddy pond to seek the clear water in the mountain. On the way she meets the hen, the duck, the cat, the dog, and the bird, who decide to join the frog in her search. Colorful illustrations. Published in the United State by L.A. Publishing Co., Long Island City, New York.

**141.** Foster, Karen Sharp. **Good Night My Little Chicks in Spanish and English = Buenas noches mis pollitos en español e inglés.** Corinth, Miss.: First Story Press, 1997. ISBN: 1-890326-12-7. unp. Adapted and illustrated by Karen Sharp Foster.

Mama calls Carlos in for bedtime, but he is not quite ready. Mama sings him the little chickie song. The illustrations are in two parts. The first part shows Mama and Carlos preparing for bed. The second part is the story of the little chicks. It is a book within a book. The song is printed on the book jacket, but does not appear in the book.

REVIEWS: *Kirkus Reviews,* October 15, 1997, p. 1581; *School Library Journal,* November 1997, p. 81.

**142.** Frasconi, Antonio. **See Again, Say Again = Guarda di nuovo, parla di nuovo = Regarde de nouveau, parle de nouveau = Mira de nuevo, habla de nuevo: A Picture Book in Four Languages.** New York: Harcourt, Brace & World, 1964. unp. Woodcuts by Antonio Frasconi.

Seventy simple words from the seasons, home and city life, fruits and vegetables, and family members are given in English (black letters), Italian (blue), French (red), and Spanish (green), with pronunciation guides. The last page lists fourteen everyday expressions. Strong, bold woodcuts.

REVIEWS: *Atlantic,* December 1964, p. 161; *Book Week,* November 1, 1964, p. 24; *Christian Century,* December 2, 1964, p. 1498; *Christian Science Monitor,*

November 5, 1964, p. 5B; *Horn Book*, October 1964, p. 495; *Library Journal*, July 1964, p. 2871; *New York Times Book Review*, November 1, 1964, pt. 2, p. 62; *Saturday Review*, November 7, 1964, p. 51.

**143.**  Frasconi, Antonio. **See and Say = Guarda e parla = Mira y habla = Regarde et parle: A Picture Book in Four Languages.** New York: Harcourt, 1955. unp. Woodcuts by Antonio Franconi.

"Beside each object pictured in this book you will find the word for it in English, Italian, French, and Spanish, together with a guide to the pronunciation. The following color key has been used throughout: Black for English words; Blue for Italian words; Red for French words; Green for Spanish words. There is also a page of everyday expressions all children use." (Introduction by the author.) Includes sixty-three words representing items that interest children, and sixteen phrases. Very colorful and bright woodcuts.

REVIEWS: *Booklist*, October 1, 1955, p. 61; *Bookmark*, November 1955, p. 39; *Chicago Sunday Tribune*, November 13, 1955, p. 10; *Christian Science Monitor*, November 10, 1955, p. 1B; *Horn Book*, October 1955, p. 362; *Horn Book*, December 1955, p. 444; *Kirkus Reviews*, July 1, 1955, p. 413; *New York Herald Tribune Book Review*, November 13, 1955, p. 4; *New York Times Book Review*, October 2, 1955, p. 34; *Saturday Review*, November 12, 1955, p. 62.

**144.**  Frasconi, Antonio. **The Snow and the Sun: A South American Folk Rhyme in Two Languages = La nieve y el sol.** New York: Harcourt, Brace & World, 1961. unp.

This cumulative rhyme is the author's own translation and a version of one published by the Education Council of Argentina in a textbook for primary schools. It is a folk rhyme that begins with five lines and then adds a new line for each stanza, repeating the first five lines and building up to a final seventeen-line rhyme. Bold, bright woodcuts.

REVIEWS: *Atlantic*, December 1961, p. 121; *Booklist*, November 1, 1961, p. 166; *Chicago Sunday Tribune*, November 12, 1961, sec. 2, p. 18; *Christian Science Monitor*, November 16, 1961, p. 2B; *Commonweal*, November 10, 1961, p. 184; *Horn Book*, October 1961, p. 435; *Kirkus Reviews*, July 1, 1961, p. 535; *Library Journal*, November 15, 1961, p. 4031; *New York Herald Tribune Books*, November 5, 1961, p. 13; *New York Times Book Review*, November 12, 1961, pt. 2, p. 44; *New Yorker*, November 18, 1961, p. 226; *San Francisco Chronicle*, October 29, 1961, p. 36; *Saturday Review*, November 11, 1961, p. 40; *Wisconsin Library Bulletin*, November 1961, p. 379.

**145.**  Galarza, Ernesto. **Poemas pe-que pe-que pe-que-ñitos = Very Very Short Nature Poems.** San Francisco: El Dorado Distributors, 1972. 64 p. (Colección mini-libros)

Short poems on flowers, fruits, vegetables, fish, worms, and small animals. Both Spanish and English rhymes are well done. Black-and-white photographs would be more effective on glossy paper. A glossary of words and phrases is provided. Galarza is well recognized by the Chicano community both as an author of children's books and as a scholar.

REVIEW: *Cartel*, December 1973, p. 88.

**146.** Galindo, Mary Sue. **Icy Watermelon = Sandía fría.** Houston: Piñata Books, 2001. ISBN: 1-55885-306-5. unp. Illustrations by Pauline Rodriguez Howard.

On Sundays grandfather and grandmother come to spend the afternoon with their three grandchildren. On this day, Mama serves everyone ice-cold watermelon; and grandfather tells them the story of how he met grandmother when he was selling watermelons from his truck. The English and Spanish texts are on the left pages with illustrations separating them. The illustrations show the watermelon field, then the whole watermelon and the individual pieces, and finally the empty rinds. The full-page illustrations on the right pages show family life in soft colors. Américas Commended List 2000.

REVIEWS: *Booklist*, December 15, 2000, p. 826; *School Library Journal*, January 2001, p. 99.

**147.** Ganz, Barbara. **Alberto y el calcetín perdido = Alberto and His Missing Sock.** Detroit: Blaine Ethridge Books, 1975. unp. Illustrated by Phyllis Noda. Translated by Agustina Santos del Favero. (A Prism Press Book)

Alberto dallies while dressing for school; his mother calls constantly for him to hurry up. First he can't find his new shoes, then he can't find one sock. He finally discovers it in an unlikely place, gets a hug from his mother, and goes off to school. Sensitive black-and-white drawings.

REVIEWS: *Booklist*, May 15, 1976, p. 1343; *Cartel*, Fall 1976, p. 1; *Proyecto Leer Bulletin*, Spring 1976, p. 11; *School Library Journal*, May 1976, p. 48.

**148.** Garaway, Margaret Kahn. **Ashkii and His Grandfather = Ashkii y el abuelo.** Tucson: Old Hogan Publishing, 1st bilingual edition, 1995. ISBN: 0-9638851-6-2. 33 p. Illustrated by Harry Warren. Translated by María Rebeca Cartes.

Ashkii is six years old and can finally go with his grandfather to the Navajo summer sheep camp. There he learns to care for the sheep, but his grandfather also encourages him to draw. Upon going to kindergarten in the fall, he and his friend Chee run away, but are soon rescued. The teacher recognizes Ashkii's talents and encourages him.

**149.** Garaway, Margaret Kahn. **The Teddy Bear Number Book = Los números con los ositos.** Tucson: Old Hogan Publishing, 1995. ISBN: 0-963881-3-8. unp. Illustrated by Sarah Garaway Butler. Translated by María Rebeca Cartes.

A counting book from one to ten. As each number is increased another teddy bear joins in the fun.

**150.**  Garcia, Maria. **The Adventures of Connie and Diego = Las aventuras de Connie y Diego.** San Francisco: Children's Book Press, 1978. ISBN: 0-89239-028-X. 22 p. Illustrated by Malaquias Montoya. Translated into Spanish by Alma Flor Ada. (Fifth World Tales: Stories for All Children from the Many Peoples of America = Cuentos del quinto mundo: cuentos de los muchos pueblos de América para todos los niños)

Twins Connie and Diego are born with different colors all over their bodies. When they grow up they run away from the mocking laughter of their family to find a land where they belong. A wise tiger helps them understand, and they return home. Bold colors.

REVIEWS: *Booklist,* September 1, 1981, p. 54; *Lector,* November/December 1983, p. 35; *Proyecto Leer Bulletin,* Fall 1980, p. 22.

**151.**  García, Richard. **My Aunt Otilia's Spirits = Los espíritus de mi tía Otilia.** San Francisco: Children's Book Press, 1978. ISBN: 0-89239-029-8. 23 p. Illustrated by Robin Cherin & Roger I. Reyes. Translated into Spanish by Jesús Guerrero Rea. (Fifth World Tales: Stories for All Children from the Many Peoples of America = Cuentos del quinto mundo: cuentos de los muchos pueblos de América para todos los niños)

A humorous story about the spirits of tall, skinny Aunt Otilia who comes to visit each summer from Puerto Rico. Demonio, her nephew, shares his bed with her and frightens Aunt Otilia and her spirits away. Illustrations use bold colors.

REVIEWS: *Booklist*, September 1, 1981, p. 54; *Proyecto Leer Bulletin*, Fall 1980, p. 27.

**152.**  García, Valerie Chellew. **The Cactus Wren and the Cholla = El reyezuelo y la cholla**. Tucson: Hispanic Books Distributors, 1997. ISBN: 0-938243-01-2. unp. Illustrator: M. Fred Barraza. A bird arrives in the Southwest and cannot find a tree to build her nest. Finally the cholla cactus offers one of her arms. The wren builds her nest, and then other trees and birds come. This is the legend of the cactus wren. Winner of the Arroz con Leche award for 1997.

**153.**  García Lorca, Federico. **The Cricket Sings: Poems and Songs for Children.** New York: New Directions, 1980. unp. Translated by Will Kirkland. Illustrated by Maria Horvath.

Includes twenty-five poems and songs García Lorca wrote especially for children. They are in the original Spanish with the English translations on the opposite pages. Expressive bold black-and-white illustrations.

REVIEWS: *Booklist*, February 1, 1981, p. 752; *Kliatt Paperback Book Guide*, Winter 1981, p. 17; *Parnassus*, Spring 1981, p. 253.

**154.**  Gardner, Lee and Gardner, Tom. **¿De quién es esta casa? = Whose House Is This?** Carmel Valley, Calif.: La Estancia Press, 1983. 31 p. Illustrated by Ayse Gilbert.

Seven different houses are illustrated, then the reader must turn the page to find out whose house it is. The animal explains who he is and how he builds his house.

REVIEW: *Booklist*, October 1, 1990, p. 349.

**155.**   Gaspar, Tomás Rodríguez. **La aventura de Yolanda = Yolanda's Hike.** Stanford, Calif.: New Seed Press, 1974. 23 p. Drawings by Sue Brown. Translated by Herminio Flores with Maurice Arancibia, Vivian Carlo, and Karen Mae.

Yolanda and three friends take a hike to a nearby hilltop for a day of adventure. Some mistakes in the Spanish version. Black-and-white drawings. Porfirio Sanchez in the *Interracial Books for Children Bulletin* says, **Yolanda's Hike** "is a step in the right direction in that it is free of racist stereotypes, but it falls short of being a story that is really relevant to the Chicano experience and truly antisexist.' (p. 15)

REVIEWS: *Booklist*, September 1, 1981, p. 54; *Interracial Books for Children Bulletin*, 6, no. 5 & 6, 1975, p. 15; *Lector*, September/October 1983, p. 49.

**156.**   Giff, Patricia Reilly. **Ho, Ho, Benjamin, Feliz Navidad.** New York: Bantam Doubleday Dell Books for Young Readers, 1995. ISBN: 0-440-41080-0. 71 p. Illustrated by DyAnne DiSalvo-Ryan. (A Yearling Book)

Benjamin Bean and Sarah Cole are getting ready for Christmas. Mrs. Halfpenny asks them to do two good deeds over the holidays. Benjamin's new neighbor in Springfield Gardens is Señora Sanchez, and Benjamin is trying to learn Spanish. Benjamin asks his mother to invite Señora Sanchez for Christmas dinner, and the Señora gives Benjamin one of the puppies her dog Bonita has just had. Before each chapter begins, there is a brief lesson in Spanish. There are two other books in this series: **Adiós Anna** and **Say Hola, Sarah.**

REVIEWS: *Children's Bookwatch*, December 1998, p. 6; *Horn Book Guide*, Fall 1998, p. 318; *School Library Journal*, October 1995, p. 37.

**157.**   Gilbert, Miriam. **Rosie, the Oldest Horse in St. Augustine: A Story Told in the Three Languages of Those Who Occupied the Oldest City in the United States.** Ft. Myers Beach, Fla.: Island Press, 1967. 48 p. Illustrated by Jean Roach.

The story of Rosie, an old horse in St. Augustine that pulls a carriage for tourists, is told in English, Spanish, and French. Her driver Carlos is unhappy because he must retire, but in the end he finds he still has youth in his heart. Some of the history of St. Augustine is told. Occasionally the illustrations are drawn over the text, making it difficult to read. There are some mistakes in both the Spanish and English versions.

**158.**   Gleiter, Jan and Thompson, Kathleen. **Diego Rivera.** Milwaukee: Raintree Publishers, 1989. ISBN: 0-8172-2908-6. 32 p. Illustrated by Yoshi Miyake.

A well-written and sympathetic biography of this Mexican artist who lived from 1886–1957. It tells of his youth, his studies in Europe, and of his great murals in Mexico and the United States. Other biographies in this series include those about Simón Bolívar, Juana Inés de la Cruz, Benito Juarez, Miguel Hidalgo y Costilla, José Martí, Luis Muñoz Marín, and Junipero Serra.

REVIEWS: *Booklist*, October 1, 1990, p. 349; *Center for Children's Books Bulletin*, November 1989, p. 56; *School Library Journal*, August 1989, p. 159.

**159.** Gonzales, Dolores. **Canciones y juegos de Nuevo México = Songs and Games of New Mexico.** South Brunswick and New York: Barnes, 1974. 128 p.

Originally published in 1942, this is a reprint in a smaller format with the same illustrations, but with a different organization of the material. The first four parts are in Spanish only: (1) for five to six-year olds, (2) for eight to ten-year olds, (3) for eleven-year olds and over, and (4) for preschool children (songs and Christmas carols). Some new games have been added, and part 4 is all new. Part 5 consists of the translations of the songs and games in English. For the second edition, the Spanish text was updated by Carolina Acosta Gonzalez.

**160.** Gonzales, Veronica Leal. **Un nombre chistoso.** Berkeley, Calif.: Center for Open Learning and Teaching, 1974. 12 p. Illustrated by Gloria Osuna.

Joaquín thinks his friend's name, Cuauhtemoc, is funny until Grandmother tells the two boys about how Cuauhtemoc, their ancestor of long ago, defended his people in Mexico until he was captured and killed by the Spaniards. Strong, forceful, and colorful illustrations.

**161.** González, Lucía M. **The Bossy Gallito: A Traditional Cuban Folktale = El gallo de bodas.** New York: Scholastic, 1994. ISBN: 0-590-46843-X. unp. Illustrated by Lulu Delacre.

The bossy rooster or un gallito mandón is going to the wedding of his uncle the parrot. On the way he gets his beak dirty, and in trying to get it clean he orders the grass to clean his beak. A cumulative tale begins involving a goat, a stick, a fire, a stream, and the sun, until the rooster gets his beak clean and can go to the wedding. Pura Belpré honor book 1996 for narrative and for illustrations. Américas Commended List 1994.

REVIEWS: *Book Links*, March 1996, p. 28; *Booklist*, May 15, 1994, p. 1680; *Center for Children's Books Bulletin*, July 1994, p. 357; *Children's Book Review Service*, May 1994, p. 111; *Entertainment Weekly*, June 17, 1994, p. 66; *Horn Book*, September 1994, p. 602–603; *Horn Book Guide*, Fall 1994, p. 347; *Publishers Weekly*, June 28, 1999, p. 81; *School Library Journal*, April 1994, p. 119; *School Library Journal*, July 1995, p. 27; *Social Education*, April 1995, p. 216; *Social Studies*, January 1997, p. 29

**162.** Gonzalez, Ralfka and Ruiz, Ana. **My First Book of Proverbs = Mi primer libro de dichos.** Emeryville, Calif.: Children's Book Press, 1995. ISBN: 0-89239-134-0. unp. Introduction by Sandra Cisneros.

Vivid illustrations and handprinted text present well-known proverbs from

*The early bird gets the worm,* to *A painting is a poem without words.* Américas Commended List 1995.

REVIEWS: *Children's Book Review Service,* Winter 1996, p. 66; *Children's Bookwatch,* October 1995, p. 5; *Horn Book Guide,* Spring 1996, p. 99; *Journal of Youth Services in Libraries,* Winter 2001, p. 36; *Publishers Weekly,* September 4, 1995, p. 69; *School Library Journal,* February 1996, p. 94; *Tribune Books (Chicago),* September 10, 1995, p. 6.

**163.** Griego, Margot C.; Bucks, Betsy L.; Gilbert, Sharon S.; and Kimball, Laurel H. **Tortillitas para Mamá: And Other Nursery Rhymes, Spanish and English.** New York: Holt, Rinehart and Winston, 1981. unp. Illustrated by Barbara Cooney.

Nursery rhymes and lullabies were collected from the Spanish communities in the Americas. Unfortunately the beautiful illustrations by Barbara Cooney, a Caldecott Medal winner, are so stereotypical, reflecting rural life in Mexico, as to negate the fine quality of the book for today's children. Reviewers differed as to the value of this book.

REVIEWS: *Booklist,* May 1, 1982, p. 1154; *Horn Book,* June 1982, p. 312; *Interracial Books for Children Bulletin,* no. 12, no. 7 & 8, 1981, p. 22; *School Library Journal,* December 1981, p. 58.

**164.** Gross, Olga Arciniega. **El Perro Guardian, the Watch Dog: An Authentic Mexican Folk Tale = El perro guardian: un cuento mexicano auténtico.** Montebello, Calif.: Montebello Unified School District, 1973. unp. Translated and adapted by Olga Arciniega Gross. Illustrated by ten children of Montebello Gardens School. Art consultant, Eleanore Bregand.

The watch dog becomes old and can no longer keep the chickens safe. A friendly coyote helps him out of his dilemma. It is interesting to note that the illustrations by the ten Chicano children show the Mexican farmers with sombreros and ponchos and the Mexican women with pigtails. The illustrations are repeated twice as the story is told first in English and then in Spanish.

REVIEW: *Cartel,* December 1973, p. 87.

**165.** Gross, Olga Arciniega. **El Zorrito, the Little Fox: An Authentic Mexican Folktale = El zorrito: un cuento mexicano auténtico.** Montebello, Calif.: Montebello Unified School District, 1973. unp. Translated and adapted by Olga Arciniega Gross. Illustrated by ten children of Montebello Gardens School. Art consultant, Eleanore Bregand.

The little fox is warned by his mother and other animals of the forest to beware of the wolf. He heeds their warnings and chases the wolf back to his lair. The children's illustrations are well done and are repeated twice, as the story is told first in English and then in Spanish.

REVIEW: *Cartel,* December 1973, p. 137.

**166.** Gunning, Monica. **The Two Georges = Los dos Jorges.** Detroit: Blaine Ethridge Books, 1976. unp. Illustrations By Veronica Mary Miracle. (A Prism Press Book)

George and Jorge, a white boy and a black boy, participate in many activities based on the alphabet from A-Z. Each activity is printed in a poetry format, although the words often do not rhyme. This means that a word in the middle of a sentence often begins with a capital letter, which might be confusing. Black-and-white sketches. The book looks like a textbook, but the text is acceptable.

REVIEWS: *Horn Book*, April 1977, p. 191; *School Library Journal*, April 1977, p. 53.

**167.** Gurney, Eric and Gurney, Nancy. **El rey, los ratones, y el queso.** New York: Beginner Books, 1967. 63 p. Translated from English by Carlos Rivera. (Yo lo puedo leer solo = Beginner Books)

The amusing story of a king who liked cheese and who finally learned to share it with the mice whom he preferred to the cats, the dogs, the lions, and the elephants. Effective use of repetition. Amusing and colorful illustrations. Cover title: **The King, the Mice, and the Cheese.**

REVIEW: *Booklist*, July 15, 1968, p. 1275.

**168.** Guy, Ginger Foglesong. **¡Fiesta!** New York: Greenwillow Books, 1996. ISBN: 0-688-14331-8. unp. Pictures by René King Moreno.

Several children go on a shopping trip to the mercado. They fill one basket (una canasta) with good things for a party including a piñata. In the process they count from one to ten.

REVIEWS: *Children's Book Review Service*, August 1996, p. 159; *Horn Book Guide*, Fall 1997, p. 338; *Journal of Youth Services in Libraries,* Winter 2001, p. 36; *Kirkus Reviews*, June 15, 1996, p. 906; *Publishers Weekly*, July 8, 1996, p. 84; *Reading Teacher*, March 1998, p. 506; *Reading Teacher*, May 1999, p. 890; *School Library Journal*, September 1996, p. 178.

**169.** Haddad, Robert J. **Mexican Tongue Twisters = Trabalenguas mexicanos.** Tempe, Ariz.: Bilingual Press, 1989. ISBN: 0-927534-02-9. 74 p. Collected and translated by Robert J. Haddad. With illustrations by Tom Graham.

A collection of 49 tongue twisters in Spanish with their English translations. In English the text may or may not be a tongue twister. Each tongue twister was collected personally by the author in the states of Michoacán, Guerrero, and the Federal District of Mexico.

**170.** Hall, Mahji. **"T" es por "terrifico": el ABC de Mahji = "T" Is for "Terrific": Mahji's ABC's.** Seattle: Open Hand Publishing, 1989. ISBN: 0-940880-22-9. 32 p. Illustrated by Mahji Hall.

Mahji, a young student, selected words that would match each letter of the alphabet in both English and Spanish. Her illustrations are in blue and pink. The complete alphabet in both languages is printed at the bottom of each page.

REVIEWS: *Booklist*, December 1, 1989, p. 752; *School Library Journal*, August 1989, p. 60; *Small Press*, June 1990, p. 34.

**171.**   Hall, Nancy Abraham and Syverson-Stork, Jill. **Los pollitos dicen: juegos, rimas y canciones infantiles de países de habla hispana = The Baby Chicks Sing: Traditional Games, Nursery Rhymes, and Songs from Spanish-Speaking Countries**. Boston: Little, Brown, 1994. ISBN: 0-316-34010-3. 31 p. Illustrated by Kay Chorao.

Seventeen songs and rhymes are included with the music in this collection. Some songs are *Tortillitas, Chocolate, Arroz con leche, Bajen la piñata,* and *De colores.*

REVIEWS: *Book Links*, July 1994, p. 7; *Booklist*, June 1, 1994, p. 1849; *Horn Book Guide*, Fall 1994, p. 347; *Publishers Weekly*, April 25, 1994, p. 81; *Publishers Weekly*, April 26, 1999, p. 85; *Reading Teacher*, April 1995, p. 605; *School Library Journal*, August 1994, p. 182.

**172.**   Hao, Kuang-ts'ai. **Dance, Mice, Dance! = ¡Bailen, ratones, bailen!** Union City, Calif.: Pan Asian Publications, 1994. ISBN: 1-57227-001-2. unp. Illustrated by Stefano Tartarotti. Spanish translation by Beatriz Zeller. Originally published by Grimm Press.

Jimmy Tune, a flute musician, loses his job twice because of alcohol. The mice he has taught to dance leave him and are trapped by a cat. Jimmy saves them, and they retire to the country to play and dance once again. The publisher says that this is based on the tale *The Pied Piper of Hamlin.*

**173.**   Hao, Kuang-ts'ai. **The Emperor and the Nightingale = El emperador y el ruiseñor**. Union City, Calif.: Pan Asian Publications, 1994. ISBN: 1-57227-019-5. unp. Illustrated by Shih-ming Chang. Spanish translation by Beatriz Zeller. Originally published by Grimm Press.

The emperor wanted to live forever so he makes a deal with the God of Heaven. The magic spell he is given helps him escape the God of Death. When the emperor becomes invisible the God of Death takes his favorite horse and the pretty girl Jade with her music. When the God of Death threatens to take the emperor's son, the emperor willingly goes to death instead. Based on a Hans Christian Andersen story.

REVIEW: *Reading Teacher*, February 1998, p. 424.

**174.**   Hao, Kuang-ts'ai. **The Giant and the Spring = El gigante y el niño primavera**. Union City, Calif.: Pan Asian Publications, 1994. ISBN: 1-57227-010-1. unp. Illustrated by Eva Wang. Spanish translation by Beatriz Zeller. Originally published by Grimm Press.

The giant who lives on top of the hill welcomes the little boy Spring to his home, and then wants to keep him there just for himself. Spring is sad and wishes to return to the world. Finally the giant patches his cloak and sends

Spring back to the rest of the world. Ever since then Spring returns once a year. Based on Oscar Wilde's tale *The Selfish Giant*.

REVIEW: *Reading Teacher*, February 1998, p. 428.

**175.**   Hao, Kuang-Tsai. **Seven Magic Brothers = Siete hermanos mágicos.** Taipei, Taiwan: Yuan-Liou Publishing, 1994. Distributed by Pan Asian Publications, Union City, Calif. ISBN: 957-32-2165-9. unp. Illustrated by Eva Wang. Spanish translation by Beatrice Zeller.

An old woman takes seven golden pills and has seven sons, each with a special power. The emperor is saved by the eldest son who has great strength. The emperor, wisely fearing this man, tries to have him killed; but at each attempt the son with the appropriate special power thwarts the killing. Thereafter the seven brothers live in peace. The illustrations are detailed and suit the story.

REVIEW: *Reading Teacher*, February 1998, p. 424.

**176.**   Harvey, Bob and Harvey, Diane Kelsay. **A Journey of Hope = Una jornada de esperanza.** Wilsonville, Ore: Beautiful America Publishing, 1991. ISBN: 0-89802-603-2. unp. Photographs by Bob Harvey and Diane Kelsay Harvey. Illustrations by Carol Johnson.

A true story of Hope, an Olive Ridley Sea Turtle, on Escobilla Beach on the south Pacific coast of Mexico. The turtle is hatched, makes its way to the sea, and after a few years returns to lay eggs. All of the journey is fraught with danger both from other animals and from man. Steps are being taken now to protect these turtles.

REVIEWS: *Booklist*, March 1, 1993, p. 1243, not recommended by the *Booklist* reviewer. *School Library Journal*, August 1992, p. 188.

**177.**   Harvey, Bob and Harvey, Diane Kelsay. **Melody's Mystery = El misterio de Melodía.** Wilsonville, Ore.: Beautiful America Publishing, 1991. ISBN: 0-89802-604-0. unp. Photography by Diane Kelsay Harvey and Bob Harvey.

The story of a monarch butterfly, from the laying of the egg on the milkweed, to birth as a caterpillar, then the change to chrysalis, and then birth again as a butterfly. The mystery is that the butterflies know each winter that they must migrate to Rosario near Mexico City. Monarch butterflies are not a threatened species, but they do have problems, and there are some groups working to protect their habitats.

REVIEW: *Instructor*, April 1997, p. 4.

**178.**   Harvey, Diane Kelsay and Harvey, Bob. **Fishing with Peter = Pescando con Pedro.** Wilsonville, Ore.: Beautiful America Publishing, 1993. ISBN: 0-89802=592-3. unp. Text and photography by Diane Kelsay Harvey and Bob Harvey. (Rivendell Nature Series)

The story of Peter, a brown pelican, who goes out on a fishing expedition. On his trip around the mangrove key he saw several other fishing birds: a black-necked stilt, a yellow-crowned night heron, a blue heron, a great blue heron, a white egret, a spoonbill, and a cormorant. After his trip, the brown pelican returns to the mangrove key. The book includes a lot of information about the plants of the keys and the need to preserve them. The photographs were taken on Cayo Rosario and Cayo Pájaro off of the coast of Belize.

**179.** Hautzig, Esther. **At Home: A Visit in Four Languages**. New York: Macmillan, 1968. unp. Illustrated by Aliki.

Friends come to visit in Chicago, Marseilles, Barcelona, and London. The story is in English, but selections of words about the home and visitors who are entertained are given in English, French, Spanish, and Russian, with phonetic pronunciations. Some additional words and the Russian alphabet are appended. Bright colorful illustrations reflect the various cultures of the four countries.

REVIEWS: *Book World*, December 29, 1968, p. 13; *Kirkus Reviews*, October 1, 1968, p. 1106; *Library Journal*, February 15, 1969, p. 861.

**180.** Hautzig, Esther. **In School: Learning in Four Languages**. New York: Macmillan, 1969. unp. Pictures by Nonny Hogrogian.

The first day in school—whether in San Francisco, San Sebastian, Cherbourg, or Odessa—is described in English text only. A few words are then selected from the text and translated into Spanish, French, and Russian with phonetic pronunciations given. Some additional words are included at the end of the book, along with the Russian alphabet. Not truly a bilingual book. Illustrations portray children in all four cultures. Two mistakes in the Spanish translation occur. A female teacher is illustrated, but the translation to Spanish is maestro instead of maestra. The librarian is also pictured as a woman, but the word librarian is translated bibliotecario instead of bibliotecaria. The science teacher, of course, is a man.

REVIEWS: *Booklist*, December 15, 1969, p. 516; *Catholic Library World*, November 1969, p. 202; *Horn Book*, December 1969, p. 669; *Kirkus Reviews*, December 15, 1969, p. 849; *Library Journal*, December 15, 1969, p. 4595; *Publishers Weekly*, October 13, 1969, p. 54.

**181.** Hautzig, Esther. **In the Park: An Excursion in Four Languages**. New York: Macmillan, 1968. unp. Pictures by Ezra Jack Keats.

A brief story in English of a visit to the park in New York, Paris, Moscow, and Madrid. Selected words about activities and animals in the park are given in English, French, Russian, and Spanish, with phonetic pronunciations. A few additional words and the Russian alphabet are appended. The illustrations, several against four-color panels, portray children and activities in all four cultures. The final illustration, showing four silhouettes against the sunset in the four cities, is very striking.

REVIEWS: *Booklist*, June 1, 1968, p. 1140; *Center for Children's Books Bulletin*, October 1968, p. 28; *Christian Science Monitor*, May 1968, p. B2; *Commonweal*, May 24, 1968, p. 309; *Kirkus Reviews*, February 15, 1968, p. 178; *Library Journal*,

July 1968, p. 2729; *New York Times Book Review*, May 5, 1968, p. 51; *Publishers Weekly*, March 11, 1968, p. 49; *Saturday Review*, September 21, 1968, p. 36.

**182.**   Hayes, Joe. **¡El cucuy!: A Bogeyman Cuento in English and Spanish**. El Paso: Cinco Puntos Press, 2001. ISBN: 0-938317-54-7. 32 p. Illustrated by Honorio Robledo.

The bogeyman carries away to his cave two little girls who refuse to help their sister as she cares for their father. A goat herder discovers them accidentally, and they return joyfully to their father. And after that they are very good indeed. Vivid illustrations designed to scare the readers.

**183.**   Hayes, Joe. **Estrellita de oro = Little Gold Star: A Cinderella cuento**. El Paso: Cinco Puntos Press, 2000. ISBN: 0-938317-49-0. 30 p. Illustrated by Gloria Osuna Perez and Lucia Angela Perez.

In a *Note for Readers and Storytellers* on the last page, Joe Hayes tells us that this Cinderella story was very popular in the mountain communities of New Mexico. He used many versions to write this story but especially relied on one by Aurora Lucero White Lea in Literary Folklore of the Hispanic Southwest. From her version he chose the name Arcía for Cinderella. The gold star which Cinderella receives on her forehead for being kind to the hawk appears in almost all of the Cinderella tales in New Mexico. Gloria Osuna Perez completed three of the very vivid paintings before she died, and her daughter Lucia Angela Perez completed the remaining twelve.

REVIEWS: *Booklist*, May 15, 2000, p. 1756; *Center for Children's Books Bulletin*, July 2000, p. 403; *Horn Book Guide*, Fall 2000, p. 340; *Newsletter of the United States Board on Books for Young People*, Spring 2001, p. [13]; *School Library Journal*, June 2000, p. 132.

**184.**   Hayes, Joe. **La Llorona = The Weeping Woman: An Hispanic Legend Told in Spanish and English**. El Paso: Cinco Puntos Press, 1987. ISBN: 0-938317-02-4. 32 p. Illustrated by Vicki Trego Hill.

This legend is the best known folk story of Hispanic America. María looks for and then marries a wealthy ranchero. She has two beautiful children. When her husband leaves her for another woman, María becomes enraged and throws her children in the river. Forever after her ghost roams the river banks looking for her children. Gloria Anzaldúa has created a new story showing La Llorona as a compassionate woman who helps a young girl find the rue needed for a medicine to cure her mother.

**185.**   Hayes, Joe. **Mariposa, mariposa: A Story in Two Languages**. Sante Fe: Trails West Publishing, 1988. ISBN: 0-939729-08-3. 32 p. Illustrated by Lucy Jelinek.

The beautiful butterfly makes a new dress and marries the mouse who is eaten by the cat. Her friends feel so sorry for her that they bring her many flowers and she spends the rest of her days going from one flower to the other.

**186.** Hayes, Joe. **Monday, Tuesday, Wednesday, Oh! = Lunes, martes, miércoles, ¡O!: A Story in Two Languages**. Santa Fe: Trails West Publishing, 1987. ISBN: 0-939729-04-0. 32 p. Illustrated by Lucy Jelinek.

A short story about a poor woman and a rich woman. The poor woman finds a pot of gold; the rich woman finds a pot of snakes and insects.

**187.** Hayes, Joe. **No Way, José! = ¡De ninguna manera, José!: A Story in Two Languages**. Santa Fe: Trails West Publishing, 1986. ISBN: 0-939779-00-8. 32 p. Illustrated by Lucy Jelinek.

A cumulative tale about a bossy little rooster named José who is going to the wedding of his Uncle Perico. He orders the grass, the sheep, the wolf, the dog, the man, and finally the ghosts in the cemetery to help him, but no one likes to be bossed around.

**188.** Hayes, Joe. **Tell Me a Cuento = Cuéntame un story: 4 Stories in English & Spanish**. El Paso: Cinco Puntos Press, 1998. ISBN: 0-938317-43-1. 63 p. Illustrated by Geronimo Garcia.

The four stories included in this collection were previously published as individual books by Trails West Publishing. They are: **Mariposa, mariposa; Monday, Tuesday, Wednesday, Oh! = Lunes, martes, miércoles, ¡Oh!; No Way, José! = ¡De ninguna manera, José!;** and **The Terrible Tragabadas = El terrible tragabadas**. On the last page you will find *Joe's Notes About the Stories*. Pages are well designed for a bilingual book, and the colorful illustrations are refreshing.

REVIEWS: *Children's Book Review Service*, February 1999, p. 79; *Children's Bookwatch*, November 1998, p. 1; *Publishers Weekly*, November 16, 1998, p. 77; *School Library Journal*, October 1998, p. 123.

**189.** Hayes, Joe. **El terrible tragadabas = The Terrible Tragadabas: A Story in Two Languages**. Santa Fe: Trails West Publishing, 1987. ISBN: 0-939729-02-4. 32 p. Illustrated by Lucy Jelinek.

Grandmother fears that the terrible tragadabas have eaten her grandchildren, the sisters Little Bitty, Middle Size, and Great Big. The bumblebee comes along and tells her that she will save them, and she proceeds to do so. They all celebrate with cakes and honey.

**190.** Hayes, Joe. **Watch Out for Clever Women! Hispanic Folktales = ¡Cuidado con las mujeres astutas!** El Paso: Cinco Puntos Press, 1994. ISBN: 0-938317-20-2. 77 p. Illustrated by Vicki Trego Hill.

These tales are a combination of traditional folklore and the author's own imagination. The following tales are all about the quiet strength of women: *In the Days of King Adobe, That Will Teach You, The Day It Snowed Tortillas, Just Say Baaaa,* and *Watch Out!*

REVIEW: *Center for Children's Books Bulletin*, December 1994, p. 130.

**191.**   Hayes, Joe. **Where There's a Will, There's a Way = Donde hay ganas, hay mañas: A Story in Two Languages**. Santa Fe: Trails West Publishing, 1995. ISBN: 0-939719-25-3. 27 p. Illustrations & design by Lucy Jelinek.

A shy boy in New Mexico finds a job as a servant with a priest who takes advantage of him. But the boy finally turns the tale around and leaves.

**192.**   Hazen, Nancy. **Grownups Cry Too = Los adultos también lloran**. Chapel Hill, N.C.: Lollipop Power, 2nd ed., 1978. 24 p. Illustrated by Nancy Hazen. Translated into Spanish by Martha P. Cotera.

A brief story told by a little boy. He describes when he and his parents cry—they could be sad, mad, tired, scared, even happy when they cry. Simple, realistic illustrations. The original edition of 1973 was in English only.

**193.**   Herrmann, Marjorie E. **Las manchas del sapo = How the Toad Got Its Spots**. Skokie, Ill.: National Textbook Company, 1978. 30, 30 p. (Fábulas bilingües = Fables in Spanish and English)

The story of a toad, Luisito, and how he got his spots by being the first toad to fly. The spots were scars from his courageous venture to the bird concert in the sky, and all toads today wear spots to honor Luisito. The amusing illustrations are repeated twice, as the story is told first in Spanish and then in English.

REVIEW: *Proyecto Leer Bulletin*, Fall 1980, p. 25.

**194.**   Herrmann, Marjorie E. **El pájaro Cú = The Cú Bird**. Skokie, Ill.: National Textbook Company, 1978. 30, 30 p. (Fábulas bilingües = Fables in Spanish and English)

A folktale from the Mexican American people of Texas about a bird, born naked, that is dressed with a red feather from the cardinal, a green one from the parrot, a black one from the crow, etc. The Cú bird becomes so beautiful that he flies away from his ugly friends. Ever since then, the owl and the roadrunner have been looking for him. The amusing illustrations are repeated twice, as the story is told first in Spanish and then in English.

REVIEW: *Proyecto Leer Bulletin*, Fall 1980, p. 25.

**195.**   Herrmann, Marjorie E. **Pérez y Martina = Pérez and Martina**. Skokie, Ill.: National Textbook Company, 1978. 30, 30 p. (Fábulas bilingües = Fables in Spanish and English)

A retelling of a well-loved Puerto Rican folktale about Martina, a beautiful ant, who is courted by the cat, the duck, the dog, the rooster, the toad, the bull, the pig, and finally Pérez the mouse, whom she decides to marry. She almost loses him in a pot of rice pudding she is preparing, but all ends happily. The illustrations are repeated twice as the story is told first in Spanish and then in English.

REVIEW: *Proyecto Leer Bulletin*, Fall 1980, p. 25.

**196.**   Herrera, Juan Felipe. **Calling the Doves = El canto de las palomas.** Emeryville, Calif.: Children's Book Press, 1995. ISBN: 0-89239-132-4. 30 p. Pictures by Elly Simmons.

The author glowingly describes the life of a campesino family as they travel up and down the valleys of California. The father Felipe sang to the doves and played the harmonica, the mother Lucha was a healer and recited poetry. There was much love among the traveling families. When Juanito is eight and it is time to go to school, the family gave up this life and moved to the city. Américas Commended List 1995.

REVIEWS: *Booklist*, January 1, 1996, p. 823; *Center for Children's Books Bulletin*, December 1995, p. 129; *Children's Book Review Service*, January 1996, p. 49; *Children's Bookwatch*, October 1995, p. 5; *Five Owls*, January 1996, p. 59; *Horn Book Guide*, Spring 1996, p. 99; *Hungry Mind Review*, Summer 1996, p. 28; *Journal of Youth Services in Libraries*, Winter 2001, p. 36; *Los Angeles Times Book Review*, December 3, 1995, p. 16; *Reading Teacher*, November 1996, p. 244; *School Library Journal*, December 1995, p. 97; *School Library Journal*, February 1996, p. 128; *Smithsonian*, November 1995, p. 170.

**197.**   Herrera, Juan Felipe. **Laughing Out Loud, I Fly: Poems in English and Spanish.** New York: HarperCollins, 1998. ISBN: 0-06-027604-3. unp. Drawings by Karen Barbour. (Joanna Cotler Books)

Herrera writes in free verse in both Spanish and English about the joy and laughter of growing up in a world where he is between two cultures and two homes. The illustrations are black and white sketches often behind the text. Many references to food such as "chorizo with nopales," are not translated into English. The author, at the age of seventeen, was inspired by Picasso's book of poems **Hunk of Skin.** Pura Belpré honor book 2000 for narrative.

REVIEWS: *Booklist*, March 15, 2000, p. 1342; *Horn Book Guide*, Fall 1998, p. 370; *Kirkus Reviews*, May 15, 1998, p. 738; *Publishers Weekly*, June 1, 1998, p. 65; *School Library Journal*, May 1998, p. 156; *Voice of Youth Advocates*, April 2000, p. 15.

**198.**   Herrera, Juan Felipe. **The Upside Down Boy = El niño de cabeza.** San Francisco: Children's Book Press, 2000. ISBN: 0-89239-162-6. 31 p. Illustrations by Elizabeth Gómez.

One day it is time for Juanito to leave the fields and go to school in the city. At first he feels awkward, like he is upside down. But the teacher discovers he has a beautiful voice, and his father gives him a harmonica. On Open House Day Juanito leads his little choir in song. Strong colorful illustrations with colored pages behind the text. The English and Spanish are either one above the other or on facing pages.

REVIEWS: *Center for Children's Books Bulletin*, April 2000, p. 282; *Children's Bookwatch*, March 2000, p. 6; *Horn Book*, September 2000, p. 595; *Horn Book*

*Guide*, Fall 2000, p. 397; *New Advocate*, Winter 2001, p. 94; *Newsletter of the United States Board on Books for Young People*, Spring 2001, p. [13]; *River Review*, Summer 2000, p. 34; *School Library Journal*, March 2000, p. 225.

**199.** Hill, Eric. **Spot's Big Book of Words = El libro grande de las palabras de Spot**. New York: Putnam, 1989. ISBN: 0-399-21689-8. unp.

Spot, the dog, and his friends, have some adventures in the kitchen, on the farm, at school, at music and dance lessons, in the garden, at the beach, and even house cleaning. They have fun in the park and have a birthday party for four-year-old Spot. They go on vacation, have fun in the winter, and have a slumber party.

REVIEWS: *Horn Book*, July 1989, p. 520–521; *School Library Journal*, February 1991, p. 102.

**200.** Hill, L. A. and Innes, Charles. **Oxford Children's Picture Dictionary = Diccionario Oxford en imágenes: inglés-español**. Oxford: Oxford University Press, 1983. ISBN: 84-85766-30 edi 6. 51 p. Illustrated by Barry Rowe.

Words in this dictionary are grouped by categories, such as the farm, the house, clothes, sports, the zoo, what time is it?, etc. English is in black type, and Spanish is in blue type. The words are numbered to correspond to the pictures. There is an index in both languages.

REVIEW: *Booklist*, October 1, 1990, p. 349.

**201.** Hodge, Ben. **Football for Fun = A divertirnos con el fútbol**. El Paso: Football Hobbies, 1978. 22 p.

This booklet explains football in three easy steps: the football field; starting play, and the team with the ball; and ready for the snap, forward passing, and punting, and officials' signals. The black-and-white illustrations add to the clear explanation of the game.

**202.** Hodge, Ben. **Good Times with Football = Momentos divertidos con el fútbol**. El Paso: Football Hobbies, 1975. 20 p.

The author describes in simple terms how the game of football is played. He includes special words to learn and diagrams of the field and of plays. A football uniform is also pictured and described. The black-and-white illustrations add clarity to the written words.

**203.** Hodge, Ben. **"Skram" Runs, Kicks, and Throws = "Skram" corre, patea y tira**. El Paso: Football Hobbies, 1978. 19 p.

An elementary reader about Skram and how he runs, kicks, and throws the football. Simple black-and-white illustrations.

**204.** Holman, Rosemary. **Spanish Nuggets**. San Antonio: Naylor, 1968. unp. Illustrated by Barbara Brigham.

Twenty-six proverbs are presented in this brief collection. Full-page sentimental sepia drawings.

REVIEW: *Library Journal*, March 15, 1969, p. 1326.

**205.**   Hupb, Loretta Burke. **Let's Play Games in Spanish: A Collection of Games, Skits & Teacher Aids**. Skokie, Ill.: National Textbook Company, 1980. 2 volumes.

Volume one includes games, skits, and songs for children in kindergarten through eighth grade, and volume two is for intermediate and advanced students. The songs and games come from all over the Hispanic world. All directions are in English. The words for the games and songs are in both languages. Includes tongue twisters and riddles. Black-and-white illustrations relate to the games to be played. These two volumes have been republished periodically, each time with a new copyright date. There is no indication in the 1980 edition as to whether there are any changes from either the 1976 or the 1974 edition.

REVIEWS: *Cartel*, June 1976, p. 156. (1974 ed.); *Proyecto Leer Bulletin*, Fall 1980, p. 13. (1976 ed.).

**206.**   Hubp, Loretta Burke. **¿Qué será? = What Can It Be?: Traditional Spanish Riddles**. New York: John Day, 1970. 63 p. Collected and arranged, with English translations, by Loretta Burke Hubp. Illustrated by Mircea Vasiliu.

Approximately two hundred riddles, most of which originated in Spain, are included in this volume. Many go far back in time; a few are from the folklore of the New World. Black-and-white whimsical illustrations.

REVIEW: *Library Journal*, May 15, 1970, p. 1943.

**207.**   Jaramillo, Nelly Palacio. **Grandmother's Nursery Rhymes: Lullabies, Tongue Twisters, and Riddles from South America = Las nanas de abuelita: canciones de cuna, trabalenguas y adivinanzas de Suramérica**. New York: Holt, 1994. ISBN: 0-8050-2555-3. unp. Illustrated by Elivia [Savadier].

A bilingual collection of rhymes, riddles, and lullabies for little children collected by the author from those she remembered from her childhood in Colombia. The book is dedicated to her children and grandchildren. Américas Commended List 1994.

REVIEWS: *Booklist*, June 1, 1995, p. 1790; *Children's Book Review Service*, November 1994, p. 27; *Horn Book Guide*, Fall 1995, p. 338; *Journal of Youth Services in Libraries*, Winter 2001, p. 36; *Publishers Weekly*, October 24, 1994, p. 63; *School Library Journal*, February 1995, p. 92; *School Library Journal*, July 1995, p. 27.

**208.**   Jaynes, Ruth. **Tell Me Please! What's That?** Glendale, Calif.: Bowmar Publishing,1968. unp. Photographed by Harvey Mandlin. (Bowmar Early Childhood Series)

Two little boys, Juan, who speaks Spanish, and David, who speaks English, go to the zoo and teach each other the Spanish and English names for the animals. The story is in English, with the names of the animals given in Spanish. Full-page color photographs portray the friendship of the two boys.

**209.**   Jiang, Wei and Jiang, Cheng An. **La heroína Hua Mulan: una leyenda de la antigua China = The Legend of Mu Lan: A Heroine of Ancient China**.

Monterey, Calif.: Victory Press, 1992. ISBN: 1-878217-01-1. 30 p. Illustrated by Wei Jiang and Cheng An Jiang.

Based on a poem written during the Song Dynasty (960-1279), the story of Mu Lan is told. Because her father is old, she takes his place in the army to defend China against invaders from the north. She is a brave soldier, wins many battles, and strategically plans the last battle to drive the invaders out, so that she can return home to her parents.

REVIEWS: *Children's Bookwatch*, October 1998, p. 2; *School Library Journal*, February 1993, p. 118.

**210.**  Jiménez, Francisco. **The Christmas Gift = El regalo de Navidad.** Boston: Houghton Mifflin, 2000. ISBN: 0-395-92869-9. unp. Illustrated by Claire B. Cotts.

Panchito hopes for a red ball for Christmas, but the migrant family has had to move again, and there is only a bag of candy for each child at Christmas. But Mama gets a beautiful handkerchief, and the whole family is pleased. Soft, delicate full-page illustrations. The story is based on an experience that the author had as a child many years ago in a farm labor tent camp. Américas Commended List 2000.

REVIEWS: *Booklist*, September 1, 2000, p. 132; *Center for Children's Books Bulletin*, December 2000, p. 148; *Children's Book Review Service*, October 2000, p. 20; *Publishers Weekly*, September 25, 2000, p. 72; *School Library Journal*, October 2000, p. 60.

**211.**  Jiménez, Juan Ramón. **Platero y yo = Platero and I.** New York: Clarion Books, 1994. ISBN: 0-395-62365-0. 47 p. Selected, translated, and adapted from the Spanish by Myra Cohn Livingston and Joseph F. Domínguez. Illustrations by Antonio Frasconi.

A wandering poet, traveling with the faithful donkey Platero, describes life in the town of Moguer, in Andalusia, Spain. The book was originally written in 1914 in 138 chapters; the distinguished poet Myra Livingston has selected 19 of these chapters for a literary and poetic translation. They cover such topics as children's games, bread, friendship, a rubber stamp, fireworks, the death of a canary, Christmas, and a carnival. Américas Commended List 1994.

REVIEWS: *Book Links*, July 1994, p. 7; *Horn Book Guide*, Fall 1994, p. 347; *Journal of Reading*, February 1995, p. 414; *Reading Teacher*, February 1998, p. 429; *School Library Journal*, July 1995, p. 27.

**212.**  Johnson, Philip. **A Probe into Mexican American Experience = Un examen sobre la experiencia de los mexicoamericanos.** New York: Harcourt Brace Jovanovich, 1973. 311 p. Spanish text by Carmen Maldonado de Johnson. With consultants Alfredo Castañeda, William Guardia, Lidia Avila Ruiz. (Searchbooks in the Social Sciences)

This is a brief, simply written history of the Mexican Americans, their background, and their present life in the United States. Illustrated with sepia drawings and photographs.

REVIEW: *Proyecto Leer Bulletin*, Spring 1976, p. 17.

**213.** Johnston, Tony. **My Mexico = México mío: Poems**. New York: Putnam, 1996. ISBN: 0-399-22275-8. 36 p. Illustrated by F. John Sierra.

A collection of eighteen poems in English and Spanish which reflect the sounds and colors of Mexico. A glossary is appended. Américas Commended List 1996.

REVIEWS: *Catholic Library World*, March 1997, p. 58; *Center for Children's Books Bulletin*, July 1996, p. 376; *Children's Book Review Service*, July 1996, p. 147; *Horn Book*, May 1996, p. 345; *Horn Book Guide*, Fall 1996, p. 368; *Reading Teacher*, February 1998, p. 427; *School Library Journal*, April 1996, p. 126; *Social Education*, April 1997, p. 12.

**214.** Jonas, Ann. **El trayecto = The Trek**. New York: Lectorum Publications, 1985. ISBN: 0-9625162-3-6. unp. Translated by Teresa Mlawer.

A little girl on her way to school sees the animals of the jungle in the trees and buildings around her.

REVIEW: *Booklist*, January 1, 1992, p. 837.

**215.** Joslin, Sesyle. **Señor Baby Elephant the Pirate**. New York: Harcourt, Brace & World, 1962. unp. Pictures by Leonard Weisgard.

Baby elephant learns some Spanish phrases from Pilar the cook. Then he sets off on a treasure hunt after saying good-bye to his mother. A glossary of Spanish words is included. The story itself is in English. Black, yellow, and gray illustrations.

REVIEWS: *Booklist*, June 1, 1962, p. 691; *Chicago Sunday Tribune*, April 29, 1962, p. 15; *Horn Book*, April 1962, p. 170; *Kirkus Reviews*, January 15, 1962, p. 54; *Library Journal*, June 15, 1962, p. 2408; *New York Herald Tribune Books*, October 21, 1962, p. 12; *San Francisco Chronicle*, May 13, 1962, p. 24; *Wisconsin Library Bulletin*, September 1962, p. 349.

**216.** Joslin, Sesyle. **There Is a Bull on My Balcony and Other Useful Phrases in Spanish and English for Young Ladies and Gentlemen Going Abroad or Staying at Home = Hay un toro en mi balcón**. New York: Harcourt, Brace & World, 1966. unp. Illustrated by Katharina Barry.

Two children travel from New York City to Mexico and experience the usual tourist activities, such as a fiesta, a boat ride, shopping, and a bullfight. Amusing black-and-white illustrations. Not all words are given in both languages; for example: "'¿Qué pasa?' means 'What's going on?' And this is when to say it." Only "Qué pasa?" is translated. The illustration then pictures the event.

REVIEWS: *Booklist*, April 1, 1966, p. 775; *Center for Children's Books Bulletin*, June 1966, p. 164; *Chicago Tribune Books Today*, April 17, 1966, p. 19; *Christian*

*Science Monitor*, May 5, 1966, p. 3B; *Horn Book*, August 1966, p. 426; *Kirkus Reviews*, January 1, 1966, p. 7; *Library Journal*, March 15, 1966, p. 1702; *New York Times Book Review*, March 27, 1966, p. 34; *Publishers Weekly*, April 4, 1966, p. 62; *School Library Journal*, January 1981, p. 33.

**217.**   Kahn, Michele. **My Everyday Spanish Word Book**. Woodbury, N.Y.: Barron's Educational Series, 1st English/Spanish ed., 1982. 41 p. Illustrated by Benvenuti. Translated by Michael Mahler and Gwen Marsh.

Everyday activities from waking up, going to school, and going to bed are illustrated with the Spanish words printed next to each of the items pictured. The story itself is in English. Occasionally sentences are given in both languages. There is a Spanish to English vocabulary at the end of this large volume. The illustrations are colorful and well done. The book was originally published in France in 1977 under the title **Mon livre de mots de tour les jours.**

**218.**   Keats, Ezra Jack and Cherr, Pat. **My Dog Is Lost**. New York: Crowell, 1960. unp.

Juanito, newly arrived from Puerto Rico and speaking only Spanish, looks for his lost dog in various parts of New York City. Many people help him, from the bank teller to a little boy in Harlem. The story is in English, but several Spanish words and phrases are used. A word list is included on the last page of the book. Black, white, and red illustrations are well done.

REVIEWS: *Booklist*, April 1, 1961, p. 500; *Catholic Library World*, April 1981, p. 390; *Christian Science Monitor*, November 3, 1960, p. 2B; *Horn Book*, February 1961, p. 44; *Kirkus Reviews*, August 15, 1960, p. 678; *Library Journal*, November 15, 1960, p. 4218; *New York Herald Tribune Books*, July 9, 1961, p. 13; *San Francisco Chronicle*, November 13, 1960, p. 14; *Saturday Review*, November 12, 1960, p. 92; *Wisconsin Library Bulletin*, March 1961, p. 49.

**219.**   Keats, Mark. **Sancho, Pronto, and the Engineer = Sancho, Pronto, y el ingeniero**. Detroit: Blaine Ethridge Books, 1976. 63 p. Translated by Raul Carrera. Illustrated by Alex Cervantes. (A Prism Press Book)

This is a moving story of a nine-year-old boy, Sancho Mendez of Oaxaca, and his mule Pronto, and of how they lead the water engineeer to a blocked mountain stream. The whole village works hard so that water once again flows from the stream. Black-and-white pedestrian drawings. The design of the book and its cover are not very attractive.

REVIEWS: *Horn Book*, April 1977, p. 191; *School Library Journal*, April 1977, p. 53.

**220.**   Keister, Douglas. **Fernando's Gift = El regalo de Fernando**. San Francisco: Sierra Club Books for Children, 1995. ISBN: 0-87156-414-9. 32 p. Spanish translation: Mario Reposo and Margaret E. Hines.

Fernando Vanegas and his family live deep inside the rain forest in Costa Rica. Fernando and his friend Carmina go to school and often have classes outside. It is Carmina's eighth birthday. Carmina takes Fernando to her favorite climbing tree only to find it cut down. Fernando's father's job is to teach people about the importance of the rain forest. He also grows trees in a plant nursery. Fernando gives Carmina a small tree for her birthday, and they go to a special safe place to plant it. The author has illustrated this book with photographs of the Vanegas family and of Costa Rica. Américas Commended List 1995.

REVIEWS: *Appraisal: Science Books for Young People*, Winter 1996, p. 33; *Booklist*, June 1, 1995, p. 1786; *Catholic Library World*, December 1995, p. 48; *Center for Children's Books Bulletin*, May 1995, p. 312; *Horn Book Guide*, Fall 1995, p. 339; *Journal of Youth Services in Libraries*, Winter 2001, p. 36; *Language Arts*, November 1995, p. 539; *Reading Teacher*, February 1997, p. 426; *School Library Journal*, July 1995, p. 64; *Smithsonian*, November 1995, p. 168.

**221.**   Kouzel, Daisy. **The Cuckoo's Reward: A Folk Tale from Mexico in Spanish and English = El premio del cuco: cuento popular de México en español e inglés**. Garden City, N.Y.: Doubleday, 1977. unp. Adapted and translated by Daisy Kouzel. Illustrated by Earl Thollander.

This legend of the cuckoo explains why her colorful feathers turned gray, how she lost her singing voice, and why other birds raise her children for her. Beautifully illustrated.

REVIEWS: *Horn Book*, April 1977, p. 191; *Kirkus Reviews*, February 15, 1977, p. 162; *Language Arts*, February 1978, p. 210; *School Library Journal*, May 1977, p. 52.

**222.**   Kraus, Robert. **José el gran ayudante**. New York: Windmill Books and Dutton, 1977. unp. Illustrations by José Aruego and Ariane Dewey. Translation by Rita Guibert.

José, a friendly octopus, likes to help his family, his friends and enemies, and the young and the old, but at suppertime he prefers to help himself. The English translation, **Herman the Helper**, is given on the dedication page at the front of the book. Colorful and attractive illustrations.

REVIEWS: *Booklist*, September 1, 1981, p. 54; *Horn Book*, December 1977, p. 686; *School Library Journal*, January 1981, p. 33.

**223.**   Kraus, Robert. **Leo el capullo tardio**. New York: Windmill Books and Dutton, 1977. unp. Illustrations by José Aruego. Translation by Rita Guibert.

Leo is a late blooming tiger, but after a winter and a spring, he finally blooms and declares to his worried parents, "I made it." The English version, **Leo, the Late Bloomer**, is included at the beginning of the book. Colorful and attractive illustrations.

REVIEWS: *Booklist*, September 1, 1981, p. 54; *Horn Book*, December 1977, p. 687; *Proyecto Leer Bulletin*, Fall 1980, p. 26; *School Library Journal*, January 1981, p. 33.

**224.**  Kraus, Robert. **Milton el madrugador**. New York: Windmill Books and Dutton, 1977. unp. Illustrated by José and Ariane Aruego. Translation by Rita Guibert.

Milton, the panda bear, is an early riser. He tries to wake everyone else, but creates havoc instead. After he works hard to put everything back together again, he falls asleep just as everyone else wakes up. The English version of **Milton the Early Riser** appears on the verso of the title page. Colorful illustrations.

REVIEWS: *Booklist*, September 1, 1981, p. 54; *Horn Book*, December 1977, p. 687; *School Library Journal*, January 1981, p. 33.

**225.**  Lachtman, Ofelia Dumas. **Big Enough = Bastante grande**, Houston: Piñata Books, 1998. ISBN: 1-55885-221-2. unp. Illustrated by Enrique O. Sánchez. Spanish translation by Yanitzia Canetti

Lupita thinks she is big enough to do many things like staying up late and helping her mother in the restaurant, but Mama doesn't think so. Only when Lupita tackles the thief who stole a special piñata does Mama think she is big enough.

REVIEWS: *Horn Book Guide*, Spring 1999, p. 56; *School Library Journal*, August 1998, p. 142.

**226.**  Lachtman, Ofelia Dumas. **Pepita Takes Time = Pepita, siempre tarde**. Houston: Piñata Books, 2001. ISBN: 1-55885-304-9. unp. Illustrated by Alex Pardo DeLange. Spanish Translation by Alejandra Balestra.

Pepita is always late, but thinks that it doesn't matter even though other people are inconvenienced. On the day the class is going to the zoo, Pepita misses the bus and must spend the day in the principal's office and in the library. Her friend Sonya had missed her. The two stop to watch a cat and her kittens, but Pepita pulls Sonya away and says "we don't want to be late." The Spanish and English texts are on the left pages with small illustrations separating them. The right pages have full colorful illustrations depicting the events in the story.

REVIEW: *School Library Journal*, January 2001, p. 102.

**227.**  Lachtman, Ofelia Dumas. **Pepita Talks Twice = Pepita habla dos veces**. Houston: Piñata Books, 1995. ISBN: 1-55885-07-5. unp. Illustrated by Alex Pardo DeLange.

Pepita is tired of speaking in two languages because it takes so much time. She announces she will only speak English, but then she wonders how will she order tacos, how will she sing the Spanish songs the family loves, how will she be able to talk to her grandmother, and what will her name be. She calls her dog Wolf instead of Lobo, but when he runs in front of a car he only responds to her call of Lobo. She decides then it is good to speak two languages.

REVIEWS: *Book Links*, March 1996, p. 26; *Horn Book Guide*, Spring 1996, p. 99.

**228.** Lachtman, Ofelia Dumas. **Pepita Thinks Pink = Pepita y el color rosado**. Houston, Piñata Books, 1998. ISBN: 1-55885-222-0. unp. Illustrated by Alex Pardo Delange.

Pepita doesn't like pink, although she likes all the other colors. When a little girl moves in next door who loves pink, Pepita is in a dilemma. She finally decides color is not important, and the two girls become friends.

REVIEWS: *Horn Book Guide*, Spring 1999, p. 56; *Publishers Weekly*, July 20, 1998, p. 222; *School Library Journal*, December 1998, p. 86.

**229.** LaMadrid-Esparza, Esther. **Humpty Dumpty and Friends in the Southwest**. Austin, Tex.: Star Light Press, 1990. 3 volumes. With illustrations by various artists and visualized by Star Light.

Volume one includes 18 tradiitonal nursery rhymes and one with a Latino flavor (*Hot Boiled Beans = Frijoles calientes*). Volume two has an additional 18 nursery rhymes, and volume three has 18 more. The art which is scanned in from many sources occasionally reflects southwestern scenes.

**230.** Lamblin, Simone. **Larousse Word and Picture Book**. New York: Larousse, 1981. 45 p. Illustration by Marianne Gaunt. Adaptation by Mary Ann Quinson.

Over 1300 words are given in English, French, and Spanish. The words are grouped into categories. Each double-page illustration includes many items. Beside each picture is a number and the name of the item in French. At the bottom of the page, the same number is given, with the words in English and Spanish. The glossary is from English to French and from English to Spanish. Many words are included that are not commonly found in children's dictionaries, such as hummingbird, ladybug, dandelion, and skyscraper, to name only a few. The illustrations are excellent, but the pages seem very crowded.

**231.** Landeen, Sharon. **When You Get Really Mad! = ¡Cuando estás muy enojado!** Tucson: Ol' Stone Press, 1996. ISBN: 1-887342-00-1. 30 p. Illustrated by Sharon Landeen. Translated by María Rebeca Cartes.

Mrs. Bird was really mad because her nest had fallen from the tree. Grandmother Bird arrives and tells her to sing a song and not say a word. Soon she is feeling better, and the other animals help her to rebuild her nest.

**232.** Laurence. **Robert and the Statue of Liberty**. Indianapolis: Bobbs-Merrill, 1968. unp. Illustrated by Laurence.

Robert invites the Statue of Liberty to visit his city, and she accepts. A fanciful tale with soft, expressive illustrations. The picture of Miss Liberty skating at Rockefeller Plaza is delightful.

REVIEWS: *Center for Children's Books Bulletin*, February 1969, p. 97; *Kirkus Reviews*, November 1, 1968, p. 1212; *Library Journal*, March 15, 1969, p. 1319; *New York Times Book Review*, November 3, 1968, p. 71; *Publishers Weekly*, November 11, 1968, p. 49.

**233.**   Lenski, Lois. **Papa Pequeño = Papa Small**. New York: Walck, 1961. 48 p. Spanish translation by María Dolores Lado.

The familiar story of Papa and Mama Small, their three children, and their activities from Monday to Sunday. Although Mama is shown in a traditional role, the whole family works together in the garden, and Papa cooks Sunday dinner. The illustrations, size, and format are the same as in the original.

**234.**   Lenski, Lois. **Vaquero Pequeño = Cowboy Small**. New York: Walck, 1960. 46 p. Spanish translationby Donald Worcester.

The favorite story of **Cowboy Small** in Spanish and English. Format and illustrations are the same as in the original.

REVIEW: *Library Journal*, October 15, 1960, p. 3853.

**235.**   Levy, Janice. **The Spirit of Tío Fernando: A Day of the Dead Story = El espírito de tío Fernando: una historia del día de los muertos**. Morton Grove, Ill.: Whitman, 1995. ISBN: 0-8075-7586-0. unp. Illustrated by Morelia Fuenmayor. Spanish translation by Teresa Mlawer.

Nando, named after his Uncle Fernando, who died six months ago, is awakened on October 31, the Day of the Dead, because his mother is taking him to the cemetery to honor the spirit of his uncle. Mother sets up an altar in the living room and then sends Nandito to the market to buy things that Uncle Fernando liked. They go to the cemetery and have a fiesta at the grave site to honor Uncle Fernando. Américas Commended List 1995.

REVIEWS: *Catholic Library World*, June 1996, p. 51; *Horn Book Guide*, Fall 1996, p. 327; *School Library Journal*, August 1996, p. 178.

**236.**   Lexau, Joan M. **José's Christmas Secret**. New York: Dial Press, 1963. 54 p. Illustrated by Don Bolognese.

José sells Christmas trees to earn enough money to buy his widowed mother a blanket for Christmas. The story is in English with only a few Spanish words. The Spanish words and the music for the song *La Terruca* are included at the end of the book. Black-and-white illustrations are sensitively drawn.

REVIEW: *Library Journal*, November 15, 1963, p. 4476.

**237.**   Lockhart, Linda Zapata and Stinson, Adele. **A es para amigo = A is for amigo**. Palo Alto, Calif.: Dos Voces Press, 1974. 48 p. Artista, John Littleboy. Editor, Charles J. Bustamente.

This alphabet book lists all of the Spanish letters, including ch, ll, ñ, and rr. Although each Spanish stanza is translated, the main word used is not. It is repeated in Spanish in the English stanza, i.e., amigo, barrio, cuento, Chicano, etc. Black-and-white illustrations are printed on cream-colored paper. Animals are an integral part of each picture.

**238.**   Lomas Garza, Carmen. **Cuadros de familia = Family Pictures**. San Francisco: Children's Book Press, 1990. ISBN: 0-89239-050-6. 30 p. Paintings by Carmen Lomas Garza. Stories as told to Harriet Rohmer. Version in Spanish: Rosalma Zubizarreta.

The author/artist has included in this series of pictures, stories about her family and life in Kingsville, Texas. Scenes represent the fair in Reynosa, Mexico; picking oranges; chicken soup for dinner; a birthday party with a piñata; a cakewalk game; picking nopal cactus; a beach scene with a hammerhead shark; rabbit for dinner; Las Posadas; making tamales; eating watermelon; the Virgin of San Juan; the healer, and rooftop dreaming. Pura Belpré honor book 1996 for illustrations. For a discussion of the art work of Lomas Garza, consult: **A Piece of My Heart = Pedacito de mi corazón: The Art of Carmen Lomas Garza**. This catalog of her paintings includes the title paper by Carmen Lomas Garza, and a critical essay by Amalia Mesa-Bains entitled *Chicano Chronicle and Cosmology: The Works of Carmen Lomas Garza*. Both of these papers are in English. This book was published by The New Press in New York in 1991 in association with the Laguna Gloria Art Museum in Austin, Texas.

REVIEWS: *Book Links*, July 1994, p. 7; *Book Links*, March 1996, p. 26; *Booklist*, June 1, 1990, p. 1907; *Bookwatch*, July 1990, p. 4; *Center for Children's Books Bulletin*, October 1990, p. 36; *Childhood Education*, Summer 1991, p. 246; *Children's Bookwatch*, August 1994, p. 2; *Instructor*, March 1993, p. 16; *Kirkus Reviews*, June 15, 1990, p. 878; *Language Arts*, April 1991, p. 324; *Learning*, February 1993, p. 62; *Los Angeles Times Book Review*, July 29, 1990, p. 8; *Newsweek*, September 9, 1991, p. 65; *Publishers Weekly*, July 13, 1990, p. 34; *Reading Teacher*, April 1991, p. 586; *School Arts*, May 1995, p. 42; *School Library Journal*, November 1990, p. 105.

**239.**   Lomas Garza, Carmen. **In My Family = En mi familia**. San Francisco: Children's Book Press, 1996. ISBN: 0-89239-138-3. unp. Paintings by Carmen Lomas Garza. As told to Harriet Rohmer. Edited by David Schecter. Spanish translation by Francisco X. Alarcón. Kingsville, Texas, is the setting for this book which lovingly tells of growing up in a traditional Mexican American community. Daily life is described and illustrated. Américas Award for 1996. Pura Belpré honor book 1998 for illustrations.

REVIEWS: *AB Bookman's Weekly*, November 18, 1996, p. 1729; *Bookbird*, Spring 1998, p. 55; *Booklist*, November 1, 1996, p. 503; *Booklist*, May 1, 1997, p. 1507; *Horn Book*, November 1996, p. 760; *Horn Book Guide*, Spring 1997, p. 108; *Hungry Mind Review*, Summer 1997, p. 28; *Journal of Youth Services in Libraries*, Winter 2001, p. 35-36; *Reading Teacher*, November 1997, p. 251; *Reading Teacher*, December 1997, p. 308; *School Library Journal*, November 1996, p. 134.

**240.**   Lomas Garza, Carmen. **Magic Windows = Ventanas mágicas**. San Francisco: Children's Book Press, 1999. ISBN: 0-89239-157-X. 30 p. Cut-paper art and stories by Carmen Lomas Garza. As told to Harriet Rohmer. Edited by David Schecter. Spanish translation by Francisco X. Alarcón.

The author/artist uses cut-paper art which seem to be magic windows through which you can see into another world. Each cut-paper design is in two different colors. Each page of text is also in a different color. The author talks about her life and the world around her including the nopal cactus, paper flowers, little tortillas, horned toads, hummingbirds, fish, deer, and turkey. She includes a short lesson on making "papel picado." Pura Belpré Award 2000 for illustrations. Américas Honorable Mention 1999. Lomas Garza has written another book which explains in English only how to create and make the papel picado/cut-paper art. The title is **Making Magic Windows: Creating Papel Picado/Cut-Paper Art**. It was published by Children's Book Press in San Francisco in 1999.

REVIEWS: *Booklist*, May 1, 1999, p. 1592; *Center for Children's Books Bulletin*, May 1999, p. 312; *Horn Book Guide*, Fall 1999, p. 360; *Hungry Mind Review*, Summer 1999, p. 43; *Journal of Youth Services in Libraries*, Winter 2001, p. 36; *New Advocate*, Winter 2000, p. 88; *Publishers Weekly*, February 22, 1999, p. 97; *School Library Journal*, July 1999, p. 87.

**241.** Lopez, Norbert C. **Bilingual ABC in Verse = Abecedario bilingüe en verso**. Fairview, N.M.: Instructional Challenges, 1974. unp. Illustrations by Diane Curnow.

Twenty-nine poems are included in each of the two languages. The verses are not meant to be translations of one another. Each verse represents a response to an illustration from a cultural and linguistic point of view. The book is based on the Spanish alphabet. The English words are not always cognates. Suitable illustrations, some in color and some in sepia. A glossary of English and Spanish words is appended. A second edition was published in 1975 with little change.

REVIEW: *Cartel*, June 1976, p. 26.

**242.** López de Mariscal, Blanca. **The Harvest Birds = Los pájaros de la cosecha**. Emeryville, Calif.: Children's Book Press, 1995. ISBN: 0-89239-131-6. 30 p. Pictures by Enrique Flores.

Juan Zanate, a young man in Mexico, wants to be a farmer, but when his father dies, there is only enough land for his two older brothers. Juan finds a wise old man who lends him land for a season. Juan plants wisely, keeping weeds around his land to prevent erosion, and plants beans, squash, and corn together. In the fall the harvest is great, and the old man gives him the land. It is the harvest birds who guide him in his work.

REVIEWS: *AB Bookman's Weekly*, November 13, 1995, p. 1888; *Book Links*, March 1996, p. 28; *Children's Book Review Service*, Spring 1995, p. 139; *Children's Bookwatch*, May 1995, p. 8; *Children's Bookwatch*, October 1995, p. 7; *EMIE Bulletin*, Fall 1995, p. 9; *Journal of Youth Services in Libraries*, Winter 2001, p. 36; *Reading Teacher*, February 1997, p. 426.

**243.** López-Rodríguez, Américo and Contreras, Richard E. **La cucarachita**. Fullerton, Calif: California State University, Fullerton Bilingual/Bicultural Education Program, [1972?]. unp. Illustrated by Thelma R. Martínez and Bea Bustamente.

The little cockroach powders her face, the bull proposes, then the dog, the rooster, the goat, and finally the mouse. Afraid of all the noises of the animals, she marries the mouse because he sleeps very quietly. An old folktale. Black-and-white sketches on yellow paper. The song *La cucaracha* is appended.

**244.** Lowell, Susan. **Los tres pequeños jabalíes = The Three Little Javelinas.** Flagstaff, Ariz.: Northland Publishing, 1992. ISBN: 0-87358-661-1. unp. Illustrated by Jim Harris.

The story of the three little pigs is told with a Southwestern flavor, as the three javelinas outwit the coyote. Unfortunately, the Spanish tranlation has a mistake on the title page.

REVIEWS: *Booklist*, November 15, 1998, p. 599; *Early Childhood Education Journal*, Fall 1997, p. 48; *Horn Book Guide*, Fall 1997, p. 339; *Journal of Youth Services in Libraries*, Winter 2001, p. 36; *School Library Journal*, November 1997, p. 136.

**245.** Loya, Olga. **Momentos mágicos = Magic Moments.** Little Rock: August House, 1997. ISBN: 0-87483-497-X. 188 p. With Spanish translations by Carmen Lizardi-Rivera.

The author is a professional storyteller, but before she started her career, she listened to stories told by her grandmother and her father. These are the stories of her childhood. They are about her family, her ancestors, East Los Angeles, her culture, and her roots. Many of the stories come from Mexico, but there are also tales from other Latin American countries. There are scary stories, stories of tricksters, stories about strong women, and myths. She concludes the book with notes about each story. Américas Commended List 1998.

REVIEWS: *Journal of Youth Services in Libraries*, Winter 2001, p. 36; *School Library Journal*, August 1999, p. 39.

**246.** Luenn, Nancy. **A Gift for Abuelita Celebrating the Day of the Dead = Un regalo para abuelita en celebración del Día de los Muertos.** Flagstaff, Ariz.: Rising Moon Books for Young Readers from Northland Publishing, 1998. ISBN: 0-87358-688-3. unp. Illustrated by Robert Chapman.

Rosita and her grandmother spend much time together. Abuelita teaches Rosita how to braid cord, hot to pat out the tortillas, and how to weed the garden. But Abuelita becomes sick and dies. Rosita is heartbroken until the Day of the Dead arrives. She goes to the grave with a braided cord, remembers the wonderful times with her grandmother, and feels her spirit there. All of the illustrations are made with cast paper: wet paper pulp dried in a mold, a technique which creates dynamic and strong illustrations. Américas Commended List 1998.

REVIEWS: *Booklist*, March 15, 1999, p. 1333; *Center for Children's Books Bulletin*, January 1999, p. 174; *Children's Book Review Service*, February 1999, p. 75; *Horn Book Guide*, Spring 1999, p. 57; *Publishers Weekly*, November 16, 1998, p. 74;

*Reading Teacher*, February 2000, p. 376; *School Library Journal*, March 1999, p. 180; *School Library Journal*, August 1999, p. 39; *Social Education*, May 1999, p. 9.

**247.**   Macaluso Rodríguez, Gina. **Green Corn Tamales = Tamales de elote**. Tucson: Hispanic Books Distributors, 1994. ISBN: 938243-00-4. unp. Illustrations by Gary Shepard.

A little girl goes to visit her grandparents over the Labor Day weekend, and the whole family joins in to make the tamales. Each person has a part, as the corn is picked, cut from the cob, ground, and made into the tamales. When they are done, they all join in eating them. Arroz con Leche Award winner for 1993.

REVIEWS: *Instructor*, November 1995, p. 49; *School Library Journal*, August 1994, p. 182.

**248.**   Marcos, Subcomandante. **The Story of Colors = La historia de los colores: A Folktale from the Jungles of Chiapas**. El Paso: Cinco Puntos Press, 1999. ISBN: 0-98317-45-8. unp. Illustrations by Domitila Dominguez. Translated by Anne Bar Din. Originally published in Guadalajara, Mexico by Ediciones Colectivo Callejero.

After seeing a macaw and a toucan, Antonio tells the Mayan legend of how colors came to the world. At first the world had only black and white, and the gray which separated them. The gods decided they wanted more colors. One god fell down and started to bleed—the third color red was born. Then other colors were found: green, brown, blue, and yellow; and the colors started to mix. The gods threw the colors around, and some splattered on the men and women, and that is why there are peoples of many different colors. Note: The Mexican government claims Marcos is Rafael Sebastián Guillén Vicente. For a discussion of this book, see "From the Jungles of Chiapas to American Bookstores: A Colorful Trip," by Elena Abós in *Horn Book*, volume 75, number 6 (November/December 1999), pages 696-704.

REVIEWS: *Bloomsbury Review*, November 1999, p. 26; *Children's Book Review Service*, August 1999, p. 161; *Children's Bookwatch*, August 1999, p. 4; *Horn Book Guide*, Fall 1999, p. 326; *New York Times Book Review*, May 16, 1999, p. 22; *Publishers Weekly*, April 5, 1999, p. 239; *School Library Journal*, May 1999, p. 110; *Whole Earth Review*, Winter 1999, p. 104.

**249.**   Markel, Michelle. **Gracias, Rosa**. Morton Grove, Ill.: Whitman, 1995. ISBN: 0-8075-3024-7. unp. Illustrated by Diane Paterson.

Kate has a new babysitter, Rosa, from Guatemala. She soon becomes friends with her. Rosa gives her a cloth Guatemalan doll and teaches Kate some Spanish words. When Rosa returns to her family and her daughter Juana in Guatemala, Kate gives her, for Juana, her doll Jessica. The story is told in English with many Spanish words.

REVIEWS: *Booklist*, June 1, 1995, p. 1787; *Childhood Education*, Spring 1996,

p. 171; *Children's Book Review Service*, July 1995, p. 148; *Horn Book Guide*, Fall 1995, p. 274; *School Library Journal*, May 1995, p. 87.

**250.**   Martel, Cruz. **Yagua Days**. New York: Dial Press, 1976. unp. Pictures by Jerry Pinkney.

Adán Riera goes with his parents on a visit to Ponce, Puerto Rico. There he discovers how fruits and vegetables grow, and he also discovers what a yagua day is. Only a few Spanish words are included, for which there is a word list at the back of the book. Very touching and sensitive black-and-white drawings. The manuscript for this book won the 1972 Council on Interracial Books for Children annual contest for unpublished third-world writers.

REVIEWS: *Babbling Bookworm*, September 1976, p. 3; *Booklist*, June 15, 1976, p. 1467; *Cartel*, November 1978, p. 52; *Catholic Library World*, April 1981, p. 389; *Center for Children's Books Bulletin*, October 1976, p. 28; *Childhood Education*, January 1977, p. 150; *Childhood Education*, April 1979, p. 262; *Choice*, November 1977, p. 1174; *Interracial Books for Children Bulletin*, 7, no. 5, 1976, p. 11; *Kirkus Reviews*, May 1, 1976, p. 531; *School Library Journal*, September 1976, p. 12; *School Library Journal*, January 1981, p. 33; *Social Education*, April 1977, p. 350.

**251.**   Martin, Patricia Preciado. **The Legend of the Bellringer of San Agustín: A Bilingual Children's Story = La leyenda del campanero de San Agustín: cuento bilingüe para niños**. Albuquerque: Pajarito Publications, 1980. unp. Dedicated to Arsenio S. Carrillo. (Special International Year of the Child Publication) (Bilingual Children's Literature = Cuentos bilingües para niños)

When the old man who always rang the bell of San Agustín in Tucson dies, the people cannot find another person to take his place. Finally a vaquero from the hills, with a song in his heart, rings the bell again. The illustrations are simple but well done.

**252.**   Martinez, Olivia; Valerio, Felipe; Apodaca, Cecilia; and Miera, Virginia. **Una luminaria para mis palomitas**. Albuquerque: Colegio de Educación, Universidad de Nuevo México, 1975. 40 p. Illustrator, Felipe Valerio.

Felipe is given two baby pigeons by the priest so that he can teach them how to fly. He builds them a wooden birdhouse. When he thinks the cat has eaten them, he builds a wooden luminaria and lights the candle to pray for their return. Sympathetic and engaging illustrations accompany the Spanish text. The English translation is on the last four pages of the book.

**253.**   Martínez Vasquéz, Ely Patricia. **La historia de Ana = The Story of Ana**. Pasadena, Calif.: Hope Publishing House, 1985. ISBN: 0-932727-15-8. 25 p. With the help of Ana Lorena Sanarabia and others.

Ely Ana Sanchez Castillos and her family travel by foot and bus from war-torn El Salvador to Los Angeles. The father finds a job, and the family begins life anew in the city. Told in simple sentences, the illustrations are by students in the author's class.

**254.**   Mascayano, Ismael. **The Daughter of the Sun = La hija del sol**. Toronto: Kids Can Press, 1978. 25 p. Written and illustrated by Ismael Mascayano after a legend from ancient Peru. (Folktale Series)

Chuqui, a daughter of the sun, finds a companion in Amaru, a shepherd of llamas in ancient Peru. Although they are punished for their disobedience and must wander forever in darkness, they find happiness in being together. Finely drawn black-and-white sketches.

REVIEW: *Booklist*, September 1, 1981, p. 54.

**255.**   Mata, Marta. **Goldilocks and the Three Bears = Ricitos de oro y los tres osos**. San Francisco: Chronicle Books, 1998. ISBN: 0-8118-2075-0. unp. Illustrations by Arnal Ballester. Spanish translation by Alis Alejandro. Originally published in Spanish by La Galera under the title **Cabellos de oro**.

The familiar story of Goldilocks and the three bears with contemporary and lively illustrations. There are three other titles in this series: *Cinderella = Cenicienta, Jack and the Beanstalk = Juan y los frijoles mágicos,* and *Little Red Riding Hood = Caperucita roja.*

REVIEWS: *Booklist*, November 15, 1998, p. 598; *Publishers Weekly*, June 1, 1998, p. 60; *School Library Journal*, August 1998, p. 154.

**256.**   Maury, Inez. **My Mother and I Are Growing Strong = Mi mamá y yo nos hacemos fuertes**. Stanford, Calif.: New Seed Press, 1978. 28 p. Illustrated by Sandy Speidel. Translated by Anna Muñoz.

Emilita tells of working with her mother Lupe in Ms. Stubblebine's garden. They are taking Daddy's place while he is in prison. One day when they visit Daddy in prison, he tells them he will be free next week. Sensitive black-and-white sketches. Elizabeth Martinez in *Interracial Books for Children Bulletin* opens her review with these words: "Once in a long time it is possible to feel really enthusiastic about a children's book—to feel that something fresh, imaginative and also rooted in today's social reality has been created. This is such a book." (p. 14)

REVIEWS: *Booklist*, September 1, 1981, p. 55; *Interracial Books for Children Bulletin*, 10, no. 3, 1979, p. 14; *Lector*, December 1982, p. 24; *Top of the News*, Summer 1981, p. 341.

**257.**   Maury, Inez. **My Mother the Mail Carrier = Mi mamá la cartera**. Old Westbury, N.Y.: Feminist Press, 1976. unp. Illustrated by Lady McCrady. Translated by Norah E. Alemany.

Lupita tells us about her mother Mariana, who is a mail carrier. She tells us her mother is tall, loves colors, likes her work, is strong and brave, gets mad, is kind and wise, is a good cook, and loves outings. Lupita, however, wants to be a jockey when she grows up. Well done illustrations are in black, brown, and yellow. This is a good example of a well-designed bilingual book, each language being given equal prominence, and the illustrations well integrated with the text.

REVIEWS: *Booklist*, September 1, 1981, p. 54; *Interracial Books for Children Bulletin*, 7, no. 7, 1976, p. 15.39; *Kirkus Reviews*, October 1, 1976, p. 1090; *School Library Journal*, March 1977, p. 134.

**258.**   McCunn, Ruthanne Lum. **Pie-Biter = Comepasteles**. Arcadia, Calif.: Shen's Books, 1998. ISBN: 1-885008-07-4. unp. Illustrated by You-shan Tang. Chinese translation by Ellen Lai-shan Yeung. Spanish translation by Teresa Mlawer.

The text is in English, Chinese, and Spanish on one page with a full-page illustration on the facing page. Hoi comes from China to the United States to help build the railroad. After more than twenty years he returns to China. In the United States, he becomes a legend because of his love of American pies. The story is based on true incidents. The pictures are dramatic and have a neon quality.

REVIEWS: *Booklist*, July 1999, p. 1959; *Children's Bookwatch*, June 1999, p. 3; *Children's Bookwatch*, October 1999, p. 6.

**259.**   **Mi primer diccionario ilustrado: edición bilingüe = My First Picture Dictionary: Bilingual Edition**. Madrid: Ediciones PLESA, 5th ed., 1981. 94 p.

The first edition was published in 1975. The English and Spanish words are printed close to the pictures, which are intended to serve as bridges to understanding. The words are grouped into categories. In many instances, several Spanish words are given for the English word. A glossary/index of the Spanish words and of the English words concludes the volume. Realistic illustrations. Except for the English introduction, which contains three misspelled words, this dictionary is well done.

**260.**   **Mi primer vocabulario de inglés**. Mexico City: Ediciones Suromex, 1990. ISBN: 968-855-091-4. 31 p.

From A to Z, words are given first in English and then in Spanish. Each word is accompanied by a picture, a sentence using the word in English, and a sentence using the word in Spanish. At the end of the book, the vocabulary is given from Spanish to English and from English to Spanish.

**261.**   Millán, Amalia and Krone, Beatrice. **Cantos de México = Folk Songs of Mexico: A Supplementary Book of Songs in Spanish for Beginning Classes**. Park Ridge, Ill.: Neil A. Kjos Music Company, 1968. 40 p. Rosita Cota, educational consultant. Illustrated by Clark Allen.

Twenty-one folk songs are included in this book. All of them are Mexican, with the exception of three. Simple accompaniments are included. The verses with the music are in Spanish. Notes on the songs and music are included for the teacher. English notes and translations are appended. The illustrations are well done.

**262.**   Miller, Carl S. **Rockabye Baby: Lullabies of Many Lands and Peoples**. New York: Chappell Music Company by arrangement with UNICEF, 1975. 72 p.

Compiled, edited, and arranged by Carl S. Miller. With the editorial assistance of the United States Committee for UNICEF through its Information Center on Children's Cultures.

Of the forty-four songs in this anthology, five are bilingual in Spanish and English. They are: *A la rue, a la me* from New Mexico; *Arrullo* from Guatemala; *Señora Santa Ana* from Mexico; *Pajarito que cantas* from Spain; and *Arrorro mi niño* from South America. The words for the music are in Spanish, and the translations into English are at the end of each selection. The book is illustrated with black-and-white photographs from the countries represented.

**263.** Miller, Carl S. **Sing, Children, Sing: Songs, Dances and Singing Games of Many Lands and Peoples**. New York: Chappell & Company by arrangement with UNICEF; distributed to the book trade by Quadrangle, 1972. 72 p. Compiled, edited, and arranged by Carl S. Miller. With the editorial assistance of the United States Committee for UNICEF through its Information Center on Children's Cultures. Introduction by Leonard Bernstein.

Of the thirty-five songs or games in this collection, seven are in Spanish with English translations. The seven are: *El tortillero* from Chile, *Bunde San Antonio* from Colombia, *Matatero-tero-la* from Guatemala, *Las mañanitas* from Mexico, *La palomita* from Paraguay, *Los maizales* from Peru, and *Matarile* from Spain. The words to the music are in Spanish, with the English translations given at the end of each selection. The book is illustrated with black-and-white photographs from each country represented.

**264.** Miller, Elizabeth I. **Just Like Home = Como en mi tierra**. Morton Grove, Ill.: Whitman, 1999. ISBN: 0-8075-4068-4. 31 p. Paintings by Mira Reisberg. Spanish translation by Teresa Mlawer.

A young girl and her family arrive in the United States in August. She compares her new life with her old life. Sometimes it is not like home; sometimes it is just like home. Colorful illustrations show family life in the United States. Each illustration is framed by a border. On the last page is a game to play—Can you find...?

REVIEWS: *Booklist*, December 1, 1999, p. 713; *Horn Book Guide*, Spring 2000, p. 47; *School Library Journal*, December 1999, p. 105.

**265.** Miller-Rogers, Janie. **Dinero bien gastado = Money Well Spent**. Carmel Valley, Calif.: La Estancia Press, 1983. 20 p. Illustrated by Linda Haggin.

Sylvia and Daniel are sent to the fish market to buy fish, but unfortunately drop their money in the water. The pelican, the seal, and the otter search for the money.

REVIEW: *Booklist*, October 1, 1990, p. 349.

**266.** Miller-Rogers, Janie. **Lizzi**. Carmel Valley, Calif.: La Estancia Press, 1983. 18 p. Illustrated by Venetia Bradfield Griggs.

Irma finds a very large egg in the hen house, but the creature which hatches is not a chicken. Named Lizzi, the creature sets out with Irma to find out what she is. They ask the librarian, but he cannot identify the animal, so he sends them to a wise professor. She identifies Lizzi as a pterodactyl and invites her to live at the museum.

REVIEW: *Booklist*, October 1, 1990, p. 349.

**267.** Mistral, Gabriela. **Crickets and Frogs: A Fable in Spanish and English = Grillos y ranas: una fábula en español e inglés.** New York: Atheneum, 1972. unp. Translated and adapted by Doris Dana. Illustrated by Antonio Frasconi. (A Margaret K. McElderry Book)

Gabriel Mistral is the pseudonym of Lucila Godoy Alcayaga, the famous Chilean poet. This well-designed book is a fable of the crickets and frogs who cannot agree in which half of the night each will sing. Bold blue, black and white, and yellow, black, and white woodcuts.

REVIEWS: *Book World*, November 5, 1972, p. 3; *Booklist*, March 1, 1973, p. 646; *Cartel*, December 1973, p. 26; *Center for Children's Books Bulletin*, March 1973, p. 110; *Childhood Education*, May 1973, p. 422; *Horn Book*, October 1972, p. 461; *Kirkus Reviews*, September 1, 1972, p. 1022; *Library Journal*, January 15, 1973, p. 255; *New York Times Book Review*, November 5, 1972, p. 47; *Publishers Weekly*, December 11, 1972, p. 35.

**268.** Mora, Francisco X. **La gran fiesta**. Fort Atkinson, Wis.: Highsmith Press, 1993. ISBN: 0-917846-19-2. unp. Illustrated by Francisco X. Mora.

The crow invites all the little birds to bring fruits and sweets to decorate his tree for Christmas. When the crow tries to put one more sweet on the tree, it crashes to the ground. However, the moon and the stars decorate the tree, and the birds enjoy the sweets. In English with many Spanish words. There is a glossary on the last page.

**269.** Mora, Francisco X. **Juan Tuza and the Magic Pouch**. Fort Atkinson, Wis.: Highsmith Press, 1994. ISBN: 0-917846-24-9. unp. Illustrated by Francisco X. Mora.

Pepe the armadillo and Juan Tuza the prairie dog work hard to keep their home in the desert. When Memo the possum comes to collect the rent which they do not have, they decide to go their separate ways to try to find a treasure. Juan rescues a coyote who gives him a magic bag. Pepe cannot sell his bag of radishes. When Memo demands the bag he gets the bag of radishes. In English with several Spanish words interspersed in the text. A glossary of Spanish words appears on the last page.

REVIEWS: *Emergency Librarian*, January 1995, p. 18; *Horn Book Guide*, Fall 1994, p. 284; *Library Talk*, May 1994, p. 16; *Wilson Library Bulletin*, May 1994, p. 94.

**270.** Mora, Francisco X. **The Legend of the Two Moons**. Fort Atkinson,

Wis.: Highsmith Press, 1992. ISBN: 0-917846-15-X. unp. Illustrated by Francisco X. Mora.

Chucho the dog is invited by Perico the parrot to sleep in his tree. Suddenly they see two moons in the sky. Perico decides to capture one of the moons for himself. It is too heavy and he falls with it into the pond. As the two go to sleep they see one moon in the sky and its reflection in the pond. In English with several Spanish words. A glossary of Spanish words appears on the last page.

**271.**   Mora, Pat. **Delicious Hullabaloo = Pachanga deliciosa**. Houston: Piñata Books, 1998. ISBN: 1-55885-246-8. unp. Illustrations by Francisco X. Mora. Spanish translation by Alba Nora Martínez and Pat Mora.

Stylized lizards call their friends to bring their appetites for a feast of mangoes, oranges, cherries, and many vegetables. In a few instances, the Spanish words are not translated into English, such as "cerezas dulces," but the illustration tells the reader what it is.

REVIEWS: *Booklist*, May 1, 1999, p. 1596; *Children's Bookwatch*, December 1998, p. 4; *Horn Book Guide*, Spring 1999, p. 133; *Journal of Youth Services in Libraries*, Winter 2001, p. 37; *Publishers Weekly*, December 14, 1998, p. 77; *School Library Journal*, March 1999, p. 199.

**272.**   Mora. Pat. **The Desert Is My Mother = El desierto es mi madre**. Houston: Piñata Books, 1994. ISBN: 1-55885-121-6. unp. Art by Daniel Lechón.

In poetic phrases, a young girl asks the desert to feed her, to tease her, to frighten her, to hold her, to heal her, to caress her, to make her beautiful, to sing to her, and to teach her. The desert provides all as a mother would. A beautifully designed bilingual book.

REVIEWS: *Booklist*, January 15, 1995, p. 932; *Children's Book Review Service*, March 1995, p. 91; Children's *Bookwatch*, September 1995, p. 1; *Horn Book Guide*, Spring 1995, p. 114; *Instructor*, November 1995, p. 49; *Publishers Weekly*, December 5, 1994, p. 76.

**273.**   Mora, Pat and Berg, Charles Ramírez. **The Gift of the Poinsettia = El regalo de la flor de nochebuena**. Houston: Piñata Books, 1995. ISBN: 1-55885-137-2. unp. Art by Daniel Lechón.

Carlos, living in the small Mexican town of San Bernardo, joins the other families on December 16 for the beginning of Las Posadas. His aunt Nina is too old and stays home. Each night he returns home with gifts for Nina, but he worries what his gift to the baby Jesus will be. Nina sends Carlos into the fields to collect a plant for his gift. As he approaches the altar on Christmas eve, his tears fall on the plant, turning it red—the poinsettia or la flor de nochebuena.

REVIEWS: *Catholic Library World*, December 1995, p. 38; *Language Arts*, March 1996, p. 209.

**274.**   Mora, Pat. **Listen to the Desert = Oye al desierto**. New York: Clarion Books, 1994. ISBN: 0-395-67292-9. unp. Illustrated by Francisco X. Mora.

In the desert, you can hear the sounds of the owl, the toad, the snake, the dove, the coyote, the mice, and the wind. The sounds in Spanish and English are different. The dove says coo, coo, coo in English. In Spanish she says currucú, currucú, currucú.

REVIEWS: *Book Links*, July 1994, p. 7; *Children's Book Review Service*, July 1994, p. 149; *Children's Book Review Service*, April 1996, p. 99; *Horn Book Guide*, Fall 1994, p. 348; *Kirkus Reviews*, May 1, 1994, p. 634.

**275.**   Mora, Pat. **Uno, dos, tres = One, Two, Three**. New York: Clarion Books, 1996. ISBN: 0-395-67294-5. 43 p. Illustrated by Barbara Lavallee.

Two little girls are shopping for Mama's birthday. Counting from one to ten they buy that number of each of the items in the market. Only the numbers are given in Spanish and English. The brief text is in English. With all their gifts the girls wish Mama "Happy Birthday." The nine little animals are representative of the alebrijas from Oaxaca, Mexico. Clothing and scenery reflect Mexican folk art.

REVIEWS: *Booklist*, June 1, 1996, p. 1736; *Children's Book Review Service*, May 1996, p. 112; *Horn Book*, May 1996, p. 327; *Horn Book Guide*, Fall 1996, p. 268; *Kirkus Reviews*, January 15, 1996, p. 139; *Los Angeles Times Book Review*, September 13, 1998, p. 8; *Reading Teacher*, November 1997, p. 251; *Reading Teacher*, May 1999, p. 890; *School Library Journal*, April 1996, p. 114.

**276.**   Morrison, Lillian. **Best Wishes, Amen: A New Collection of Autograph Verses**. New York: Crowell, 1974. 195 p. Illustrated by Loretta Lustig.

Includes a section, ¿Escribo yo en tu libro?, pp. 175-193, which contains eighteen bilingual autograph verses collected by the author in New York City from albums lent by children and other friends. Black-and-white amusing sketches. The size of the book is similar to the size of an autograph album.

REVIEWS: *Booklist*, February 1, 1975, p. 572; *Center for Children's Books Bulletin*, April 1975, p. 135; *Horn Book*, February 1975, p. 63; *Kirkus Reviews*, December 1, 1974, p. 1257; *New Yorker*, December 1, 1975, p. 185; *Publishers Weekly*, November 11, 1974, p. 49; *School Library Journal*, March 1975, p. 100; Teacher, April 1975, p. 32.

**277.**   Morton, Lone. **Goodnight Everyone = Buenas noches a todos**. Hauppauge, N.Y.: Barron's Educational Series, 1994. ISBN: 0-8120-6452-6. unp. Pictures by Jakki Wood. Spanish by Rosa Martín. (I Can Read Spanish: Language Learning Story Books)

Mamá puts Marta to bed with all her animals. A note on pronouncing Spanish is included.

REVIEWS: *Books for Keeps*, September 1998, p. 9; *Horn Book Guide*, Spring 1995, p. 114.

**278.**   **My First Spanish & English Dictionary**. Lincolnwood, Ill.: Passport Books, 1992. ISBN: 0-8442-0055-7. 64 p.

This is not a dictionary in the usual sense. The words, both in Spanish and English, are presented around topics, such as: the family, the house and the rooms in it, food, the body, school, the city and the country, the seasons, and animals. Illustrations are realistic.

**279.** Nardelli, Robert R. **The Cat in the Hat Beginner Book Dictionary in Spanish**. New York: Beginner Books, 1966. 133 p. Adapted into beginner's Spanish by Robert R. Nardelli.

This large-format dictionary is from English to Spanish only. After the words are listed, they are given in an English sentence and a Spanish sentence. The dictionary includes a basic vocabulary of more than one thousand Spanish words. A brief pronunciation guide is given on the last two pages. Although the illustration of Dr. Seuss's cat in the hat appears on the cover, the cat is not used for the illustrations in the dictionary. Instead there is a dog with a hat. The colorful and amusing illustrations are not by Dr. Seuss but by an unnamed illustrator.

REVIEWS: *Christian Science Monitor*, November 3, 1966, p. B5; *Library Journal*, December 15, 1966, p. 6209; *Saturday Review*, November 19, 1966, p. 51.

**280.** Neruda, Pablo. **Bestiary = Bestiario: A Poem**. New York: Harcourt, Brace & World, 1965. unp. Translated by Elsa Neuberger. With woodcuts by Antonio Frasconi. Introduction by Angel Flores.

Pablo Neruda's poem *Bestiario* was originally published in Buenos Aires in 1958. The poem shows the author's intimacy with an infinite variety of life. The woodcuts in black and red are striking pictures, both simple and strong. The introduction by Angel Flores is in English. This book has been beautifully printed on specially made paper from hand-set type in a limited edition of 3,500 copies. The English and Spanish versions of the poem are on opposite pages.

REVIEW: *Library Journal*, November 15, 1965, p. 4986.

**281.** Nims, Bonnie. **Yo quisiera vivir en un parque de juegos = I Wish I Lived at the Playground**. Chicago: J. Philip O'Hara, 1972. 48 p. Translated by Ramón S. Orellana. Illustrated by Ramón F. Orellana.

Poems about merry-go-rounds, balloons, sandpiles, swings, seesaws, and slides. The black-and-white drawings of the children playing are sensitively and realistically drawn. In the copy I examined four titles of poems, unfortunately, were printed upside down.

REVIEW: *Library Journal*, March 15, 1973, p. 995.

**282.** Nye, Naomi Shihab. **The Tree Is Older Than You Are: A Bilingual Gathering of Poems & Stories from Mexico with Paintings by Mexican Artists**. New York: Simon & Schuster Books for Young Readers, 1995. ISBN: 0-689-80297-8. 111 p.

Ms. Nye in the introduction to this book says: "Some of the writers in this collection are names well known and legendary—José Juan Tablada, Rosario

Castellanos, and Octavio Paz among them. Others belong to a younger generation of voices." The poems, in English and Spanish, are arranged in two groups: People, and Earth and Animals. Notes on the contributors, a note on the folktales, a note on the translations and translators, acknowledgments, an index of titles (English), an index of titles (Spanish), an index of writers and artists, and a list of illustrations conclude the volume. Américas Commended List 1995.

REVIEWS: *Book Links*, March 1996, p. 29; *Booklist*, March 15, 1996, p. 1276; *Center for Children's Books Bulletin*, November 1995, p. 101; *Emergency Librarian*, September 1996, p. 24; *Horn Book*, March 1996, p. 218; *Horn Book Guide*, Spring 1996, p. 136; *Hungry Mind Review*, Summer 1996, p. 28; *Journal of Youth Services in Libraries*, Winter 2001, p. 37; *New York Times Book Review*, March 10, 1996, p. 21; *Publishers Weekly*, April 13, 1998, p. 77; *Reading Teacher*, February 1997, p. 425; *Reading Teacher*, March 1997, p. 477; *School Library Journal*, October 1995, p. 150; *Voice of Youth Advocates*, December 1995, p. 333; *Voice of Youth Advocates*, August 1998, p. 228.

**283.** Ohara, Maricarmen. **Adivinanzas, fábulas y refranes populares**. Ventura, Calif.: Alegría Hispana Publications, 1990. ISBN: 0-44356-06-0. 77 p. English version of the fables by Ken Knowlton. Illustrations by Rubén Darío Acevedo.

Over 25 riddles, fables, and proverbs are included in this collection in both English and Spanish. Some well-known ones include: *Belling the Cat*, *The Boy Who Cried Wolf*, and *The Goose with the Golden Eggs*.

**284.** Ohara, Maricarmen. **Aventuras infantiles = Adventures for Kids**. Ventura, Calif.: Alegría Hispana Publications, 1989. ISBN: 0-944356-04-04. 79 p. Ilustrado por Rubén Darío Acevedo.

Ten fairy tales and stories are included in this collection in both English and Spanish: *The Fisherman and His Wife*, *The Shirt of the Happy Man*, *The Two Hunchbacks*, *The Squirrels*, *The Magic Drum*, *Three Questions*, *Like Cat and Dog*, *The Eyes of the Tiger*, *The Paraguayan Bell Bird*, and the *Incompatible Roommates*.

**285.** Ohara, Maricarmen. **Cuentos favoritos = Favorite Tales**. Ventura, Calif.: Alegría Hispana Publications, 1987. ISBN: 0-944356-01-X. 80 p. Illustrated by Monica Estill.

Ten short stories are included in this bilingual collection. Cultural information, legends, and fables are woven into the stories. The Spanish and English are on opposite pages, and a vocabulary listing is given at the end of each story.

REVIEW: *Booklist*, October 1, 1990, p. 349.

**286.** Ohara, Maricarmen. **Cuentos matemáticos = Math Tales**. Ventura, Calif.: Alegría Hispana Publications, 1989. ISBN: 0-944356-06-0. 77 p. Ilustrado por Rubén Darío Acevedo.

Seven folk tales with mathematical themes are included in this collection: *The House of Joe Frog Maracas*, *The Tailor from Salta*, *The Last Will*, *Don Leonardo's Horseshoe*, *The Magic Thread*, *The Fried Eggs*, and *The Pharmacist's Accounting*.

**287.** Ohara, Maricarmen. **Fantasía bilingüe = Bilingual Fantasy**. Ventura, Calif.: Alegría Hispana Publications, 1987. ISBN: 0-944356-02-8. 80 p. Illustrated by Monica Estill.

Ten short stories are included in this collection. After each story is a listing of vocabulary words in both Spanish and English. The collection has themes taken from fairy tales, myths, and legends.

REVIEW: *Booklist*, October 1, 1990, p. 349.

**288.** Ohara, Maricarmen. **Tesoro de refranes populares = A Treasure of Popular Proverbs**. Ventura, Calif.: Alegría Hispana Publications, 1990. ISBN: 0-944356-10-9. 144 p. Illustrated by Rubén Darío Acevedo.

This collection includes the most popular proverbs of the Spanish language. The author has translated them almost literally. If the translation is awkward, she has included brief explanations.

**289.** Ormsby, Virginia. **What's Wrong with Julio?** Philadelphia: Lippincott, 1965. unp. Illustrated by the author.

The children at school teach each other some Spanish words and some English words, except for Julio, who won't talk. Maria finds out he is lonely, so the children donate their dessert money so that he can call his parents by long distance. He thanks them in English. All of the school signs are in both languages, and the endpapers include small sketches of animals and other familiar items with their names in both languages. The library is translated "librería" instead of "biblioteca." Symphathetic and amusing illustrations.

REVIEWS: *Center for Children's Books Bulletin*, April 1966,p. 135; *Interracial Books for Children Bulletin*, 5, no. 7 & 8, 1975, p. 11; *Library Journal*, December 15, 1965, p. 5504.

**290.** Orozco, José-Luis. **De colores and Other Latin-American Folk Songs for Children**. New York: Dutton Children's Books, 1994. ISBN: 0-525-45260-5. 56 p. Selected, arranged, and translated by José-Luis Orozco. Illustrated by Elisa Kleven.

The author has collected 27 songs, chants, and rhymes from many countries of Latin America. The music for each song is given along with the verses in both Spanish and English. Illustrations are colorful and present everyday activities of children. Each page has a right and left border of various designs. Américas Commended List 1994.

REVIEWS: *Book Links*, March 1996, p. 29; *Booklist*, December 15, 1994, p. 750; *Horn Book*, January 1995, p., 66-67; *Publishers Weekly*, August 23, 1999, p. 61.

**291.** Orozco, José-Luis. **Diez deditos = Ten Little Fingers and Other Play Rhymes and Action Songs from Latin America**. New York: Dutton Children's Books, 1997. ISBN: 0-525-45736-4. 56 p. Selected, arranged and translated by José-Luis Orozco. Illustrated by Elisa Kleven.

Orozco learned these rhymes and action songs from his mother and grand-mother in Mexico City and from families he lived with while traveling as a singer with the Mexico City Children's Choir. Some songs and rhymes are his own creation. Many of the rhymes have the music included and pictures show-ing the finger motions. There are wonderful, busy illustrations, many of them full page. Borders on the top and bottom of textual pages add color and inter-est. Each rhyme is preceded by a brief history of the song. The last page has a subject index. Américas Commended List 1997.

REVIEWS: *Booklist*, January 1, 1998, p. 819; *Center for Children's Books Bul-letin*, March 1998, p. 254; *Children's Bookwatch*, December 1998, p. 4; *Early Childhood Education Journal*, Winter 1998, p. 105; *Horn Book*, March 1998, p. 231; *Horn Book Guide*, Spring 1998, p. 148; *Journal of Youth Services in Libraries*, Winter 2001, p. 37; *Kirkus Reviews*, December 15, 1997, p. 1837; *Publishers Weekly*, December 8, 1997, p. 74; *Reading Teacher*, September 1998, p. 62; *School Library Journal*, February 1998, p. 132; *Social Education*, April 1998, p. 9.

**292.**  Palmer, Helen. **Un pez fuera del agua**. New York: Beginner Books, 1967. 64 p. Illustrated by P. D. Eastman. Translated from the English by Car-los Rivera. (Yo lo puedo leer solo = Beginner Books)

A humorous story of a little goldfish that is fed too much by his owner and soon outgrows his fishbowl, all the pots and pans in the house, the bathtub, and even the town swimming pool. Mr. Carp from the pet shop saves the day by making Otto small again. Amusing illustrations. The cover title is: **A Fish Out of Water**.

REVIEW: *Booklist*, July 15, 1968, p. 1275.

**293.**  Patiño, Ernesto. **A Boy Named Paco = Un niño llamado Paco**. San Antonio: Naylor, 1974. 43 p. Spanish translation by Herlinda P. Olivas. Illus-trations by Arturo Perez Torres.

The English text is on pp. 1-25, and the Spanish text is on pp. 27-42. Paco loves to play the bull in mock bullfights, but this passion keeps him from hold-ing a job. Scolded by his parents, he runs away by stealing a ride on a truck, which ends up at Don Luis Ortega's ranch. He proves his worth by hard work, after which he unexpectedly is selected to play the bull for Alfredo. Paco has finally found his niche in the world. Brief vocabulary is included. Black-and-white sketches, only one of which is with the Spanish text.

REVIEWS: *Cartel*, Fall 1976, p. 6; *Center for Children's Books Bulletin*, May 1975, p. 152.

**294.**  Paulsen, Gary. **Sisters = Hermanas**. San Diego: Harcourt Brace, 1993. ISBN: 0-15-275324-9. 65 + 63 p. Translated into Spanish by Gloria de Aragón Andújar.

The author alternately tells the story of Rosa and Traci, two fourteen-year-old girls. Rosa is Mexican American and a prostitute. Traci is an Anglo who is trying to be a model. Traci sees Rosa in a shop, and suddenly realizes that they are the same—both selling their bodies and their looks. The English version is from the beginning of the book to the middle. When you flip the book over, the Spanish version is also from the beginning of the book to the middle. This is a book for young adults by a well-known author.

REVIEWS: *Horn Book*, March 1994, p. 206; *Kliatt Young Adult Paperback Book Guide*, May 1994, p. 11.

295.   Paz, Elena. **Favorite Spanish Folksongs: Traditional Songs from Spain and Latin America**. New York: Oak Publications, 1965. 96 p. Compiled and edited by Elena Paz. Foreword by Pru Devon.

A selection of regional songs from several countries in Latin America: Argentina, Bolivia, Chile, Cuba, Mexico, Peru, Puerto Rico, and Spain. The music for voice is accompanied by the Spanish words. Then the stanzas in Spanish and English are given side by side. The descriptions are in English. The expressive black-and-white illustrations, including some nudes, were selected and positioned by Moses Asch. This collection is not designed particularly for children, although some of the songs might be useful.

REVIEWS: *Booklist*, October 1, 1965, p. 129; *Library Journal*, April 1, 1965, p. 1723.

296.   Paz, Elena and García Travesi, Carlos. **Las Posadas, a Mexican Christmas: A Playlet with Music in Spanish and English**. Melville, N.Y.: Belwin Mills Publishing, 1962. 24 p.

Directions for this Christmas play designed to be used by music or language classes are given in Spanish and English, and the dialog of the play is also in both languages. However, the words of ten of the eleven songs included are in Spanish only, and one song is in English only. A simple guide to Spanish pronunciation is given on the last page. Instructions are included for the teacher. The music for voices and piano is included. There are no other illustrations.

297.   Pearce, T. M. **Stories of the Spanish Southwest: In English and Spanish = Cuentos de los niños chicanos**. Albuquerque: The Author, 1973. 54 p. Translated by Catherine Delgado Espinosa. Illustrations by Skeeter Leard.

Six stories are included in this collection, dedicated to both children and their elders who are young in heart. The stories are: *The Fried Buns of Euphemia, The Burro and the Wise Men, A Faithful Friend, The Piñata, The Grandfather,* and *Patient Pepita*. Small black-and-white illustrations appear at the beginning of four of the stories. The Spanish title on the paper covers was: **Cuentos de nuestros niños**. Printed by Aiken Printing Company and sold through the Quivira Bookshop in Albuquerque.

298.   Pellowski, Anne; Sattley, Helen R.; and Arkhurst, Joyce C. **Have You Seen a Comet? Children's Art and Writing from Around the World**. New York: John Day, in cooperation with the U.S. Committee for UNICEF, 1971. 120 p.

This collection of children's original art and writing was gathered from seventy-five countries of the world. The child authors and artists range in age from six to sixteen. There are only three Spanish/English selections: (1) *Sadness in the Rain* by Esmeralda de la O, age eleven, p. 31; (2) *I Speak Your Name with Respect* by Margarita de Bedout, age nine, p. 45; and (3) *My Mother* by Carlos Eduardo Amador, age nine, p. 50. All three selections are from Costa Rica. The children's art work is in color.

REVIEWS: *Book World*, November 7, 1971, p. 12; *Booklist*, January 1, 1972, p. 394; *Center for Children's Books Bulletin*, December 1971, p. 64; *Childhood Education*, April 1972, p. 380; *Horn Book*, February 1972, p. 67; *Kirkus Reviews*, October 1, 1971, p. 1076; *Library Journal*, January 15, 1972, p. 284; *Saturday Review*, November 13, 1971, p. 60; *Teacher*, April 1977, p. 32; *Top of the News*, April 1972, p. 310.

**299.** Peña, Sylvia Cavazos. **Kikiriki: Stories and Poems in English and Spanish for Children.** Houston; Revista Chicano-Riqueña/Arte Público Press, 1981. 112 p. Illustrated by Narciso Peña.

The selections included in this issue for children from kindergarten to sixth grade reflect various aspects of Latino life in the United States, in addition to Latino history, traditions, imagination, and fantasy. Thirteen selections are in Spanish, and fifteen selections are in English. A few black-and-white sketches are included.

**300.** Peña, Sylvia Cavazos. **Tun-ta-ca-tun: More Stories and Poems in English and Spanish for Children.** Houston: Arte Público Press, 1986. ISBN: 0-934770-43-3. 191 p. Illustrated by Narcisco Peña.

This collection includes fifteen poems in English, eight stories in English, twelve poems in Spanish, and eight stories in Spanish. The English versions are given first and then the Spanish. Some of the verse selections have been collected from the Hispanic comunity of Houston.

REVIEW: *Booklist*, October 1, 1990, p. 349.

**301.** Pérez, Amada Irma. **My Very Own Room = Mi propio cuartito.** San Francisco: Children's Book Press, 2000. ISBN: 0-89239-164-2. 30 p. Illustrations by Maya Christina Gonzalez.

A nine-year old girl shares a bedroom with her five little brothers. All she wants is a room of her own. Based on a family story, the little girl finds a storage room in their tiny house, and everyone helps her move the "stuff" in it to the porch. Tio Pancho brings her a bed. Mama has enough stamps for a lamp. And the little girl goes to the library for six books to fill her room. Colorful bright illustrations. Américas Honorable Mention 2000.

REVIEWS: *Booklist*, July 2000, p. 2042; *Center for Children's Books Bulletin*, November 2000, p. 116; *Horn Book*, November 2000, p. 749; *Newsletter of the United States Board on Books for Young People*, Spring 2001, p. [13]; *Publishers*

*Weekly*, Fall 2000, p. 71; *River Review*, Fall 2000, p. 31; *School Library Journal*, August 2000, p. 163.

**302.**   Perl, Lila. **Piñatas and Paper Flowers: Holidays of the Americas in English and Spanish = Piñatas y flores de papel: fiestas de las Américas en inglés y español.** New York: Clarion Books, 1983. 91 p. Illustrated by Victoria DeLarrea. Spanish version by Alma Flor Ada.

Eight holidays are described in detail, along with the customs in both North America and South America, especially in the United States, Puerto Rico, and Mexico. The holidays are New Year's Day, Epiphany, Mardi Gras and Easter, St. John the Baptist, Columbus Day, Halloween, Festival of the Sun, and Christmas. In an attempt to describe parallel holidays on the two continents, some important Latin American holidays are omitted. The black-and-yellow illustrations are well done. The reviewer in *Lector* does not recommend this title.

REVIEWS: *Interracial Books for Children Bulletin*, 14, no. 5, 1983, p. 27; *Lector*, September 1983, p. 48.

**303.**   Pietrapiana. **Tomasa the Cow = La vaca Tomasa.** Houston: Piñata Books, 1999. ISBN: 1-55885-284-0. unp.

Tomasa desires freedom, and César, a little bird, releases her. On her journey, she discovers that she does not like the city. She ends up swimming with Lucas, the whale. The Spanish and English texts are on the left pages, and the right pages are filled with strong, bold illustrations.

REVIEWS: *Horn Book Guide*, Spring 2000, p. 49; *School Library Journal*, September 1999, p. 200.

**304.**   Politi, Leo. **Juanita.** New York: Scribners, 1948. unp.

A beautifully told story in English of Antonio and Maria Gonzalez and their daughter Juanita, for whom they named their shop on Olvera Street in old Los Angeles. Juanita receives a white dove for her birthday and carries it in the procession for "The Blessing of the Animals." Sensitive and beautiful illustrations. Only a few Spanish words and phrases are included in the story. A Caldecott Honor Book, 1949.

REVIEWS: *Booklist*, May 1948, p. 302; *Chicago Sun Times*, April 10, 1948, p. 19; *Commonweal*, November 19, 1948, p. 146; *Elementary English*, April 1968, p. 451; *Horn Book*, May 1948, p. 173; *Horn Book*, July 1950, p. 272; *Kirkus Reviews*, April 1, 1948, p. 169; *Library Journal*, May 1, 1948, p. 716; *New York Herald Tribune Weekly Book Review*, March 21, 1948, p. 6; *New York Times Book Review*, March 28, 1948, p. 33; *New Yorker*, December 11, 1948, p. 125; *Saturday Review of Literature*, April 10, 1948, p. 34; *Social Education*, October 1979, p. 476.

**305.**   Politi, Leo. **Song of the Swallows.** New York: Scribners, 1949. unp.

Only a few Spanish words are included in this lovely story about Juan and the swallows that return each spring on St. Joseph's Day to the Mission of San Juan Capistrano. Beautiful, soft illustrations. Caldecott medal, 1950.

REVIEWS: *Book World*, September 13, 1981, p. 12; *Booklist*, April 15, 1949, p. 285; *Catholic World*, December 1949, p. 212; *Chicago Sun Times*, April 16, 1949, p. 37; *Christian Science Monitor*, November 15, 1949, p. 11; *Commonweal*, November 18, 1949, p. 189; *Elementary English*, April 1968, p. 451; *Horn Book*, May 1949, p. 209; *Horn Book*, July 1950, p. 272; *Kirkus Reviews*, March 15, 1949, p. 149; *Library Journal*, April 15, 1949, p. 667; *New York Herald Tribune Weekly Book Review*, May 8, 1949, p. 12; *New York Times Book Review*, May 15, 1949, p. 22; *San Francisco Chronicle*, November 13, 1949, p. 7; *Saturday Review of Literature*, April 9, 1949, p. 36; *Wisconsin Library Bulletin*, June 1949, p. 107.

**306.** Pomerantz, Charlotte. **The Tamarindo Puppy: And Other Poems.** New York: Greenwillow Books, 1980. 31 p. Pictures by Byron Barton.

In the first poem of 119 words, only nine words are in Spanish. In another poem of 86 words, 51 are in Spanish. This pattern of mixing Spanish and English is followed throughout the thirteen poems in this collection. Some of the resulting rhymes are very interesting and might be useful as nonsense verses to use in story hour. Colorful illustrations.

REVIEWS: *Booklist*, February 15, 1980, p. 836; *Booklist*, September 1, 1981, p. 55; *Catholic Library World*, April 1981, p. 390; *Center for Children's Books Bulletin*, November 1980, p. 62; *Childhood Education*, September 1981, p. 51; *Children's Book Review Service*, March 1980, p. 74; *Horn Book*, August 1980, p. 423; *Kirkus Reviews*, June 1, 1980, p. 711; *New York Times Book Review*, April 27, 1980, p. 47; *School Library Journal*, March 1980, p. 124; *School Library Journal*, January 1981, p. 33; *Top of the News*, Summer 1981, p. 342.

**307.** Prieto, Mariana. **Ah Ucu and Itzu: A Story of the Mayan People of Yucatán = Ah Ucu e Itzo: un cuento de la gente Maya de Yucatán.** New York: John Day, 1964. 48 p. Illustrations by Lee Smith.

A well-told Mayan legend about the little people who help the corn grow, and about a little boy, Ah Ucu, and his pet mouse Itzo. Strong two-color (red and black or green and black) illustrations faithfully reflect the story.

REVIEWS: *Center for Children's Books Bulletin*, December 1965, p. 67; *Elementary English*, January 1967, p. 9; *Library Journal*, May 15, 1964, p. 2221.

**308.** Prieto, Mariana. **Johnny Lost.** New York: John Day, 1969. 48 p. Illustrations by Catherine Hanley.

Juanito, a little Cuban boy, makes a habit of getting lost. After arriving in a large city in the United States, he gets lost at the Thanksgiving day parade, along with an Italian boy and an American black girl. They are all rescued by a policewoman and are reunited with their parents. Sympathetic and realistic illustrations. The half-title page includes the parallel title: **Juanito Perdido**.

REVIEWS: *Library Journal*, July 1969, p. 2673.

**309.** Prieto, Mariana. **A Kite for Carlos = Un papalote para Carlos.** New York: John Day, 1966. 48 p. Illustrations by Lee Smith.

Carlos's grandfather makes him a kite for his ninth birthday. After a birthday party, Grandfather takes the children to the park to fly the kite. When Carlos tries to fly it by himself in disobedience, the kite ends up in the top of the poinciana tree. Carlos learns an important lesson. Illustrations are well done, especially the portrayal of the grandfather.

REVIEWS: *Center for Children's Books Bulletin*, September 1966, p. 18; *Elementary English*, January 1967, p. 10; *Kirkus Reviews*, April 1, 1966, p. 372; *Library Journal*, April 15, 1966, p. 2213.

310. Prieto, Mariana. **Play It in Spanish: Spanish Games and Folk Songs for Children.** New York: John Day, 1973. 43 p. Music by Elizabeth Colwell Nielson. Illustrated by Regina and Haig Shekerjian.

Seventeen Spanish folk songs and games, many of them old, were selected for the elementary school child. Verses for the songs are in opposite columns in English (freely translated) and Spanish, but the directions for the games are in English only. The melody is for the Spanish words and is separated from the piano music for easier reaading.

REVIEWS: *Cartel*, December 1974, p. 121; *Library Journal*, September 15, 1973, p. 2643; *Proyecto Leer Bulletin*, Winter 1974, p. 9.

311. Prieto, Mariana. **The Wise Rooster = El gallo sabio.** New York: John Day, 1962. unp. Illustrations by Lee Smith.

This is a lovely Latin American legend of Christmas Eve, when the animals learn they can talk until the vain donkey breaks the spell. Beautiful single-color illustrations. Brief vocabulary at the end.

REVIEWS: *Booklist*, July 15, 1968, p. 1275; *Elementary English*, January 1967, p. 9; *Library Journal*, September 15, 1962, p. 3205.

312. Provensen, Alice and Provensen, Martin. **El libro de las estaciones = A Book of Seasons.** New York: Random House, 1982. unp. Translated into Spanish by Pilar de Cuenca and Inés Alvarez.

The seasons in a northern climate are portrayed in picture and story. Lovely illustrations show children in various activities throughout the year.

313. Puig Zaldívar, Raquel. **Robert Goes Fishing = Roberto va de pesca.** New York: Lectorum Publications, 1992. ISBN: 1-880507-00-5. unp. Illustrations by Saundra Smith Rubiera.

Robert wakes up one morning and decides to go fishing. But it is raining, so he pretends he is fishing from his bed. The sun finally comes out, and Robert and his mother can go fishing. Full-page illustrations face the bilingual text.

314. Reed, Lynn Rowe. **Pedro, His Perro and the Alphabet Sombrero.** New York: Hyperion Books for Children, 1995. ISBN: 0-7868-0071-2. unp.

Pedro gets a dog and a sombrero for his birthday. Because the hat is too plain, Pedro fixes it up by adding an avión, gato, huevo, etc. On each page are three or four new words in Spanish, in alphabetical order ending with *zorrillo.* Each page is filled with bold colors. A glossary is included on the last page.

REVIEWS: *Booklist,* April 15, 1995, p. 1507; *Children's Book Review Service,* Spring 1995, p. 137; *Emergency Librarian,* November 1995, p. 55; *Horn Book Guide,* Fall 1995, p. 339; *Kirkus Reviews,* April 1, 1995, p. 474; *School Library Journal,* April 1995, p. 114.

315.   Reiser, Lynn. **Margaret and Margarita = Margarita y Margaret.** New York: Greenwillow Books, 1993. ISBN: 0-688-12239-6. unp.

Two little girls go to the park. One speaks Spanish and the other one speaks English. Even though they do not understand each other, they manage to play together, have a party, and take a nap. They each learn a few of the other's words.

REVIEWS: *Book Links,* July 1994, p. 7; *Booklist,* September 15, 1993, p. 160; *Center for Children's Books Bulletin,* October 1993, p. 56; *Childhood Education,* Summer 1994, p. 248; *Kirkus Reviews,* August 15, 1993, p. 1078; *Library Talk,* March 1994, p. 20; *Reading Teacher,* May 1994, p. 654; *Reading Teacher,* April 1995, p. 637; *School Library Journal,* August 1994, p. 182.

316.   Reiser, Lynn. **Tortillas and Lullabies = Tortillas y cancioncitas.** New York: Greenwillow Books, 1998. ISBN: 0-688-14628-7. 40 p. Pictures by "Corazones Valientes." Coordinated and translated by Rebecca Hart.

Divided into four sections: tortillas, flowers, washing, and lullabies. The stories are told from great-grandmother, to grandmother, to mother, to child, and to the child's doll. Music for one lullaby is included. There is also an author's note. The artists, taught by a Peace Corps volunteer in San José, Costa Rica, were six women from the ages of 19-42: Viria Salas, Ivannia Zambrana Ríos, Toribia Mairena Guido, Esmeralda Rivera Ruíz, Luz Ríos Duarte, and Marina Méndez Cruz (the Corazones Valientes).

REVIEWS: *Booklist,* April 1, 1998, p. 1333; *Children's Book Review Service,* July 1998, p. 150; *Early Childhood Education Journal,* Fall 1999, p. 39; *Horn Book,* May 1998, p. 335; *Horn Book Guide,* Fall 1998, p. 370; *Journal of Youth Services in Libraries,* Winter 2001, p. 37; *Kirkus Reviews,* April 1, 1998, p. 501; *New York Times Book Review,* September 20, 1998, p. 32; *Publishers Weekly,* February 23, 1998, p. 78; *Reading Teacher,* May 1999, p. 866; *Reading Teacher,* May 1999, p. 890; *School Library Journal,* April 1998, p. 108.

317.   Resnick, Seymour. **Selections from Spanish Poetry.** Irvington-on-Hudson, N.Y.: Harvey House, 1962. 96 p. Illustrated by Anne Marie Jauss.

The thirty-eight selections of Spanish poetry, arranged in chronological order in this volume, are favorite classics from the twelfth century to today. Twenty-two poems have literal prose translations. The others have verse translations. The notes are in English. In the preface the editor groups the poems by level of difficulty (simple, average, difficult). Black-and-white sketches.

REVIEW: *Library Journal,* January 15, 1963, p. 355.

**318.**   Resnick, Seymour. **Spanish-American Poetry: A Bilingual Selection.** Irvington-on-Hudson, N.Y.: Harvey House, 1964. 96 p. Illustrated by Anne Marie Jauss.

Includes forty selections of Spanish-American poetry. Twenty of the selections have literal prose translations, and the others have verse translations. The selections, arranged in chronological order, range from the time of the Spanish conquest and colonial period to the twentieth century. A list of the poems arranged by difficulty level (simple, average, and difficult) is included in the preface. Notes on the poets are in English. Black-and-white sketches.

**319.**   Retana, María Luisa. **Born into the Pack = Nacer en la manada.** Bisbee, Ariz.: High Desert Productions, 1997. ISBN: 0-9652920-4-5. unp. Illustrated by Marian Weaver. Translated by Guillermo Retana.

The story of five little puppies born in the high desert. They are Mexican gray wolves. The puppies grow up. On one page the English version is first, and on the next page the Spanish version is first.

**320.**   Retana, María Luisa. **The Pig That Is Not a Pig = El cerdo que no es cerdo.** Bisbee, Ariz.: High Desert Productions, 1997. ISBN: 0-9652920-8-8. unp. Illustrated by Marian Weaver.

The story of a family of javelinas in the desert. On one page the English version is first, and on the next page the Spanish version is first.

**321.**   Rey, H. A. **Jorge el curioso = Curious George.** Boston: Houghton Mifflin, 1961. 56 p. Translated into Spanish for young readers by Pedro Villa Fernandez.

The first adventures of Curious George, on his trip from Africa to a zoo in the United States. The text is in Spanish, with a few phrases translated at the bottom of each page and a complete vocabulary at the end. Designed for American children who want to learn Spanish. The familiar illustrations are very colorful. Yolanda Rivas in the *Horn Book* review says: "Unfortunately, the text shows some of the undesirable characteristics of literal translations, which not only tend to be formal and dry but also lead to errors in grammar and usage in general."

REVIEWS: *Horn Book*, April 1977, p. 192; *Library Journal*, February 15, 1962. p. 844; *Teacher*, May 1977, p. 115.

**322.**   Ribes Tovar, Federico. **Puerto Rico en mi corazón.** New York: Plus Ultra Educational Publishers, 1972. 30 p.

Bits and pieces of Puerto Rican history and culture are presented in this brief text. Back cover title is **Puerto Rico in My Heart.** Two-color illustrations are stong and expressive.

REVIEWS: *Booklist*, February 1, 1976, p. 794; *Cartel*, June 1976, p. 214; *Interracial Books for Children*, 5, no. 5, 1974, p. 6.

**323.**   Rice, James. **Vaqueros: In Spanish and English.** Gretna, La.: Pelican

Publishing, 1998. ISBN: 1-56554-309-2. unp. Illustrated by James Rice. Translation by Ana Smith.

Chi Chi, a chihuahua, tells the story of the vaqueros and describes their special skills. Their history from the arrival of the first cattle brought by the Spanish in the early 1500s up to the Civil War is related. Illustrations portray much of the action of both men and animals.

REVIEW: *Horn Book Guide*, Fall 1998, p. 370.

**324.** Rider, Alex. **We Say Happy Birthday = Decimos feliz cumpleaños.** New York; Funk & Wagnalls, 1967. 45 p. Pictures by Betty Fraser. (A Learn-a-language Book in English and Spanish)

In this series, nouns that occur in the text of both languages appear in color, red in this volume. This is a pleasant story about a little girl's birthday party. The illustrations for the English version show a blond girl in a northern setting, and the illustrations for the Spanish version show a dark-haired girl in a southern environment. Pronunciation guide and vocabulary list are included.

REVIEW: *Library Journal*, February 15, 1968, p. 872.

**325.** Rider, Alex. **We Take a Saturday Walk = Vamos a pasear el sábado.** New York: Funk & Wagnalls, 1968. 45 p. Pictures by Peter Madden. (A Learn-a-language Book in English and Spanish)

The nouns in the text of both languages are in orange typeface, and there is a pronunciation guide and a vocabulary list in this volume. Father takes his two children on a Saturday trip, this time to the zoo. In the illustrations for the English version the children are blond, and in the illustrations for the Spanish version they are dark haired.

REVIEW: *Library Journal*, November 15, 1968, p. 4398.

**326.** Rider, Alex. **When We Go to Market = Cuando vamos al mercado.** New York: Funk & Wagnalls, 1968. 45 p. Pictures by Gioia Fiammenghi. (A Learn-a-language Book in English and Spanish)

Two children, Pedro and Roberta, are sent to the market to shop before going to school. The nouns that appear in the text of both languages are in green type. The illustrations portray an urban environment for the English version of the story and a Mexican rural environment for the Spanish version. A pronunciation guide and a vocabulary list are included.

REVIEW: *Library Journal*, October 15, 1969, p. 3813.

**327.** Rider, Alex. **When We Go to School = Cuando vamos a la escuela.** New York: Funk & Wagnalls, 1967. 45 p. Pictures by Peter Madden. (A Learn-a-language Book in English and Spanish)

John and Juan return to school in the fall. This is the story of one day's activities. Nouns that occur in the text of both languages are in red typeface. There is a pronunciation guide and a vocabulary list at the back of the book.

The illustrations for John's story reflect an American setting, those for Juan's story a Hispanic setting.

**328.**   Rios, Edwin T. **Abecedario = Alphabet.** San Jose, Calif.: Educational Factors, 1980. 56 p. Learning consultant, Juanita C. Strick. Teaching consultant, Evelyn D. Rios. Illustrator, William E. Hubbard.

A large-format alphabet book told from the point of view of a little boy. Each letter of the alphabet is represented by the same object in both languages, and the letters ñ, q, w, x, and z are creatively presented. An excellent alphabet book.

**329.**   Rivera, Susana Madrid. **El piojo y la liendre.** Berkeley, Calif.: Quinto Sol Publications, 1974. unp.

The cover includes the English title: **The Nit and the Louse.** A very old poem recorded by the author as told to her by her father, with two additional stanzas. Synonymous ideas are presented in the English version rather than a word-for-word translation. Simple music with the Spanish words has been provided on the last page. The story is about the nit and the louse who cannot marry because the cat ate the mouse who was to have been the best man. The busy, vibrant illustrations almost overwhelm the text. Good use of repetition.

REVIEW: *Cartel*, December 1974, p. 120.

**330.**   Roa, Anina. **Pedro Pelícano = Peter Pelican.** Fort Myers Beach, Fla.: Island Press, 1964. unp.

Peter Pelican, who lives on one of the Florida Keys, is nearsighted, so he learns to dance for his supper. There are some mistakes in the Spanish version of the story. The large illustrations are humorously drawn.

**331.**   Robins, Lewis and Harris, Reed. **A "Picture-practice Book" for Learning to Speak Spanish with Our Friends in Spain.** New York: William Sloan Associates, 1962. 47 p. Illustrated by Kirschen.

Cover title is **Our Friends in Spain.** Words and short sentences in both languages about daily activities and a quick trip to Spain are included in this volume. There is a great deal of repetition of the 300-word Spanish vocabulary in the book. Illustrations are colorful caricatures.

REVIEWS: *Christian Science Monitor*, June 28, 1962, p. 11; *Commonweal*, November 16, 1962, p. 212; *Library Journal*, September 15, 1962, p. 3206; *New York Times Book Review*, November 11, 1962, p. 53.

**332.**   Rockwell, Anne. **El toro pinto and Other Songs in Spanish.** New York: Macmillan, 1971. 52 p. Illustrated by Anne Rockwell.

The thirty songs in this collection were gathered from the many countries where Spanish is spoken. Music and guitar chords are included. English translations, not intended for singing, are at the end of the book. Humorous colorful illustrations.

REVIEWS: *Booklist*, October 15, 1971, p. 106; *Cartel*, June 1976, p. 266; *Childhood Education*, December 1971, p. 150; *Horn Book*, February 1972, p. 65; *Kirkus Reviews*, July 15, 1971, p. 744; *Library Journal*, September 15, 1971, p. 2909; *Proyecto Leer Bulletin*, Winter 1974, p. 9; *Top of the News*, January 1972, p. 204.

**333.**   Rockwell, Anne. **El toro pinto and Other Songs in Spanish.** New York: Aladdin Paperbacks, 1995. ISBN: 0-689-71880-2. 52 p. Illustrated by Anne Rockwell. Originally published in 1971.

The songs in this collection have been gathered from almost all the countries where Spanish is spoken. Music is included, and guitar chords have been added. The illustrations suggest what the song is about. English translations, not intended for singing, are provided on pages 41-52. Favorite songs, such as *Arroz con leche, El rancho grande,* and *Cielito lindo,* are included.

**334.**   Rodríguez, David and Rodríguez, Lisa. **Bopo Joins the Circus = Bopo se une al circo.** Marietta, Georgia: BOPO Bilingual Books, 1998. ISBN: 0-9665575-0-6. unp. Written and illustrated by Lisa M. Rodríguez. Edited and translated by David A. Rodríguez.

Spanish translations in this book reflect Spanish spoken in the Caribbean. Elizabeth F. Moreno and Jesús M. Rodríguez contributed to the editing of the translation. Bopo and his friends rush to join the circus, but find more work there than at home. They learned a lesson the hard way. Bopo and his friends are illustrated as stylized animals. The rabbit is in a wheelchair.

**335.**   Rodríguez, Doris. **Diego Wants to Be = Diego quiere ser.** Fort Atkinson, Wis.: Highsmith Press, 1994. ISBN: 0-917846-35-5. unp. Illustrated by Doris Rodríguez.

Diego doesn't want to be a boy, a fish, a bird, or a dog. He wants to be a man. But when he gets old he would like to be a boy again, and it is too late. Winner of the Multicultural Publishers Exchange Children's Book Award.

REVIEWS: *Children's Book Review Service*, Winter 1995, p. 68; *Horn Book Guide*, Spring 1995, p. 115.

**336.**   Rodriguez, Luis J. **It Doesn't Have to Be This Way: A Barrio Story = No tiene que ser así: una historia del barrio.** San Francisco: Children's Book Press, 1999. ISBN: 0-89239-161-8. 31 p. Illustrations by Daniel Galvez.

Based on his experiences in barrio gangs, the author tells the story of Monchi, who is asked to join a gang. At first Monchi is admired, but then is asked to steal a bicycle and become involved in a fight with another gang. His cousin is wounded. Uncle Rogelio tells him that it doesn't have to be this way, and Monchi refuses to join the gang. Colorful realistic illustrations. Américas Commended List 1999.

REVIEWS: *Booklist*, August 1999, p.2059; *Booklist*, January 1, 2000, p. 929; *Children's Bookwatch*, July 1999, p. 3; *Horn Book Guide*, Spring 2000, p. 70; *Hungry Mind Review*, Fall 1999, p. 35; *Kirkus Reviews*, August 1, 1999, p. 1230;

*Publishers Weekly*, August 16, 1999, p. 85; *School Library Journal*, October 1999, p. 124; *School Library Journal*, August 2000, p. 38.

**337.**   Roe, Eileen. *Con mi hermano = With My Brother.* New York: Bradbury Press, 1991. ISBN: 0-02-777373-6. unp. Illustrations by Robert Casilla.

A story of a little boy and his older brother as they play together. The little boy wants to grow up just like his brother, go to school on the bus, deliver newspapers, and play ball in the park.

REVIEWS: *Book Links*, July 1994, p. 7; *Booklist*, March 1, 1993, p. 1242; *Horn Book*, May 1991, p. 359; *School Library Journal*, April 1991, p. 101.

**338.**   Rohmer, Harriet and Guerrero Rea, Jesús. **Atariba & Niguayona.** San Francisco: Children's Book Press, 1976. ISBN: 0-89239-026-3. 23 p. Illustrated by Consuelo Mendez Castillo. (Fifth World Tales: Legends in Spanish and English for All the Children of North America = Cuentos del quinto mundo: leyendas en español e inglés para todos los niños de Norteamérica)

This legend from the Taino people of Puerto Rico tells the moving story of the young boy Niguayona's quest for the tall caimoni tree whose fruit will save the life of the ailing Atariba. His search is successful, Atariba recovers, and there is a fiesta with many songs and dances. Niguayona becomes a great man and Atariba a strong woman. Bold colors in sensitive illustrations.

REVIEWS: *Booklist*, September 1, 1981, p. 53; *Horn Book*, June 1979, p. 331; *Lector*, November/December 1983, p. 39; *Proyecto Leer Bulletin*, Fall 1980, p. 23.

**339.**   Rohmer, Harriet and Guerrero Rea, Jesús. **Cuna Song = Canción de los Cunas.** San Francisco: Children's Book Press, 1976. 23 p. Illustrated by Irene Perez. (Fifth World Tales: Legends in Spanish and English for All the Children of North America = Cuentos del quinto mundo: leyendas en español e inglés para todos los niños de Norteamérica)

A Cuna boy from Panama is drowned and wanders underwater in search of a way back to his mother's house. The wise ones sing the story of his travels and his final acceptance of the fact that his human days are over. Vivid, colorful illustrations.

REVIEWS: *Booklist*, September 1, 1981, p. 54; *Horn Book*, June 1979, p. 331; *Proyecto Leer Bulletin*, Fall 1980, p. 24.

**340.**   Rohmer, Harriet and Anchondo, Mary. **The Headless Pirate = El pirata sin cabeza.** San Francisco: Children's Book Press, 1976. 19 p. Illustrated by Ray Rios. (Fifth World Tales: Legends in Spanish and English for All the Children of North America = Cuentos del quinto mundo; leyendas en español e inglés para todos los niños de Norteamérica)

A story told by the old fishermen of Costa Rica about the English pirate Captain William Dampier, who plundered a Spanish treasure ship in the Caribbean. His excessive greed cost him his life as he drowned trying to escape the wrath of the headless pirate called Son-of-the Devil. Bold colors are used in the illustrations.

REVIEW: *Booklist*, September 1, 1981, p. 54.

341. Rohmer, Harriet and Anchondo, Mary. **How We Came to the Fifth World = Cómo vinimos al quinto mundo.** San Francisco: Children's Book Press, 1976. ISBN: 0-89239-024-7. 23 p. Illustrated by Graciela Carrillo de Lopez.

An Aztec legend about the destruction of the four worlds or historical ages by the gods of water, air, fire, and earth. After this destruction, the present fifth world is reached. Colors in the illustrations are extremely vivid.

REVIEWS: *Booklist*, September 1, 1981, p. 54; *Horn Book*, June 1979, p. 331; *Proyecto Leer Bulletin*, Fall 1980, p. 26.

342. Rohmer, Harriet; Chow, Octavio; and Vidaure, Morris. **The Invisible Hunters: A Legend from the Miskito Indians of Nicaragua = Los cazadores invisibles: una leyenda de los indios miskitos de Nicaragua.** San Francisco: Children's Book Press, 1987. ISBN: 0-89239-031-X. 32 p. Illustrated by Joe Sam. Version in Spanish, Rosalma Zubizaretta & Alma Flor Ada.

This is a Miskito Indian legend from Nicaragua. It portrays three brothers from the village of Ulwas on the Coco River. They are successful hunters who are persuaded to sell their meat to the traders. Eventually they succumb to greed and are banished from the village.

REVIEWS: *Booklist*, April 1, 1988, p. 1358; *Center for Children's Books Bulletin*, November 1987, p. 55; *Children's Bookwatch*, August 1994, p. 2; *Horn Book*, January 1988, p. 89; *Journal of Youth Services in Libraries*, Winter 1989, p. 160; *Kirkus Reviews*, November 15, 1987, p. 1633; *Language Arts*, October 1990, p. 610; *Los Angeles Times Book Review*, May 22, 1988, p. 10; *Newsweek*, September 9, 1991, p. 65; *Publishers Weekly*, November 27, 1987, p. 79; *Reading Teacher*, April 1990, p. 589; *School Library Journal*, November 1987, p. 111; *Wilson Library Bulletin*, September 1988, p. 61.

343. Rohmer, Harriet and Guerrero Rea, Jesús. **Land of the Icy Death = Tierra de la muerte glacial.** San Francisco: Children's Book Press, 1976. 23 p. Illustrated by Xavier Viramontes. (Fifth World Tales: Legends in Spanish and English for All the Children of North America = Cuentos del quinto mundo: leyendas en español e inglés para todos los niños de Norteamérica)

A Chilean legend of the Yahgan people, the story tells about the bravery of their ancestor Na Ha. He saves them from the monsters of the sea but in so doing loses his own life. Colorful brilliant illustrations.

REVIEWS: *Booklist*, September 1, 1981, p. 54; *Horn Book*, June 1979, p. 331; *Lector*, September 1983, p. 49; *Proyecto Leer Bulletin*, Fall 1980, p. 26.

344. Rohmer, Harriet. **The Legend of Food Mountain = La montaña del alimento.** San Francisco: Children's Book Press, 1982. ISBN: 0-89239-022-0.

23 p. Illustrated by Graciela Carrillo. Translated into Spanish by Alma Flor Ada and Rosalma Zubizarreta.

This legend, which has several levels of meaning, tells of the discovery of corn. It was adapted from the Chimalpopocatl Codice of Mexico. The illustrations are in vibrant colors. The hand-lettered Spanish text is on the left page, and the English text is on the right page.

REVIEWS: *Booklist*, August 1983, p. 1459; *Lector*, June 1983, p. 19.

**345.**   Rohmer, Harriet and Anchondo, Mary. **The Little Horse of Seven Colors = El caballito de siete colores.** San Francisco: Children's Book Press, 1976. 23 p. Illustrated by Roger I. Reyes. (Fifth World Tales: Legends in Spanish and English for All the Children of North America = Cuentos del quinto mundo; leyendas en español e inglés para todos los niños de Norteamérica)

A Nicaraguan fairy tale about a poor boy, a princess, and a horse of many colors. Bold, colorful illustrations.

REVIEW: *Booklist*, September 1, 1981, p. 54.

**346.**   Rohmer, Harriet and Anchondo, Mary. **The Magic Boys = Los niños mágicos.** San Francisco: Children's Book Press, 1975. unp. Illustrated by Patricia Rodriguez. (Fifth World Tales: Legends in Spanish and English for All the Children of North America = Cuentos del quinto mundo: leyendas en español e inglés para todos los niños de Norteamérica)

This story is from the Popol Vuh or Book of the Community—the bible of the Maya Quiché Indians of Guatemala. It is a humorous tale of how Hunahpú and Ixbalanqué trick their older brothers and turn them into monkeys so they can live in grandmother's house.

REVIEWS: *Booklist*, September 1, 1981, p. 54; *Horn Book*, June 1979, p. 331; *Lector*, September 1983, p. 50; *Proyecto Leer Bulletin*, Fall 1980, p. 26.

**347.**   Rohmer, Harriet and Anchondo, Mary. **The Mighty God Viracocha = El díos poderoso Viracocha.** San Francisco: Children's Book Press, 1976. 19 p. Illustrated by Mike Rios and Richard Montez. (Fifth World Tales: Legends in Spanish and English for All the Children of North America = Cuentos del quinto mundo: leyendas en español e inglés para todos los niños de Norteamérica)

A retelling of the story of the creation of the world and the different peoples in it, as told by the Aymara Indians of Peru and Bolivia. Bold, colorful illustrations picture angular space-age robots as the gods.

REVIEWS: *Booklist*, September 1, 1981, p. 54; *Horn Book*, June 1979, p. 331; *Lector*, March 1984, p. 38.

**348.**   Rohmer, Harriet and Wilson, Dornmather. **Mother Scorpion Country: A Legend from the Miskito Indians of Nicaragua = La tierra de la madre escorpión: una leyenda de los indios miskitos de Nicaragua.** San Francisco: Children's Book Press, 1987. ISBN: 0-89239-032-8. 32 p. Illustrated by Virginia Stearns.

Kati and her husband Naklili are Miskitos who live in Nicaragua. When Kati dies, her husband follows her to the land of Mother Scorpion. Where Kati sees beauty, Naklili sees only death. He returns home, but soon dies from a snake bite and is reunited with Kati.

REVIEWS: *Booklist*, April 1, 1988, p. 1358; *Center for Children's Books Bulletin*, November 1987, p. 55; *Horn Book*, January 1988, p. 89; *Journal of Youth Services in Libraries*, Winter 1989, p. 160; *Kirkus Reviews*, November 15, 1987, p. 1633; *Publishers Weekly*, November 27, 1987, p. 79; *School Library Journal*, December 1987, p. 96; *Small Press*, October 1989, p. 80.

349.   Rohmer, Harriet and Gomez, Cruz. **Mr. Sugar Came to Town = La visita del Sr. Azúcar.** San Francisco: Children's Book Press, 1989. ISBN: 0-89239-045-X. 32 p. Illustrated by Enrique Chagoya.

Although Grandma Lupe makes the best tamales, the children Alicia and Alfredo are lured outside by Mr. Sugar, who persuades them to buy his sweets. The children eat and eat, get fatter, and fall asleep at their desks. Finally Grandma unmasks Mr. Sugar. Based on a puppet show produced by the Watsonville, California Health Clinic.

REVIEWS: *Booklist*, November 15, 1989, p. 662; *Bookwatch*, September 1989, p. 3; *Horn Book*, May 1990, p. 362; *Hungry Mind Review*, November 1989, p. 28; *School Library Journal*, November 1989, p. 136.

350.   Rohmer, Harriet and Anchondo, Mary. **Skyworld Woman = La mujer del mundo-cielo.** San Francisco: Children's Book Press, 1975. 21 p. Illustrated by Roger I. Reyes. (Fifth World Tales: Legends in Spanish and English for All the Children of North America = Cuentos del quinto mundo: leyendas en español e inglés para todos los niños de Norteamérica)

A legend from the Philippines, this is the story of Bugan, a young goddess from the fourth skyworld. The story, which represents the creation cycle, comes from the Kiagan Ifugao mountain people of northern Luzon. Tagalog and Ilocano translations are also available. Illustrations are in bold colors.

REVIEW: *Lector*, November 1983, p. 39.

351.   Rohmer, Harriet and Guerrero Rea, Jesús. **The Treasure of Guatavita = El tesoro de Guatavita.** San Francisco: Children's Book Press, 1976. 22 p. Illustrated by Carlos Loarca. (Fifth World Tales: Legends in Spanish and English for All the Children of North America = Cuentos del quinto mundo: leyendas en español e inglés para todos los niños de Norteamérica)

A legend from Colombia, this tale describes three different stages in the civilization of the Chibcha people—the prehistoric time of the goddess Bachue and her son, the pre-conquest period of cultural development, and the final period of conquest and post-conquest. Bold colors are used in the abstract illustrations.

REVIEWS: *Booklist*, September 1, 1981, p. 54; *Horn Book*, June 1979, p. 331; *Proyecto Leer Bulletin*, Fall 1980, p. 28.

352.   Rohmer, Harriet. **Uncle Nacho's Hat = El sombrero del tío Nacho.** San Francisco: Children's Book Press, 1989. ISBN: 0-89239-043-3. 31 p. Illustrated by Veg Reisberg.

Uncle Nacho has an old hat full of holes. Although his niece Ambrosia brings him a new hat, Uncle Nacho can't seem to get rid of the old one. Ambrosia tells him to introduce his new hat to his neighbors. Based on a Nicaraguan folk-tale performed by the Puppet Workshop of Nicaraguan National Television.

REVIEWS: *Book Links*, July 1994, p. 7; *Booklist*, November 15, 1989, p. 662; *Bookwatch*, September 1989, p. 4; *Center for Children's Books Bulletin*, December 1989, p. 94; *Children's Bookwatch*, August 1994, p. 2; *Horn Book*, May 1990, p. 362; *Hungry Mind Review*, November 1989, p. 28; *Kirkus Reviews*, August 1, 1989, p. 1166; *Library Talk*, November 1990, p. 37; *Publishers Weekly*, August 11, 1989, p. 458; *Reading Teacher*, April 1990, p. 588; *School Library Journal*, February 1990, p. 118; *Utne Reader*, January 1990, p. 104; *Village Voice Literary Supplement*, December 1989, p. 34; *Wilson Library Bulletin*, February 1990, p. 83.

353.   Rosario, Idalia. **Idalia's Project ABC: An Urban Alphabet Book in English and Spanish = Proyecto ABC.** New York: Holt, Rinehart and Winston, 1981. unp.

An alphabet book with emphasis on city sights and sounds. In the Spanish alphabet, ch, ll, and ñ are included. Translation is not always parallel. Reviews of this book varied from positive to negative. Realistic illustrations.

REVIEWS: *Center for Children's Books Bulletin*, June 1981, p. 202; *Children's Book Review Service*, June 1981, p. 92; *Curriculum Review*, June 1981, p. 244; *Horn Book*, October 1981, p. 556; *Interracial Books for Children Bulletin*, 12, no. 4 & 5, 1981, p. 37; *Kirkus Reviews*, May 15, 1981, p. 37; *Language Arts*, October 1981, p. 845; *School Library Journal*, August 1981, p. 59.

354.   Rosenberg, Joe, editor. **¡Aplauso! Hispanic Children's Theater.** Houston: Piñata Books, 1995. ISBN: 1-55885-127-5. 274 p.

Joe Rosenberg formed the first university bilingual theater company in Kingsville, Texas in 1972. This company in 1980 formed the professional Bilingual Theater Company of Corpus Christi. In this collection Mr. Rosenberg includes five plays in English, two bilingual plays, and four plays in Spanish. The bilingual plays are *El gato sin amigos = The Cat Who Had No Friends*, by Joe Rosenberg; and *Song of the Oak = El canto del roble*, by Roy Conboy. By Hispanic theater is meant theater that touches on Puerto Rican, Cuban American, and Mexican American life, and Hispanic intercultural life of various descriptions.

REVIEW: *Children's Bookwatch*, August 1995, p. 1.

355.   Ross, Patricia Fent. **The Hungry Moon: Mexican Nursery Tales.** New York: Knopf, 1946. 72 p. Illustrated by Carlos Mérida.

"Although these stories are original, they are all based on authentic and well-known old Mexican nursery rhymes, which are printed here in the original form.

English versions of the rhymes are by the author." (Note from verso.) The thirteen short stories are in English, but each story is prefaced by the nursery rhyme in both English and Spanish. Two songs are included, with the words in English and Spanish. The illustrations are representative of folk art. This is a good example of a publication of this decade.

REVIEWS: *Booklist*, January 1, 1947, p. 139; *Horn Book*, January 1947, p. 32; *Kirkus Reviews*, October 1, 1946, p. 492; *Library Journal*, December 15, 1946, p. 1810; *Wisconsin Library Bulletin*, March 1947, p. 57.

**356.**   Rossi, Joyce. **The Gullywasher = El chaparrón torrencial.** Flagstaff: Rising Moon Books for Young Readers from Northland Publishing, 1998. ISBN: 0-87358-607-7. unp. Illustrated by Joyce Rossi. Spanish translation by Patricia Hinton Davison.

Grandfather tells Leticia a story about his days as a cowboy. In the telling, the story becomes more and more exaggerated, as a gullywasher transforms Abuelito from a strong young man into the grandfather Leticia knows. Soft, delicate illustrations. A short glossary of Spanish words is appended.

**357.**   Rothman, Joel and Palacios, Argentina. **This Can Lick a Lollipop: Body Riddles for Kids = Esto goza chupando un caramelo: las partes de cuerpo en adivinanzas infantiles.** Garden City, N.Y.: Doubleday, 1979. unp. English words by Joel Rothman. Spanish words by Argentina Palacios. Photographs by Patricia Ruben.

Each of the fifteen riddles, both in English and Spanish, appears on one page. The answer is then given on the next page in both languages, along with a photograph that illustrates the answer. The black-and-white photographs of children are charming.

REVIEWS: *Babbling Bookworm*, August 1979, p. 1; *Book World*, April 8, 1979, p. L5; *Booklist*, April 1, 1979, p. 1220; *Childhood Education*, January 1980, p. 172; *Curriculum Review*, October 1979, p. 308; *Horn Book*, August 1979, p. 448; *Kirkus Reviews*, March 15, 1979, p. 331; *School Library Journal*, May 1979, p. 54; *School Library Journal*, January 1981, p. 33.

**358.**   Ruiz, Jesse N. **El gran César.** Menlo Park, Calif.: Educational Consulting Associates, 1973. 83 p.

With photographs and autobiographical commentary, the reader sees the barrio through the eyes of a ten-year-old boy, César, and learns about his Mexican heritage and traditions as well as his daily activities. José Taylor states in the *Proyecto Leer Bulletin* review: "Not very imaginatively presented, but useful because it presents a positive acceptance of being a Chicano child in an urban situation." (p. 17) Black-and-white photographs.

REVIEWS: *Cartel*, December 1973, p. 50; *Proyecto Leer Bulletin*, Fall 1976, p. 17.

**359.**   Sáenz, Benjamin Alire. **A Gift from Papá Diego = Un regalo de Papá**

**Diego.** El Paso: Cinco Puntos Press, 1998. ISBN: 0-938317-33-4. 39 p. Illustrations by Geronimo Garcia.

Little Diego, who lives in El Paso, misses his grandfather who lives in Chihuahua, Mexico. His father gives him Superman comics, and Diego dreams of flying to see his grandfather. He gets a Superman suit for his birthday, but that doesn't help. However, when the birthday celebration starts, his grandfather is actually there. He has come to visit by bus. The artist made the illustrations by shaping clay into figures and painting them with acrylic. There is a brief glossary and notes about the author and artist.

REVIEWS: *Bloomsbury Review*, November 1999, p. 26; *Booklist*, May 1, 1998, p. 1522; *Children's Book Review Service*, June 1998, p. 128; *Children's Bookwatch*, March 1998, p. 1; *Horn Book*, July 1998, p. 178; *Journal of Youth Services in Libraries*, Winter 2001, p. 37; *Kirkus Reviews*, April 15, 1998, p. 585; *Publishers Weekly*, January 19, 1998, p. 378.

**360.** Sáenz, Benjamin Alire. **Grandma Fina and Her Wonderful Umbrellas = La abuelita Fina y sus sombrillas maravillosas.** El Paso: Cinco Puntos Press, 1999. ISBN: 0-938317-46-6. 31 p. Illustrated by Geronimo Garcia. Spanish translation by Pilar Herrera.

Grandma Fina talks a walk with her tattered yellow parasol, her yellow purse, and her yellow shoes. She loves her parasol but as she meets Mrs. Byrd, her daughter Cecilia, Mrs. García, Mr. López, her three grandchildren, Tommy on his skateboard, Mr. Johnson, Mrs. Wong and her dog, and her son Rubén, each in turn thinks how tattered the parasol is. The next day, Grandma goes to her daughter's house and is surprised by a birthday party. She opens her gifts to find nine new umbrellas. The next day Rubén takes her to the Community Center. Grandma gives an umbrella to each of her nine friends, and they all go out for a walk. Grandma keeps her yellow parasol. A simulated sidewalk serves as an illustrated backdrop on each page showing the activities.

REVIEWS: *Bloomsbury Review*, November 1999, p. 26; *Children's Bookwatch*, December 1999, p. 5; *Horn Book Guide*, Spring 2000, p. 52; *Newsletter of the United States Board on Books for Young People*, Spring 2001, p. [14]; *School Library Journal*, October 1999, p. 125.

**361.** Sagel, Jim. **Where the Cinnamon Winds Blow = Donde soplan los vientos de canela.** Santa Fe: Red Crane Books, 1993. ISBN: 1-878610-32-5. 156 p.

Ten-year-old Tomás has a special relationship with his wise aunt Zulema. He has one adventure after another as he seeks to come to grips with his feelings after the loss of his father. Magical eyeglasses and a deck of playing cards help him.

REVIEWS: *Book Report*, January 1995, p. 29; *Book Report*, May 1995, p. 42.

**362.** Salas-Porras, Pipina. **El ratoncito pequeño = The Little Mouse.** El Paso: Cinco Puntos Press, 2001. ISBN: 0-938317-56-3. 30 p. A nursery rhyme in Spanish and English as remembered by Pipina Salas-Porras. Illustrated by José Cisneros.

On the left pages are short phrases in both Spanish and English telling the story of the little mouse who was eaten by the cat. On the right pages are large illustrations of the mouse and the cat. The cat looks more like a dog and looks quite ferocious. There are more illustrations of the cat than the mouse. The publishers note that the English is not a literal translation of the Spanish. They tested the text with many children and Spanish-speakers.

**363.**   Salinas, Bobbi. **The Three Pigs = Los tres cerdos: Nacho, Tito, and Miguel.** Alameda, Calif.: Piñata Publications, 1998. ISBN: 0-934925-05-4. 28 p. Retold and illustrated by Bobbi Salinas. Spanish version by Amapola Franzen and Marcos Guerrero.

Nacho builds a house of straw, but the wolf José blows it down when Nacho won't let him in. Tito builds a house of wood, and José blows that down too. Miguel builds his house of adobe bricks and outwits the wolf. Illustrations have a touch of humor. Miguel is shown working at his computer or reading a book by Cesar Chavez. The calendar on the wall is from the Barelas Coffee Shop in Albuquerque. A one-page glossary and costume ideas are included.

**364.**   San Souci, Robert D. **The Little Seven-Colored Horse: A Spanish American Folktale.** San Francisco: Chronicle Books, 1995. ISBN: 0-8118-0412-7. unp. Illustrated by Jan Thompson Dicks.

Diego, Pedro, and Juanito are brothers of a farmer. The two older brothers leave the farm to go off and make their fortune. Juanito follows them, but the brothers push him into the river. A beautiful seven-colored horse saves him. In the village lives a beautiful young woman whose father is the alcalde. They all fight for the honor of marrying her. Juanito must accomplish three tasks successfully before he can claim her as his bride. The brothers are sent off to Spain. In English with only a few Spanish words. There is a glossary of the Spanish words used. There is also appended a note on sources used and on the settings of the story. A male version of the Cinderella theme.

REVIEWS: *Booklist*, December 1, 1995, p. 624; *Children's Book Review Service*, November 1995, p. 28; *Horn Book Guide*, Spring 1996, p. 94; *Kirkus Reviews*, October 15, 1995, p. 1501; *Publishers Weekly*, November 13, 1995, p. 61; *School Library Journal*, January 1996, p. 105.

**365.**   San Xavier Mission School First and Second Grade Pupils and Sister M. Antoninus Hubatch. **Our Book = T-O'ohana = Nuestro libro.** Tucson: San Xavier del Bac, 1969. 50 p. Papago translation compiled by Dean Saxton. Spanish translation compiled by Brother Lawrence Hogan.

Everyday activities are recorded in simple language in Papago, Spanish, and English by the school children. The photographs, by an unnamed photographer, are excellent and show the daily life of the children and their families. Printed by the Carmel Print Shop, Salpointe High School in Tucson.

**366.**   Sandoval, Ruben. **Games, Games, Games = Juegos, juegos, juegos: Chicano Children at Play—Games and Rhymes.** New York: Doubleday, 1977. 78 p. Photographs by David Strick. Introduction by Julian Nava.

The introduction and preface are in English and are written for the adult. The photo captions and directions for the games are in English. The songs for the games are in Spanish. The translations for the directions (to Spanish) and for the songs (to English) are in the appendix. Excellent black-and-white photographs of children playing in an urban neighborhood.

REVIEWS: *Horn Book*, December 1977, p. 687; *School Library Journal*, March 1978, p. 133; *Teacher*, April 1978, p. 30.

**367.**   Santos, Richard G. **Diarios de vacaciones = Vacation Diaries.** San Antonio: Intercultural Development Research Association,1979. 46 p. Photographs by Cynthia Ann Santos and Deborah Ann Zamora. Illustrations by Jesús María "Chista" Cantú.

Gloria visits her cousin Anita in San Antonio, and Anita visits her cousin Gloria in Taos, New Mexico. On each trip the girls and their families visit various historical sites in the Southwest, and each girl keeps a diary, one in English and one in Spanish. The photographs are in black and white and in color and are repeated for each diary. The content of the two diaries varies somewhat, although the major events are the same. A vocabulary list and brief explanations about selected events and places conclude each section.

**368.**   Santos, Richard G. **Tejanitos.** San Antonio: Intercultural Development Research Association, 1978. 131 p.

Five stories are included in this volume. They are presented first in Spanish and then in English. There are also two poems in Spanish only. Two of the stories are folklore, one is an animal tale, one is a historical fictional story, and another is a cowboy story. There are only a few black-and-white sketches.

**369.**   Santos, Richard G. **Viaje a las pirámides mexicanas = Trip to the Pyramids.** San Antonio: Intercultural Development Research Association, 1980. 58 p. Photographs by Cynthia Ann Santos and Deborah Ann Zamora.

Using a fictional framework, two cousins, one writing in English and the other in Spanish, keep a diary of their trip to see the pyramids of Mexico. The historical sites, events, and personalities are seen through the eyes of the two girls. The photographs are in color and in black and white and are repeated for each diary. A vocabulary list and brief information about selected events and places conclude each section. Some variations occur in the content of the two stories.

**370.**   Sauvageau, Juan. **Fábulas para siempre = Fables Are Forever.** Kingsville, Tex.: Twin Palms Editorial, 1979. 4 volumes.

In the first volume of a four-volume set, the author retells twelve fables, many of them familiar to children. After each story there is a brief English-to-

Spanish vocabulary and a series of questions to use with children. Black-and-white sketches, some large and some very small. Marred by some typographical errors.

**371.**   Sauvageau, Juan. **Stories That Must Not Die.** Austin, Tex.: Oasis Press, 1975-1978. 4 volumes.

A collection of forty folkloric stories from the Southwest, ten in each volume. English and Spanish appear in parallel columns. After each story there are two lists of questions, the first related directly to the text and intended for younger students, the second suggested by the text and designed for more advanced students. At the end of each volume lists of vocabulary words and cognates for each story are included. *La Llorona*, a legend that appears often in Chicano literature, is included in volume one. The black-and-white sketches in the first three volumes are by Roel Montalvo; in the fourth volume they are by Servando Hinojosa.

REVIEWS: *Booklist*, September 1, 1981, p. 55; *Cartel*, June 1976, p. 251; *Proyecto Leer Bulletin*, Fall 1976, p. 19.

**372.**   Schon, Isabel and Chalquest, R. R. **Doña Blanca and Other Hispanic Nursery Rhymes and Games.** Minneapolis: Denison, 1983. ISBN: 513-01768-2. 41 p.

Eighteen nursery rhymes and games are included in this collection. The Spanish version is given first and then the English version. If it is a game, the directions for playing it are included. Illustrated with simple brown and white drawings.

REVIEWS: *Booklist*, December 1, 1985, p. 583; *Reading Teacher*, March 1985, p. 669.

**373.**   Schrade, Arlene O. **Gabriel, the Happy Ghost, in Mexico = Gabriel, el fantasmita simpático, en México.** Skokie, Ill.: National Textbook Company, 1979. 29 p.

Gabriel shows his friend Chucho a Halloween festival in the United States, and Chucho shows his friend "The Day of the Dead" festival in Mexico. The orange-and-black illustrations are repeated twice, as the story is presented first in English and then in Spanish.

**374.**   Schrade, Arlene O. **Gabriel, the Happy Ghost, in Pamplona = Gabriel, el fantasmita simpático, en Pamplona.** Skokie, Ill.: National Textbook Company, 1979. 28 p.

Gabriel is reading a book in the library about the festival of San Fermín in Pamplona. Suddenly he takes off for Spain to join in the fun of the dancing, the parades, and the running of the bulls. Amusing two-color illustrations which are repeated twice, as the English version of the story is presented first and then the Spanish version. The 1983 printing of this story has the title: **Gabriel, el fantasmita simpático, en España = Gabriel, the Happy Ghost, in Spain.**

**375.**  Schrade, Arlene O. **Gabriel, the Happy Ghost, in the Caribbean = Gabriel, el fantasmita simpático, en el Caribe.** Skokie, Ill.: National Textbook Company, 1979. 29 p.

Gabriel takes a trip to Puerto Rico and goes skin diving with a dolphin. He visits Indian Cave and a phosphorescent bay, "La Parguera." The blue-and-white illustrations are repeated twice, as the English text is presented first and then the Spanish text. A new printing of this story has the title: **Gabriel, el fantasmita simpático, en Puerto Rico = Gabriel, the Happy Ghost, in Puerto Rico.**

**376.**  Schultz, Clara Peck. **Grasshopper Grump And Other Poems of Wonder.** Grand Junction, Colo.: Juventud Multilingual Press, 2001. ISBN: 0-9707775-0-7. 112 p. Albino Gonzalez, Editor-Translator.

A collection of poetry presented through two characters, the children Iliana (for Spanish) and Christopher (for English). Some of the poems are short, such as "Rain Promises," and some of them are long, such as "El Grasshopper Grump," which tells a story. A teacher's guide "Using El Grasshopper Grump in K-8 Classrooms" is appended. No illustrations.

**377.**  Serfozo, Mary. **Welcome, Roberto! = ¡Bienvenido, Roberto!** Chicago: Follett, 1969. 32 p. Photographs by John Serfozo.

An excellent photographic story in black and white of one school day in the life of a five-year-old boy.

REVIEWS: *Library Journal*, July 1969, p. 2673; *Proyecto Leer Bulletin*, Fall 1976, p. 11.

**378.**  Seuss, Dr. **El gato ensombrerado.** New York: Random House, 1967. 63 p. Translated by Carlos Rivera. (Yo lo puedo leer solo = Beginner Books)

The familiar story about the cat in the hat who entertains Sally and her brother while Mother is out. In the Spanish translation the story loses some of its rhythm and bounce. The beloved Dr. Seuss illustrations are the same as in the original edition. The cover title is **The Cat in the Hat.**

REVIEW: *Booklist*, July 15, 1968, p. 1274.

**379.**  Shannon, Terry. **A Trip to Mexico = Un viaje a México.** Chicago: Childrens Press, 1961. 30 p. Pictures by Charles Payzant.

Peter and Ann accompany their parents on a trip to Mexico City, where they visit some tourist attractions. The story is presented at the bottom of each page in English, but selected words and phrases are given above the story in Spanish and English with phonetic pronunciations. Illustrations are stereotypical.

REVIEWS: *Library Journal*, October 15, 1961, p. 3675; *Saturday Review*, September 23, 1969, p. 46.

**380.**  Sheheen, Dennis. **A Child's Picture Dictionary: English/Spanish.** New York: Adama Books, 1984. Distributed by Watts. ISBN: 0-915361-11-6. 44 p. Illustrated by Dennis Sheheen.

Each letter of the English alphabet is illustrated by two to five words, and the Spanish translations are given along with the correct articles.

REVIEW: *School Library Journal*, October 1985, p. 150.

**381.**   Silva, María Luisa. **Versos and Verses.** Santiago, Chile: Editorial Los Andes, 1995. ISBN: 956-7014-75-2. unp. English version by Valerie Moir. Illustrations by René Moya.

A collection of poems from a talented poet of Chile. This book was an honor book at the IBBY Congress in the Netherlands in 1996.

**382.**   Silva Lee, Alfonso. **Coquí y sus amigos: los animales de Puerto Rico = Coquí & His Friends: The Animals of Puerto Rico.** Saint Paul: Pangaea, 2000. ISBN: 1-929165-03. 95 p.

After a series of short essays, including "An Island Is Born," individual animals, insects, birds, snakes, and fish are described. All of them are clearly shown in excellent photographs. The coquí is the most popular frog in Puerto Rico. A map of the island is included. The author is also the photographer. He is a Caribbean biologist living in the mountains of Puerto Rico.

REVIEW: *Bookwatch*, July 2000, p. 10.

**383.**   Simon, Norma. **Cuando me enojo.** Chicago: Whitman, 1976. 40 p. Illustrated by Dora Leder. Spanish version by Alma Flor Ada. (A Concept Book)

Boys and girls get mad from time to time, and the author humorously presents a variety of these situations. But the children are told, "It's not bad to be angry—once in a while." The illustrations are well done in black and orange. The story accompanying the illustrations is told in the Spanish equivalent of the informal English text, rather than in a word-by-word translation. The English text, **I Was So Mad,** is given at the back of the book.

**384.**   Simon, Norma. **What Do I Do?** Chicago: Whitman, English/Spanish ed., 1969. unp. Pictures, Joe Lasker.

In simple everyday language the author describes the activities of a little girl from morning to night in answer to the repeated question, What do I do? Expressive illustrations. The name of the little girl should be Consuelo instead of Consuela.

REVIEWS: *Center for Children's Books Bulletin*, October 1970, p. 33; *Interracial Books for Children*, Spring 1972, p. 4; *Library Journal*, July 1970, p. 2530; *Proyecto Leer Bulletin*, Winter 1974, p. 9.

**385.**   Simon, Norma. **What Do I Say?** Chicago: Whitman, English/Spanish ed., 1967. unp. Pictures, Joe Lasker.

The author describes the activities of a little boy from morning, when he says "Good morning = Buenos días" to night, when he says "Good night = Buenas noches." Realistic illustrations.

REVIEWS: *Booklist*, January 1, 1968, p. 548; *Center for Children's Books Bulletin*, November 1967, p. 48; *Christian Science Monitor*, November 2, 1967, p.

B4; *Interracial Books for Children*, Spring 1972, p. 4; *Kirkus Reviews*, May 15, 1967, p. 597; *Library Journal*, September 15, 1967, p. 3180; *Saturday Review*, October 21, 1967, p. 42.

**386.** Sisyphus. **Carrusel: una fábula para niños en español e inglés = Carrousel: A Fable for Children in Spanish and English.** New Orleans: Royal Editions, 1981. 14 p. Illustrated by Leticia Tarrago.

The bee envies the bird her freedom to fly high in the sky. One day she tries flying high even though she is afraid, and then turns into a beautiful butterfly. Exquisite line drawings. The author's real name is J. M. Calonico.

REVIEW: *Booklist*, October 1, 1990, p. 349.

**387.** Smith, MaryLou M. **Grandmother's Adobe Dollhouse.** Santa Fe: New Mexico Magazine, 1984. ISBN: 0-937206-07-5. 32 p. Illustrated by Ann Blackstone.

Matt, a little boy, visits his grandmother in New Mexico, and takes the readers on a tour of his grandmother's adobe dollhouse. He explains how adobe is made and tells about many of the items in the dollhouse. The story is in English with some Spanish words, which are explained in the text.

REVIEW: *Booklist*, January 15, 1967, p. 1612.

**388.** Sopena. **Sopena inglés de los niños: diccionario infantil ilustrado español-inglés = English for Children: An Illustrated Children's Dictionary in Spanish and English.** Barcelona: Editorial Ramon Sopena, 1982. ISBN: 84-303-0893-8. 63 p.

Spanish words are listed in alphabetical order. They are identified as to part of speech, the English word is given, and then there is a sentence in both Spanish and English. Some words are illustrated.

REVIEW: *Booklist*, October 1, 1990, p. 349.

**389.** Soto, Gary. **Chato's Kitchen.** New York: Putnam, 1995. ISBN: 0-399-22658-3. unp. Illustrated by Susan Guevara.

Chato, a low-riding cat in East Los Angeles, has new neighbors—a whole family of mice. He invites them to dinner and with his friend Novio Boy, they begin to prepare the tortillas, fajitas, enchiladas, carne asada, chiles rellenos, a pitcher of tamarindo, and a sweet flan. The mice ask permission to bring their friend Chorizo along; he just happens to be a big dog. So instead of mice for dinner, they all have the wonderful food from Chato's kitchen. Many Spanish words in addition to the names of the foods are mixed in with the story, which is in English. First Pura Belpré Award 1996 for illustrations. Américas Honorable Mention 1995.

REVIEWS: *Book Links*, March 1996, p. 26; *Booklist*, March 1, 1995, p. 1250; *Booklist*, March 15, 1996, p. 1288; *Children's Book Review Service*, May 1995, p. 112; *Christian Science Monitor*, May 25, 1995, p. B1; *Early Childhood Education Journal*, Spring 1997, p. 176; *Horn Book*, September 1995, p. 591; *Horn Book*

Guide, Fall 1995, p. 283; *Kirkus Reviews*, March 15, 1995, p. 395; *Library Journal*, March 1996, p. 204; *Los Angeles Times Book Review*, July 2, 1995, p. 8; *Publishers Weekly*, February 6, 1995, p. 84; *Reading Teacher*, February 1997, p. 426; *School Library Journal*, July 1995, p. 69; *Tribune Books* (Chicago), February 12, 1995, p. 6.

**390.**   Stevens, Cat. **Teaser and the Firecat: A Book in English, French, and Spanish.** New York: Four Winds Press, 1972. unp. Illustrated by Cat Stevens.

A whimsical tale of Teaser, his cat, and a journey with the moon. Illustrations complement the tone of the story.

REVIEWS: *Babbling Bookworm*, February 1975, p. 2; *Booklist*, October 15, 1974, p. 247; *Kirkus Reviews*, September 15, 1974, p. 1006; *Library Journal*, December 15, 1974, p. 3265; *Publishers Weekly*, October 21, 1974, p. 52.

**391.**   Stevens, Jan Romero. **Carlos and the Carnival = Carlos y la feria.** Flagstaff, Ariz.: Rising Moon Books for Young Readers from Northland Publishing, 1999. ISBN: 0-87358-733-2. unp. Illustrated by Jeanne Arnold.

Carlos and Gloria go to a fair in the Española Valley of northern New Mexico. Carlos spends all his birthday money, but then wins the first prize of $5.00 for his pet rabbit. At the fair they eat sopaipillas. The recipe is included.

REVIEWS: *Booklist*, August 1999, p. 2066; *Booklist*, January 1, 2000, p. 929; *Horn Book Guide*, Spring 2000, p. 55; *Journal of Youth Services in Libraries*, Winter 2001, p. 37; *School Library Journal*, July 1999, p. 81.

**392.**   Stevens, Jan Romero. **Carlos and the Cornfield = Carlos y la milpa de maíz.** Flagstaff, Ariz.: Northland Publishing, 1995. ISBN: 0-87358-596-8. unp. Illustrated by Jeanne Arnold. Spanish translated by Patricia Davison. Spanish edited by Ana Consuelo Matiella.

Carlos is in a hurry to plant the corn seeds because he wants to buy a pocket knife. He puts in more than three seeds. Then at harvest time some of the corn does not come up. He returns the knife and buys new corn seed. When that corn is harvested, his mother serves him blue corn cakes. His father then gives him back the knife. Carlos had bought blue corn seed instead of yellow. A recipe for cornmeal pancakes is included. A note on the Spanish language used is also appended.

REVIEWS: *Booklist*, January 1, 1996, p. 854; *Journal of Youth Services in Libraries*, Winter 2001, p. 37; *Reading Teacher*, February 1997, p. 426.

**393.**   Stevens, Jan Romero. **Carlos and the Skunk = Carlos y el zorrillo.** Flagstaff, Ariz.: Rising Moon Books for Young Readers from Northland Publishing,1997. ISBN: 0-87358-591-7. unp. Illustrated by Jeanne Arnold.

Carlos shows off for his friend Gloria by catching a skunk, but then he gets more than he bargained for. In the dedication, the author says: "This story is based on a true incident, which was told to me by DeWitt and Patty Reed." Américas Commended List 1997.

REVIEWS: *Booklist*, May 15, 1997, p. 1581; *Horn Book Guide*, Spring 1998, p. 118; *Journal of Youth Services in Libraries*, Winter 2001, p. 37; *Reading Teacher*, October 1998, p. 169.

**394.** Stevens, Jan Romero. **Carlos and the Squash Plant = Carlos y la planta de calabaza.** Flagstaff, Ariz.: Northland Publishing, 1993. ISBN: 0-87358-559-3. unp. Illustrated by Jeanne Arnold.

Carlos loves to work in the garden in the fertile Española Valley in Northern New Mexico, but he hates to take a bath. The dirt accumulates on his hands, under his fingernails, and in his ears. One morning he wakes up with a squash plant growing out of his ear, the next morning it is bigger, and the following morning even bigger. Finally Carlos takes a bath, and the squash plant disappears. That evening the family has calabacitas for dinner. The recipe for the squash is included in the book.

REVIEWS: *Horn Book Guide*, Spring 1994, p. 115; *Journal of Youth Services in Libraries*, Winter 2001, p. 37.

**395.** Strumpen-Darrie, Robert; Berlitz, Charles; Berlitz, Valerie; and the Staff of the Berlitz Schools of Languages. **Berlitz Spanish Zoo Animals for Children.** New York: Grosset & Dunlap, 1963. unp. Illustrations by Art Seiden.

Each page has a picture of a different animal, a sentence or two in Spanish, the phonetic pronunciation, and the English translation. A word list is included at the back of the book. Realistic illustrations are alternately in color and in black and white.

**396.** Suarez-Rivas, Maite. **Latino Read-Aloud Stories.** New York; Black Dog & Leventhal Publishers, 2000. ISBN: 1-57912-09-1. 368 p.

A collection created for children who want to learn about the stories of various Latino cultures. The countries represented range from Cuba, Mexico, Puerto Rico, and Bolivia to Peru, Nicaragua, Colombia, Chile, and Spain. Each story is first presented in English and then in Spanish. Stories include myths and legends of pre-Columbian cultures, fables and riddles, and historical tales from the empires of pre-Columbian Latin America, to the conquistadors and settlers, and the nation builders. There is also a section devoted to Spanish American literature of more recent times.

**397.** Tabor, Nancy María Grande. **Somos un arco iris = We Are a Rainbow.** Watertown, Mass.: Charlesbridge Publishing, 1995. ISBN: 0-88106-813-6. unp. Written and illustrated by Nancy María Grande Tabor.

A family is moving to a new country where there are different customs. Although people are different, they are also much the same. The Spanish is at the top of the page, the English is at the bottom of the page, with the illustrations representing paper cutouts in between. Nancy Tabor has written three other books, but they are not easily available: **Albertina anda arriba: el abecedario = Albertina Goes Up: An Alphabet Book, Cincuenta en la cebra:**

contando con los animales = Fifty on the Zebra: Counting with the Animals, and **El gusto del mercado mexicano = A Taste of the Mexican Market.**

REVIEWS: *Booklist*, June 1, 1995, p. 1791; *Center for Children's Books Bulletin*, January 1998, p. 179; *Horn Book Guide*, Spring 1998, p. 49.

398. Tafolla, Carmen. **Baby Coyote and the Old Woman: A Bilingual Celebration of Friendship and Ecological Wisdom = El coyotito y la viejita: una celebración bilingüe de la amistad y sabiduría ecológica.** San Antonio: Wings Press, 2000. ISBN: 0-930324-48-X. 24 p. Illustrated by Matt Novak.

The baby coyote teaches an old woman in the desert to recycle her papers, cans, and bottles. Then they both sit down and enjoy the view of their desert. Full-page colorful illustrations.

399. Talbot, Toby. **Coplas: Folk Poems in Spanish and English.** New York: Four Winds Press, 1972. 79 p. Illustrated with woodcuts by Rocco Negri.

This collection includes 134 coplas—songs of a few lines—under the following categories: coplas and guitars, nature, fiesta, work and play, people, love, gossip, life and death, farewell, and nanas or lullabies. Expressive woodcuts.

400. Tallon, Robert. **ABCDEFGHIJKLMNOPQRSTUVWXYZ in English and Spanish.** New York: Lion Press, 1969. unp. Illustrated by Robert Tallon.

The title of this book as given on the spine is **ABC's in English and Spanish.** The ABC's are based on the English alphabet. The Spanish letters ch, ll, and ñ are omitted, and the English w is included. A guide to pronunciation appears at the end of the book. Whimsical and colorful illustrations.

401. Tarbox, Todd. **María.** Skokie, Ill.: National Textbook Company, 1973. 26, 26 p. Edited by María Medina Swanson. (¡Hola, amigos!: The Bilingual Series)

An average day in the life of eight-year old María, who lives in Acopilco, a small town near Mexico City. The black-and-white photographs show many scenes of city life and expressive portraits of María's family and friends. The story is told first in Spanish and then in English.

REVIEW: *Cartel*, December 1973, p. 53.

402. Tarbox, Todd. **Teresa.** Skokie, Ill.: National Textbook Company, 1973. 26, 26 p. Edited by María Medina Swanson. (¡Hola, amigos!: The Bilingual Series)

Teresa lives in Mexico City. This is a photographic essay of a day in Chapultepec Park that Teresa shares with her family and friends. The black-and-white photographs are very expressive. The story is told in Spanish in the first half of the book, and in English in the second half of the book.

REVIEW: *Cartel*, December 1973, p. 53.

403. Tardy, Gene and Jackson, Al. **Soccer: World's Most Popular Sport = Fútbol soccer: el deporte más popular del mundo.** LaPuente, Calif.: Jay Alden

Publishers, 1975. 31 p. Written and photographed by Gene Tardy and Al Jackson. Spanish translation by Maria Consuelo Perez.

A brief explanation of the game of soccer, how it is played, and how it differs from football and basketball. Good color action photographs. To read the alternate language, it is necessary to flip the book and turn it over.

**404.** Tardy, William T. **Bedtime Stories in Spanish.** Dallas: Banks Upshaw, 1960. 178 p. Illustrated by Dorothy Hearon.

The twelve stories included in this collection were published in *La Luz* during the previous twenty-nine years. They were republished in the same format with different illustrations by the National Textbook Company in 1969. The illustrations in this edition are black-and-white drawings and sketches.

**405.** Tibo, Gilles. **Simon and His Boxes = Simón y las cajas.** Union City, Calif.: Pan Asian Publications, 1996. ISBN: 1-57227-033-0. unp. Spanish translation by Beatriz Zeller. Originally published by Tundra Books of Montreal.

Simon likes to play with boxes but he can find no one else who wants his boxes. All the animals have homes of their own. He decides to use them for his collections.

**406.** Treviño, Elizabeth Borton de. **A Carpet of Flowers = Una alfombra de flores.** Detroit: Blaine Ethridge Books, 1975. 117 p. Translated from the English by Maria Ana Murillo Peralta. Illustrated by Cyril Miles. (A Prism Press Book)

Traditionally the people of Huamantla journey to the basilica of Our Lady of Guadalupe in Mexico City to weave a carpet of flowers for the great nave of the church. One year a blind boy participates in the devotion and brings pansies for the eyes of the Virgin, overcoming many difficulties to do so. Miraculously, he regains his sight, and the withered pansies he carried so far appear fresh. A moving story, well told by a Newbery medal winner (*I, Juan de Pareja*, 1966), which could be read out loud for a religious celebration. There are a few errors in the Spanish text. There are only three small stylized black-and-white illustrations.

REVIEWS: *Booklist*, September 1, 1981, p. 55; *Cartel*, June 1976, p. 44; *Horn Book*, April 1977, p. 190; *Proyecto Leer Bulletin*, Spring 1976, p. 21; *School Library Journal*, May 1976, p. 48.

**407.** Trez, Denise and Trez, Alain. **El gato travieso = The Mischievous Cat.** Cleveland: World, 1967. unp.

A naughty cat pesters all the other animals in the garden until he makes friends with another cat. Humorous but simple drawings. The Spanish text is from the front of the book to the middle, and the English text is from the back page to the middle of the book.

REVIEWS: *Book World*, December 17, 1967, p. 12; *Library Journal*, November 15, 1967, p. 4255.

**408.**  **Trictionary**, English-Chinese-Spanish, As Spoken on the Lower East Side of Manhattan, New York City: Including Sections on the Important People, Famous Places, and Traditional Holidays of the Caribbean and China. New York: Art Resources for Teachers and Students, 1982. 111, 151, 108 p.

An additional title is given on the cover: **Triccionario, español-chino-inglés.** The title is also given in Chinese. This project was funded by a grant from the National Endowment for the Humanities. The project staff includes the names of Mary Scherbatskoy and Jane Shapiro as project directors. Credits are also given to Virginia Swift, branch librarian at the Chatham Square Library, and to Phyllis R. Winant, lexicographer. The first section of the book lists important people from China and the Caribbean; famous places from China, the Caribbean, and New York; and traditional holidays from the Chinese and Hispanic cultures. Part II is the English-Chinese-Spanish section on blue paper. Part III is the Chinese-English-Spanish section on yellow paper. Part IV is the Spanish-Chinese-English section on pink paper. Each section includes an introduction. Black-and-white sketches are included.

**409.**  Tufiño de Breitman, Nitza. **Borinquen before Columbus.** New York: Amigos del Museo del Barrio, 1974. unp. Illustrations and research, Nitza Tufiño de Breitman. Editor, Mary Segarra de Diaz. Transcription, Hilda Arroyo de Gillis.

Includes a brief history of Puerto Rico before Columbus, as well as the letters of the alphabet illustrating indigenous words. Large brown drawings, some turned sideways. Suggestions for teachers appear on the last page. Designed more for the teacher's use than for the child's.

REVIEW: *Booklist*, February 1, 1976, p. 794.

**410.**  Ulibarrí, Sabine R. **Mi abuela fumaba puros y otros cuentos de tierra amarilla = My Grandma Smoked Cigars and Other Stories of Tierra Amarilla.** Berkeley, Calif.: Quinto Sol Publications, 1977. ISBN: 0-88412-105-4. 167 p.

Includes the following stories by this talented storyteller who combines oral tradition with a personal approach: *My Grandma Smoked Cigars, Witcheries or Tomfooleries?, My Uncle Cirilo, El negro aguilar, Elacio Was Elacio, La Kasa KK, Mano fashico, El apache, He Went for Nails,* and *The Penitentes.* The author at the time of publication of the book was Chairman of the Department of Modern and Classical Languages at the University of New Mexico in Albuquerque.

**411.**  VanLaan, Nancy. **La Boda: A Mexican Wedding Celebration**. Boston: Little, Brown, 1996. ISBN: 0-316-89626-8. unp. Illustrated by Andrea Arroyo.

Alfonso and Luisa are being married in Oaxaca. Their Zapotec wedding is a mixture of ancient customs and Catholic tradition. The story is told in rhythmic verse with only a few words in Spanish. A glossary of the Spanish words used is on the verso. Américas Commended List 1996.

REVIEWS: *Center for Children's Books Bulletin*, May 1996, p. 318; *Children's Book Review Service*, July 1996, p. 151; *Horn Book Guide*, Fall 1996, p. 280; *Junior Bookshelf*, December 1996, p. 242; *Kirkus Reviews*, April 15, 1996, p. 608; *Observer (London)*, July 21, 1996, p. 17; *School Library Journal*, May 1996, p. 101.

**412.**  VanStone, Mary R. **Spanish Folk Songs of the Southwest.** Fresno, Calif.: Academy Guild Press, 1963. 44 p. Collected and transcribed by Mary R. VanStone. Foreword by Merle Armitage.

"The songs range from a lullabye from the 17th century New Mexican miracle play, *Los Pastores*, to a bootlegger's ballad, product of the prohibition era" (p. 2). The first edition of this collection was published in 1928. Music for twenty-five songs is included, with the stanzas in Spanish. The English translations are on the last five pages of the book. Only three black-and-white illustrations are in the book.

**413.**  Vigil, Angel. **The Corn Woman: Stories and Legends of the Hispanic Southwest = La mujer del maíz: cuentos y leyendas del sudoeste hispano.** Englewood, Colo.: Libraries Unlimited, 1994. ISBN: 1-56308-194-6. 234 p. Retold by Angel Vigil. Translated by Jennifer Audrey Lowell and Juan Francisco Marín. (World Folklore Series no. 4)

Many of the stories in this collection are in English only. The following stories which follow one another are in English and Spanish: *The Weeping Woman = La Llorona, Our Lady of Guadalupe = Nuestra Señora de Guadalupe, The Three Branches = Las tres ramas, The Gifts of the Holy Family = Los regalos de la Sagrada Familia, The True Path to Happiness = El camino verdadero a la felicidad, One for You, One for Me = Una para tú, una para mí, Like Father, Like Son = De tal palo, tal astilla, The Three Simpletons = Los tres simplones, The Three Pieces of Good Advice = Los tres buenos consejos, The Boy Who Killed the Giant = El muchacho que mató al gigante, The Rabbit and the Coyote = El conejo y el coyote, The Foolish Coyote = El coyote loco, The Dust Devil = El diablo de polvo*, and *The Corn Woman = La mujer del maíz*. Appended are a "Glossary of Spanish Words," a "Bibliography," and a section titled "About the Author and Biographies of Contributing Latino Storytellers."

**414.**  Vigna, Judith. **Gregorio y sus puntos.** Chicago: Whitman, 1976. unp. Illustrations by Judith Vigna. Spanish version by Alma Flor Ada.

This Spanish edition is a well-done colloquial translation of the original English story, which is reprinted on the last page of the book. As each friend passes on the news of how Gregory got the six stitches on his forehead, the story changes and Gregory becomes a hero. Action-oriented, colorful illustrations.

REVIEWS: *Hispania*, December 1977, p. 1041; *Horn Book*, April 1977, p. 192.

**415.**  Vogan, Grace Dawson. **Merry-go-round of Games in Spanish.** Skokie, Ill.: National Textbook Company, rev. ed. 1974. 29 p. Originally published in Dallas by Upshaw in 1941.

A brief collection of vocabulary-building games arranged around basic vocabulary groups such as professions, numbers, animals, clothing, food, etc. Directions are in English; the games are in Spanish with the English translations included. Small black-and-white illustrations.

**416.**   Volkmer, Jane Anne. **Song of the Chirimia: A Guatemalan Folktale = La música de la chirimia: folklore guatemalteco.** Minneapolis: Carolrhoda Books, 1990. ISBN: 0-87614-423-7. unp. Illustrated by Jane Anne Volkmer. Translated by Lori Ann Schatschneider.

King Clear Sky has a daughter whom he names Moonlight. As she grows up she becomes very sad. The king brings many suitors to her, but she only smiles when a poor young man sings a lovely song. She agrees to marry him if he can learn to sing like the birds. His name is Black Feather, and he goes into the woods, where he meets the Great Spirit of the Woods. From a branch of a tree, the spirit fashions a chirimia, a long, hollow pipe. Black Feather learns to play it, returns to Moonlight, and they marry.

REVIEWS: *Childhood Education*, Summer 1991, p. 247; *Children's Book Review Service*, February 1991, p. 79; *Horn Book*, May 1991, p. 359-360; *Kirkus Reviews*, November 15, 1990, p. 1606; *School Library Journal*, March 1991, p. 190; *Social Education*, April 1991, p. 257; *Social Studies*, January 1997, p. 29.

**417.**   Wahl, Jan. **La Dama y Juan Diego = Juan Diego and the Lady.** New York: Putnam, 1974. 48 p. Spanish translation by Dolores Janes Garcia. Illustrated by Leonard Everett Fisher.

A simple but beautiful retelling of the story of the Christian Indian Juan Diego and the miracle of Our Lady of Guadalupe. Illustrations convey the pathos and joy of the story.

REVIEWS: *Cartel*, December 1974, p. 86; *Library Journal*, February 15, 1974, p. 583.

**418.**   Wakefield, Charito Calvachi. **Navidad latinoamericana = Latin American Christmas.** Lancaster, Pa.: Latin American Creations, 1997. 80 p. Introduction and novena prayers by Marco Vinicio Rueda. Translation: Grace Catalina Wintemute.

Includes the words of the most popular Christmas carols in Latin America; nine days of prayers before Christmas with illustrations; and a brief description of Christmas traditions in twenty-five Latin American countries. A compact disc with twelve of the songs in Spanish is available.

**419.**   Ward, Mary Dodson. **I'm Going to California = Yo voy a California.** Houston: Colophon House, 1997. ISBN: 1-882539-21-4. unp. Illustrator: Virginia Marsh Roeder. Translator: Juan M. Aguayo.

A little girl goes to California to see the sights of Hollywood, San Francisco, Capistrano, the zoo, and the redwood trees. On the last two pages there is a list of sights to see.

**420.**   Ward, Mary Dodson. **I'm Going to Texas = Yo voy a Tejas.** Houston: Colophon House, 1995. ISBN: 1-882539-17-6. unp. Translated by Guadalupe C. Quintanilla. Illustrated by Virginia Marsh Roeder.

The story and the illustrations are designed for young readers. At the bottom of each page are boxes with descriptive and historical information about places and events in Texas. This information is for parents.

**421.**   Webber, Irma E. **Esta cosa se ve así: el libro de los puntos de vista = It Looks Like This: A Point-of-view Book.** San Francisco; International Society for General Semantics, 1976. unp. Spanish translation by Maria Urquidi.

A humorous story of four mice who live in different parts of the barn and see the cow, the donkey, the pig, and the cat from four different points of view: front, back, side, and top. Simple black-and-white sketches show all four views.
REVIEW: *School Library Journal*, March 1983, p. 90.

**422.**   Weissman, Anne. **El castillo de Chuchurumbel = The Castle of Chuchurumbel.** Tucson: Hispanic Books Distributors, 1987. ISBN: 968-6217-00-2. 24 p. Illustrated by Susan Bailyn.

A cumulative tale told in Mexico and the southwestern United States, although the writer states that it may have originated in Spain. Whimsical illustrations will appeal to young children.
REVIEWS: *Booklist*, October 1, 1990, p. 349; *Childhood Education*, May 1990, p. 314.

**423.**   West, Patricia M. **Hispanic Folk Songs of the Southwest: For Bilingual Programs.** Denver: Center for Teaching International Relations, University of Denver, updated ed., 1982. 33 p. (Bilingual/Bicultural Foreign Language Series)

Words in Spanish and English are given for three lullabies and four other songs. Definitions of terms and song types are included. Background notes on the songs are also given. No music is included. Spanish proficiency level for the songs is listed as beginning to intermediate. Songs are suitable for grades K-3. An audiocassette tape with the songs sung in Spanish accompanies the booklet. This book is labeled Part II. The title of Part I is **Hispanic Folk Songs of the Southwest: An Introduction**.

**424.**   Willford, Robert W. **A Knowledge Aid Picture Dictionary = Diccionario pictórico para ayudar el conocimiento.** Niles, Ill.: Knowledge Aid, 1969. 39 p. Ronald E. Reed, associate author. Jim Hsieh, illustrations. Margaret A. Lowery, Gloria L. Gonzales, Spanish consultants.

A brief picture dictionary of words in English and Spanish in the following categories: letters, colors, numbers, toys, animals, food, people, clothes, money, weather, house and garden, days of the week, and months of the year. Color illustrations are quite ordinary.

**425.**   Williams, Letty. **The Little Red Hen = La pequeña gallina roja.** Englewood Cliffs, N.J.: Prentice-Hall, 1969. unp. Pictures by Herb Williams. Translated by Doris Chávez and Ed Allen. (Treehouse Paperbacks)

The little red hen found the corn, ground it, made the tortillas, and ate
them. The cat did not like tortillas. The pig and the dog were lazy, so got no
tortillas to eat. The author makes effective use of repetition. The illustrations
are amusing but stereotypical.

REVIEWS: *Cartel,* November 1978, p. 25; *Library Journal,* February 15, 1970,
p. 776; *School Library Journal,* January 1981, p. 33.

**426.**   Williams, Letty. **The Tiger! = ¡El tigre!** Englewood Cliffs, N.J.: Prentice-Hall, 1970. unp. Pictures by Herb Williams. Translated by Doris Chaves
[sic], William Tasca, and Mary Ann Nancarrow.

Maria and her dog Pancho wander into the jungle and are kidnapped by a
tiger. Maria cooks a pot of beans with very hot peppers in an attempt to escape.
However, the tiger likes the dish, and Maria sets up a stand to get rich by selling hot beans to the tigers in the jungle. Bright Illustrations.

REVIEW: *Library Journal,* October 15, 1970, p. 3624.

**427.**   Winter, Jeanette. **Josefina.** San Diego: Harcourt Brace, 1996. ISBN: 0-
15-201091-2. unp.

"This story was inspired by Josefina Aguilar, a beloved Mexican folk artist
who is still creating her painted clay figures in the village of Ocotlán today."
Josefina grew up watching her mother and father make clay figures. She continued the tradition with her nine children. The book ends with a counting
story. The text is in English. Only the counting words are in Spanish, such as:
un sol, dos ángeles, tres casas, etc. Illustrations are in the style of Mexican folk
art. Américas Commended List 1996.

REVIEWS: *Center for Children's Books Bulletin,* October 1996, p. 80; *Children's
Book Review Service,* November 1996, p. 29; *Horn Book Guide,* Spring 1997, p.
54; *Kirkus Reviews,* September 15, 1996, p. 1409; *Reading Teacher,* March 1998,
p. 510; *School Library Journal,* October 1996, p. 109.

**428.**   Winter, Jonah. **Diego: In English and Spanish.** New York: Knopf,
1991. ISBN: 0-679-81987-8. unp. [Illustrations] by Jeanette Winter. Translated
from the English by Amy Prince.

A brief biography of Diego Rivera, from his birth in Guanajuato, his heal-
ing in the mountains after the death of his twin brother Carlos, his schooling,
his study in Paris and Italy, and finally his painting of the wonderful murals
showing the people of Mexico.

REVIEWS: *Booklist,* January 1, 1992, p. 837; *Center for Children's Books Bul-
letin,* November 1991, p. 79; *Childhood Education,* Winter 1991, p. 110; *Children's
Bookwatch,* November 1991, p. 3; *Five Owls,* November 1991, p. 36; *Five Owls,*
May 1999, p. 98; *Hungry Mind Review,* Spring 1992, p. C12; *Instructor,* October

1991, p. 14; *Kirkus Reviews*, July 15, 1991, p. 940; *New York Times Book Review*, November 3, 1991, p. 38; *Publishers Weekly*, August 9, 1991, p. 23; *School Library Journal*, January 1992, p. 107; *Social Education*, April 1992, p. 253.

**429.** Work Projects Administration. **The Spanish-American Song and Game Book.** New York: Barnes, 1942. 87 p. Illustrated and compiled by workers of the writers' program, music program, and art program of the Work Projects Administration in the state of New Mexico. Sponsored by the University of New Mexico and State Superintendent of Public Instruction of New Mexico.

Both the songs and the directions are in English and Spanish. The songs have been translated freely into English, so the stanzas might differ from the Spanish. The Spanish stanzas are sometimes grammatically incorrect, but that is the way they are sung. These are games and songs that have been sung in New Mexico for generations and are stil in use. Part 1 is for children from five to seven years; part 2 is for those from eight to ten; and part 3 is for those eleven and over. The foreword and introduction are in English. Black-and-white stereotypical illustrations. This title was reprinted in 1973 as **Canciones y juegos de Nuevo México = Songs and Games of New Mexico**.

**430.** World Association of Girl Guides and Girl Scouts. **Canciones de nuestra cabaña.** New York: Girl Scouts of the U.S.A., 1980. 100 p.

A song book for girl guides and girl scouts that includes camp-fire openings and greetings, songs for festivals and ceremonies, graces, rounds and canons, singing games and action songs, part songs, vespers and closings, and other favorites. All songs include the music for voice. For many songs, the stanzas are in English and in Spanish. Some songs are in English only or in Spanish only. There are also a few songs in other languages. There is a glossary of musical terms in Italian, English, and Spanish, and a title index to the songs. A few stick figures are used to illustrate the singing games.

**431.** Yolen, Jane. **Sleep Rhymes Around the World.** Honesdale, Pa.: Wordsong, 1994. ISBN: 1-56397-243-3. 39 p. Illustrated by 17 international artists.

A collection of 21 sleep rhymes from 17 countries. Each rhyme is presented in its native language along with a translation in English. If the language is in a non-Roman alphabet, phonetic translations have been provided. The following languages are represented: Thai, Italian, Yoruba, Welsh, Ukrainian, Slovenian, Abenaki, Spanish, Afghan, Finish, Korean, Farsi, Luganda, Czech, Turkish, and English. Lullabies from Puerto Rico and Venezuela are presented in Spanish and English.

REVIEWS: *Christian Science Monitor*, May 6, 1994, p. 12; *Horn Book Guide*, Fall 1994, p. 378; *Library Talk*, March 1994, p. 27; *Reading Teacher*, May 1994, p. 649.

**432.** Yolen, Jane. *Street Rhymes Around the World*. Honesdale, Pa.: Wordsong, 1992. ISBN: 1-878093-53-3. 39 p. Illustrated by 17 international artists.

A collection of 32 street rhymes from 17 countries. Each rhyme is presented in its native language along with a translation in English. If the language is in a non-Roman alphabet, phonetic translations have been provided. The following languages are represented: Portuguese, Tamil, Hebrew, Japanese, Russian, Chinese, Spanish, Greek, German, Zambia (language not indicated), Danish, Cheyenne, French, Armenian, Dutch, and English. Only one song from Mexico is presented in Spanish and English.

REVIEWS: *American Book Review*, August 1993, p. 11; *Booklist*, May 15, 1992, p. 1684; *Children's Book Review Service*, April 1992, p. 104; *Come-All-Ye*, Winter 1994, p. 7; *Five Owls*, March 1992, p. 73; *Hungry Mind Review*, Summer 1992, p. C17; *Kirkus Reviews*, May 1, 1992, p. 619; *Language Arts*, December 1992, p. 628; *Library Talk*, January 1993, p. 31; *Publishers Weekly*, April 27, 1992, p. 270; *School Library Journal*, May 1992, p. 110.

**433.**   Yurchenco, Henrietta. **A Fiesta of Folk Songs from Spain and Latin America.** New York: Putnam, 1967. 88 p. Illustrated by Jules Maidoff.

Includes songs about animals and nature, singing games and dances, songs about people, and songs for Christmas. Attractive illustrations. This is a well-designed book.

REVIEWS: *Booklist*, October 1, 1967, p. 201; *Horn Book*, October 1967, p. 607; *Kirkus Reviews*, June 1, 1967, p. 647; *Library Journal*, July 1967, p. 2646; *Library Journal*, December 15, 1967, p. 4580; *Young Readers Review*, October 1967, p. 2.

# Appendix A: Publishers and Numbers of Bilingual Children's Titles

# Apéndice A: Editoriales y números de títulos bilingües para los niños

| Publisher/Editorial | 40s | 50s | 60s | 70s | 80s | 90s | 2000s | Total |
|---|---|---|---|---|---|---|---|---|
| Abrams | | | | | | 1 | | 1 |
| Academy Guild Press | | | 1 | | | | | 1 |
| Adama Books | | | | | 1 | | | 1 |
| Aladdin Paperbacks | | | | | | 1 | | 1 |
| Alegría Hispana Publications | | | | | 4 | 2 | | 6 |
| All of Us, Inc. | | | | 1 | | | | 1 |
| Amigos del Museo del Barrio | | | | 2 | | | | 2 |
| Anaya | | | | 3 | | | | 3 |
| Art Resources for Teachers and Students | | | | | 1 | | | 1 |
| A.R.T.S., Inc. | | | | | 1 | | | 1 |
| Atheneum | | | | 2 | | | | 2 |
| August House | | | | | | 2 | | 2 |
| Author | | | | 1 | | | | 1 |
| Banks Upshaw | | | 2 | | | | | 2 |
| Bantam Doubleday Dell | | | | | | 1 | | 1 |
| Barnes | | | | 1 | | | | 1 |
| Barron's Educational Series | | | | | 1 | 1 | | 2 |
| Beautiful America Publishing | | | | | | 3 | | 3 |
| Beginner Books | | | 4 | | | | | 4 |
| Belwin Mills Publishing | | | 2 | | | | | 2 |
| Bilingual Educational Services | | | | | 1 | | | 1 |
| Bilingual Press | | | | | 1 | | | 1 |
| Black Dog & Leventhal | | | | | | | 1 | 1 |
| Blaine Ethridge Books | | | | 7 | | | | 7 |
| Bobbs-Merrill | | | 1 | | | | | 1 |
| BOPO Bilingual Books | | | | | | 1 | | 1 |

| Publisher/Editorial | 40s | 50s | 60s | 70s | 80s | 90s | 2000s | Total |
|---|---|---|---|---|---|---|---|---|
| Bowmar Publishing | | | 1 | | | | | 1 |
| Bradbury Press | | | | | | 2 | | 2 |
| California State University, Fullerton | | | | | 1 | | | 1 |
| Caribbean World Communications | | | | 1 | | | | 1 |
| Carolrhoda Books | | | | | | 1 | | 1 |
| Center for Open Learning & Teaching | | | | 1 | | | | 1 |
| Center for Teaching Internat'l Relations | | | | | 1 | | | 1 |
| Chappell Music Company | | | | 2 | | | | 2 |
| Charlesbridge Publishing | | | | | | 1 | | 1 |
| Children's Book Press | | | | 12 | 6 | 18 | 4 | 40 |
| Childrens Press | | | 1 | | | | | 1 |
| Chronicle Books | | | | | | 3 | | 3 |
| Cinco Puntos Press | | | | | 1 | 5 | 3 | 9 |
| Clarion Books | | | | | 1 | 3 | | 4 |
| Colophon House | | | | | | 2 | | 2 |
| Crowell | | | 1 | 1 | | | | 2 |
| Delair Publishing | | | | | 1 | | | 1 |
| Delacorte Press | | | | | | 1 | | 1 |
| Denison | | | | | 1 | | | 1 |
| Derrydale Books | | | | | 1 | | | 1 |
| Dial Press | | | 1 | 1 | | | | 2 |
| Dos Voces Press | | | | 1 | | | | 1 |
| Doubleday | | | | 4 | | 1 | | 5 |
| Dutton/Windmill | | | | 3 | | 4 | | 7 |
| Eakin Press | | | | 1 | | | | 1 |
| Ediciones PLESA | | | | | 1 | | | 1 |
| Ediciones Suromex | | | | | | 1 | | 1 |
| Editorial Los Andes | | | | | | 1 | | 1 |
| Editorial Patria | | | | | 7 | | | 7 |
| Editorial Ramon Sopena | | | | | 1 | | | 1 |
| Editorial Sigmar | | | | | 1 | | | 1 |
| Educational Consulting Associates | | | | 1 | | | | 1 |
| Educational Factors | | | | | 1 | | | 1 |
| El Dorado Distributors | | | | 1 | | | | 1 |
| Feminist Press | | | | 1 | | | | 1 |
| First Story Press | | | | | | 1 | | 1 |
| Follett | | | 1 | | | | | 1 |
| Football Hobbies | | | | 3 | | | | 3 |
| Four Winds Press | | | | 2 | | | | 2 |
| Friendship Press | | | 1 | | | | | 1 |
| Fry-Innovations | | | | | | 1 | | 1 |
| Funk & Wagnalls | | | 4 | | | | | 4 |
| Girl Scouts of the U.S.A. | | | | | 1 | | | 1 |
| Greenwillow Books | | | | | 1 | 3 | | 4 |
| Grosset & Dunlap | | 1 | 1 | | | | | 2 |
| Hampton-Brown Books | | | | | | 1 | | 1 |
| Harcourt Brace (Jovanovich) | | 1 | 5 | | 1 | 2 | 5 | 14 |
| HarperCollins & HarperTrophy | | | | | | 3 | | 3 |
| Harvey House | | | 2 | | | | | 2 |
| High Desert Productions | | | | | | 2 | | 2 |
| Highlights for Children | | | | 1 | | | | 1 |
| Highsmith Press | | | | | | 4 | | 4 |
| Hispanic Books Distributors | | | | | 1 | 2 | | 3 |

| Publisher/Editorial | 40s | 50s | 60s | 70s | 80s | 90s | 2000s | Total |
|---|---|---|---|---|---|---|---|---|
| Holt (Rinehart and Winston) | | | | | 2 | 4 | | 6 |
| Hope Publishing House | | | | | 1 | | | 1 |
| Houghton Mifflin | | | 1 | | | | 1 | 2 |
| Hyperion Books for Children | | | | | | 2 | | 2 |
| Instructional Challenges | | | | 1 | | | | 1 |
| Intercultural Develop Research Association | | | | 2 | 2 | | | 4 |
| Internat'l Society for General Semantics | | | | 1 | | | | 1 |
| Island Press | | | 2 | | | | | 2 |
| J. Philip O'Hara | | | | 1 | | | | 1 |
| Jay Alden Publishers | | | | 1 | | | | 1 |
| JJ Publications | | | | 1 | | | | 1 |
| John Day | | | 4 | 2 | | | | 6 |
| Juventud Multilingual Press | | | | | | | 1 | 1 |
| Kids Can Press | | | | 1 | | | | 1 |
| Knopf | 1 | | | | | 2 | | 3 |
| Knowledge Aid | | | 1 | | | | | 1 |
| La Estancia Press | | | | | 3 | | | 3 |
| Larousse | | | | | 1 | | | 1 |
| Latin American Creations | | | | | | 1 | | 1 |
| Lectorum Publications | | | | | 1 | 2 | | 3 |
| Lee & Low Books | | | | | | 2 | | 2 |
| Leslie Press | | | | 1 | | | | 1 |
| Libraries Unlimited | | | | | | 1 | | 1 |
| Lion Press | | | 1 | | | | | 1 |
| Lippincott | | | 1 | | | | | 1 |
| Little Brown | | | 1 | | 1 | 6 | | 8 |
| Lollipop Power/Carolina Wren | | | | 3 | | 1 | | 4 |
| Lothrop, Lee & Shepard | | | | | | 2 | | 2 |
| Macmillan | | | 3 | 1 | | | | 4 |
| McGraw Hill | | | 1 | 1 | | | | 2 |
| Mediaworks | | | | 1 | | | | 1 |
| Mills Music | 1 | | | | | | | 1 |
| Montebello Unified School District | | | | 2 | | | | 2 |
| Morrow Junior Books | | | | | | 1 | | 1 |
| National Textbook Company | | | 1 | 16 | 2 | | | 19 |
| Naylor | | | 1 | 2 | | | | 3 |
| Neil A. Kjos Music Company | | | 1 | | | | | 1 |
| New Directions | | | | | 1 | | | 1 |
| New Mexico Magazine | | | | | 1 | | | 1 |
| New Seed Press | | | | 2 | | | | 2 |
| Northland & Rising Moon | | | | | | 9 | | 9 |
| Oak Publications | | | 1 | | | | | 1 |
| Oasis Press | | | | 1 | | | | 1 |
| Ol' Stone Press | | | | | | 1 | | 1 |
| Old Hogan Publishing | | | | | | 2 | | 2 |
| Open Hand Publishing | | | | | 1 | 1 | | 2 |
| Orchard Books | | | | | | 1 | | 1 |
| Organization of American States | | | | 1 | | | | 1 |
| Ottenheimer | | | | | | 1 | | 1 |
| Oxford University Press | | | | | 1 | | | 1 |
| Pajarito Publications | | | | | 1 | | | 1 |
| Pan American Book Company | | 1 | | | | | | 1 |
| Pan Asian Publications | | | | | | 5 | | 5 |

| Publisher/Editorial | 40s | 50s | 60s | 70s | 80s | 90s | 2000s | Total |
|---|---|---|---|---|---|---|---|---|
| Pangaea | | | | | | | 1 | 1 |
| Passport Books | | | | | | 2 | | 2 |
| Pelican Publishing | | | | | | 1 | | 1 |
| Piñata Books & Arte Público | | | | | 2 | 13 | 3 | 18 |
| Piñata Publications | | | | | | 1 | | 1 |
| Plus Ultra Educational | | | | 1 | | | | 1 |
| Prentice Hall | | | 1 | 1 | | | | 2 |
| Putnam | | | 1 | 1 | 1 | 2 | | 5 |
| Quinto Sol Publications | | | | 2 | | | | 2 |
| Raintree Publishers | | | | | 1 | 2 | | 3 |
| Random House | | | 2 | | 4 | | | 6 |
| RD Communications | | | | 1 | | | | 1 |
| Red Crane Books | | | | | | 1 | | 1 |
| Regents Publishing | | | | 1 | | | | 1 |
| Royal Editions | | | | | 1 | | | 1 |
| San Xavier del Bac | | | 1 | | | | | 1 |
| Scholastic | | | | | 1 | 4 | | 5 |
| Scott, Foresman | | | | 1 | | | | 1 |
| Scribners | 2 | | | | | | | 2 |
| Shen's Books | | | | | | 1 | | 1 |
| Sierra Club | | | | | | 1 | | 1 |
| Simon & Schuster | | | | | | 1 | | 1 |
| Star Light Press | | | | | | 1 | | 1 |
| Totinem Publications | | | | 1 | | | | 1 |
| Trails West Publishing | | | | | 4 | 1 | | 5 |
| Troll Associates | | | | | 1 | | | 1 |
| Tundra Books | | | | 1 | | | | 1 |
| Twin Palms Editorial | | | | 1 | | | | 1 |
| U.S. Indian Service/Bureau of Indian Affairs | 2 | 1 | | | | | | 3 |
| Universidad de Nuevo Mexico | | | | 1 | | 1 | | 2 |
| Vantage Press | | | | 1 | | | | 1 |
| Victory Press | | | | | | 1 | | 1 |
| Voluntad Publishers | | | | | 1 | | | 1 |
| Walck | | | 2 | | | | | 2 |
| Watts | | | | 2 | 1 | | | 3 |
| Westminster Press | | | | 1 | | | | 1 |
| Whitman | | | 2 | 2 | | 3 | | 7 |
| William Sloan Associates | | | 1 | | | | | 1 |
| Willowisp Press | | | | | | 1 | | 1 |
| Wings Press | | | | | | | 1 | 1 |
| Work Projects Administration | 1 | | | | | | | 1 |
| Wordsong | | | | | | 2 | | 2 |
| World | | | 1 | | | | | 1 |
| Yuan-Liou Publishing | | | | | | 2 | | 2 |
| TOTAL | 7 | 4 | 58 | 113 | 74 | 162 | 15 | 433 |

# Appendix B:
# Review Journals Cited

# Apéndice B:
# Revistas críticas citadas

| Journal/Revista | Number of Reviews/ Número de críticas |
|---|---|
| AB Bookman's Weekly | 3 |
| America | 1 |
| American Book Review | 2 |
| Appraisal: Science Books for Young People | 1 |
| Atlantic | 2 |
| Babbling Bookworm | 3 |
| Belles Lettres | 1 |
| Bloomsbury Review | 6 |
| Book Links | 22 |
| Book Report | 4 |
| Book Week | 1 |
| Book World | 7 |
| Bookbird | 1 |
| Booklist | 177 |
| Bookmark | 1 |
| Books for Keeps | 1 |
| Bookwatch | 8 |
| Business Week | 1 |
| Cartel | 32 |
| Catholic Library World | 9 |
| Catholic World | 1 |
| Center for Children's Books Bulletin | 60 |
| Chicago Sun Times | 2 |
| Chicago Sunday Tribune (Books Today) | 4 |
| Childhood Education | 16 |
| Children's Book Review Service | 40 |

| *Journal/Revista* | *Number of Reviews/*<br>*Número de críticas* |
|---|---|
| Children's Bookwatch | 36 |
| Choice | 1 |
| Christian Century | 1 |
| Christian Science Monitor | 14 |
| Come-All-Ye | 1 |
| Commonweal | 5 |
| Curriculum Review | 3 |
| Day Care & Early Childhood Education | 1 |
| Early Childhood Education Journal | 8 |
| Elementary English | 8 |
| Emergency Librarian | 5 |
| EMIE Bulletin | 1 |
| Entertainment Weekly | 1 |
| Five Owls | 11 |
| Hispania | 9 |
| Horn Book | 84 |
| Horn Book Guide | 76 |
| Hungry Mind Review | 13 |
| Instructor | 14 |
| Interracial Books for Children | 13 |
| Journal of Reading | 3 |
| Journal of Youth Services in Libraries | 32 |
| Junior Bookshelf | 2 |
| Kirkus Reviews | 82 |
| Kliatt Young Adult Paperback Book Guide | 2 |
| Language Arts | 15 |
| Learning | 2 |
| Lector | 11 |
| Library Journal | 51 |
| Library Talk | 13 |
| Los Angeles Times Book Review | 8 |
| Multicultural Review | 1 |
| Music Educators Journal | 2 |
| New Advocate | 4 |
| New Directions for Women | 1 |
| New York Herald Tribune (Weekly) Book Review/Books | 6 |
| New York Times Book Review | 19 |
| New Yorker | 5 |
| Newsletter of the United States Board on Books for Young People | 9 |
| Newsweek | 3 |
| Observer (London) | 1 |
| Parents' Choice | 1 |
| Parents Magazine | 2 |
| Parnassus | 1 |
| Proyecto Leer Bulletin | 25 |

| Journal/Revista | Number of Reviews/<br>Número de críticas |
|---|---|
| Publishers Weekly | 71 |
| Reading Teacher | 54 |
| River Review | 2 |
| San Francisco Chronicle | 3 |
| Saturday Review/Saturday Review of Literature | 10 |
| School Arts | 1 |
| School Library Journal | 149 |
| Scientific American | 1 |
| Small Press | 5 |
| Small Press Book Review | 1 |
| Smithsonian | 3 |
| Social Education | 19 |
| Social Studies | 6 |
| Teacher | 4 |
| Times Educational Supplement | 1 |
| Top of the News | 5 |
| Tribune Books (Chicago) | 3 |
| Utne Reader | 1 |
| Village Voice Literary Supplement | 2 |
| Voice of Youth Advocates | 4 |
| Whole Earth Review | 1 |
| Wilson Library Bulletin | 6 |
| Wisconsin Library Bulletin | 4 |
| Young Readers Review | 2 |
| Total Number of Reviews | 1370 |
| Total Number of Books | 433 |
| Average Number of Reviews Per Book | 3.16 |

# Index of Coauthors, Illustrators and Translators

# Índice de co-autores, ilustradores y traductores

*References are to entry numbers.*

*Los números se refieren a los números de cada entrada.*

Abós, Elena 248
Accardo, Anthony 31
Acevedo, Rubén Darío 283, 284, 286, 288
Acosta Gonzalez, Carolina 159
Ada, Alma Flor 150, 302, 342, 344, 383, 414
Aguayo, Juan M. 419
Aguilar, Josefina 427
Alarcón, Francisco X. 239, 240
Alejandro, Alis 255
Alemany, Norah E. 257
Aliki 179
Allen, Clark 261
Allen, Ed. 425
Alvarez, Inés 1, 41, 125, 312
Alvarez Lecuona, Consuelo 21
Amador, Carlos Eduardo 298
American Folklore Society 135
Anchondo, Mary 340, 341, 345, 346, 347, 350
Andersen, Hans Christian 173
Andújar, Gloria de Aragón 127, 294
Apodaca, Cecilia 252
Aponte de Zacklin, Lyda *see* Zacklin, Lyda
  Aponte de
Aragón Andújar, Gloria de *see* Andújar,
  Gloria de Aragón
Arancibia, Maurice 155
Arkhurst, Joyce C. 298
Armitage, Merle 412

Arnold, Jeanne 391, 392, 393, 394
Arnold, Sandra Martin 17
Arroyo, Andrea 411
Arroyo de Gillis, Hilda 409
Aruego, Ariane 222, 224
Aruego, José 222, 223, 224
Asch, Moses 295
Atene, Ann 90
Auclair, Joan 71
Avery, Charles E. 30
Avila Ruiz, Lidia 212

Bailyn, Susan 422
Baker, Charlotte 15, 16
Baker, Donald 91
Baker, Marguerite Arguedas 91
Balestra, Alejandra 226
Ballester, Arnal 56, 255
Ballesteros, María Del Carmen 32
Barbour, Karen 197
Bar Din, Anne 248
Barnett, Moneta 55
Barraza, M. Fred 152
Barry, Katharina 216
Barton, Byron 306
Bedout, Margarita de 298
Bellm, Dan 51
Belpré, Pura 77

Benedetto, Armando Sabino de 39
Benitez, Emerito 38
Benvenuti 217
Berenstain, Jan 41
Berg, Charles Ramírez 273
Berlitz, Charles F. 395
Berlitz, Valerie 395
The Berlitz Schools of America 42, 395
Bernstein, Leonard 263
Bertrand, Diane Gonzales 44, 45
Bilingual Theater Company of Corpus
    Christi 354
Bishop, Dorothy Sword 37
Blackstone, Ann 387
Bolognese, Don 236
Borja, Robert 37
Borton de Treviño, Elizabeth *see* Treviño,
    Elizabeth Borton de
Bregand, Eleanore 164, 165
Breitman, Nitza Tufiño de *see* Tufiño de
    Breitman, Nitza
Brigham, Barbara 204
Brown, Richard 58, 59
Brown, Sue 155
Brunhoff, Laurent de 61
Brusca, María Cristina 62
Bucks, Betsy L. 163
Bustamente, Bea 243
Bustamente, Charles J. 237
Butler, Sarah Garaway 149

Calonico, J. M. 386
Canetti, Yanitzia 225
Cantú, Jesús María "Chista" 367
Carlo, Vivian 155
Carlson, Lori Marie 76
Carrera, Raul 219
Carrillo, Arsenio S. 251
Carrillo, Graciela 344
Carrillo de Lopez, Graciela 341
Cartes, María Rebeca 148, 149, 231
Casilla, Robert 337
Castañeda, Alfredo 212
Castedo, Elena 77
Castellanos, Rosario 282
Castilla, Julia Mercedes 31, 44, 80
Castillo, Consuelo Mendez *see* Mendez
    Castillo, Consuelo
Cavazos Peña, Sylvia *see* Peña, Sylvia Cavazos
Cervantes, Alex 219
Chagoya, Enrique 349
Chalquest, R. R. 372
Chang, Shih-ming 173
Chapman, Robert 246

Chávez, Doris 425, 426
Cherin, Robin 151
Chermayeff, Jane Clark 81
Cherr, Pat 218
Chesneau, Eva V. 99
Chorao, Kay 171
Chow, Octavio 342
Cisneros, José 362
Cisneros, Sandra 162
Collier-Morales, Roberta 88
Conboy, Roy 354
Connelly, Gwen 18
Contreras, Richard E. 243
Cooney, Barbara 163
"Corazones Valientes" 316
Cota, Rosita 261
Cotera, Martha P. 110, 192
Cotts, Claire B. 210
Cruz, Manuel 95
Cruz, Marina Méndez *see* Méndez Cruz,
    Marina
Cruz, Ruth 95
Cruz Martinez, Alejandro 96
Cuenca, Pilar A. de 1, 41, 125, 312
Curnow, Diane 241

Dana, Doris 267
Darío Acevedo, Rubén *see* Acevedo, Rubén
    Darío
Dávalos, Felipe 5
Davison, Patricia 392
Davison, Patricia Hinton 63, 93
de Brunhoff, Laurent *see* Brunhoff, Laurent
    de
de Cuenca, Pilar A. *see* Cuenca, Pilar A. de
Delacre, Lulu 161
DeLange, Alex Pardo 45, 226, 227, 228
Delano, Irene 53, 54
Delano, Jack 53, 54
de la O, Esmeralda 298
DeLarrea, Victoria 302
Delgado Espinosa, Catherine 297
DeOnís, Harriet 53, 54
Deru, Myriam 14
Devon, Pru 295
Dewey, Ariane *see* Aruego, Ariane
Diaz, Mary Segarra de *see* Segarra de Diaz,
    Mary
Diaz Valcárcel, Emilio 113
Dicks, Jan Thompson 364
Diez, Richard A. 39
Dinhofer, Al 116
DiSalvo-Ryan, DyAnne 156
Dominguez, Domitila 248

Dominguez, J. A. 118
Domínguez, Joseph F. 211
Dominguez, Juanita 118
Dominguez, Roberto 118
Dominguez, Zarife 118
Dorros, Sandra Marulanda 121
Duarte, Luz Ríos *see* Ríos Duarte, Luz
DuBois, William Pène 123

Eastman, P. D. 124, 292
Eber, Christina Engla 28
Elivia 207
Espinosa, Catherine Delgado *see* Delgado
   Espinosa, Catherine
Estill, Monica 285, 287
Eyzaguirre, Roberto 61

Favero, Agustina Santos del 147
Fernandez, Pedro Villa *see* Villa Fernandez,
   Pedro
Fiammenghi, Gioia 326
Fisher, Leonard Everett 417
Flores, Angel 280
Flores, Enrique 242
Flores, Herminio 155
Foster, Karen Sharp 141
Fox, Herbert 117
Franzen, Amapola 363
Frasconi, Antonio 97, 142, 143, 211, 267,
   280
Fraser, Betty 324
Fuenmayor, Morelia 235

Galvez, Daniel 336
Garcia, Dolores Janes 417
Garcia, Geronimo 188, 359, 360
García Moliner, María Dolores *see* Moliner,
   María Dolores García
García Lorca, Federico 77, 153
Garcia Travesi, Carlos 296
Gardner, Tom 154
Garza, Carmen Lomas *see* Lomas Garza,
   Carmen
Gaspar, Tomás Rodríguez 155
Gaunt, Marianne 230
Gilbert, Ayse 154
Gilbert, Sharon S. 163
Gillis, Hilda Arroyo de *see* Arroyo de Gillis,
   Hilda
Girl Guides 430
Girl Scouts 430
Godoy Alcayaga, Lucila *see* Mistral,
   Gabriela
Gomez, Cruz 349

Gómez, Elizabeth 26, 198
Gonzales Bertrand, Diane *see* Bertrand,
   Diane Gonzales
Gonzalez, Albino 376
Gonzalez, Carolina Acosta *see* Acosta Gon-
   zalez, Carolina
Gonzalez, Christina 25
Gonzalez, Gloria 424
Gonzalez, Maya Christina 9, 10, 11, 12, 301
Graham, Tom 169
Griggs, Venetia Bradfield 266
Guardia, William 212
Guerrero, Marcos 363
Guerrero Rea, Jesús 151, 338, 339, 343, 351
Guevara, Susan 389
Guibert, Rita 222, 223, 224
Guido, Toribia Mairena *see* Mairena Guido,
   Toribia
Guillén Vicente, Rafael Sebastian *see* Mar-
   cos, Subcomandante
Gurney, Nancy 167
Gutiérrez, Marta 40

Haddad, Robert J. 169
Haggin, Linda 265
Hall, Mahji 170
Hampares, Katherine 138, 139, 140
Hanley, Catherine 308
Harper, Piers 57
Harris, Jim 244
Harris, Reed 331
Harris, Violet J. 4
Hart, Rebecca 316
Harvey, Bob 176, 177, 178
Harvey, Diane Kelsay 176, 177, 178
Hayes, Joe 135
Hazen, Nancy 192
Hearon, Dorothy 404
Herrera, Pilar 360
Herrera, Velino 85
Hijuelos, Oscar 75, 77
Hill, Vicki Trego 184, 190
Hines, Margaret E. 220
Hogan, Brother Lawrence 365
Hogrogian, Nonny 180
Hopkins, Lee Bennett 4
Horvath, Maria 153
Howard, Kim 6
Howard, Pauline Rodriguez 44, 146
Hsieh, Jim 424
Hubatch, Sister M. Antoninus 365
Hubbard, William E. 328

Innes, Charles 200

Jackson, Al 403
Jaramillo, Nelly Palacio 207
Jauss, Anne Marie 317, 318
Jefferson, Cheri Lynn 73
Jelinek, Lucy 185, 186, 187, 189, 191
Jenkins, Cristina M. 83, 84, 85
Jiang, Cheng An 209
Jiang, Wei, 209
Johnson, Carmen Maldonado de *see* Maldonado de Johnson, Carmen
Johnson, Carol 176
Johnson, Celeste 19

Kaltovich, Edith Rusconi 74
Karas, G. Brian 137
Keats, Ezra Jack 181
Kilb, Anne Marie 20
Kilgore, Susi 87
Kimball, Laurel H. 163
Kirkland, Will 153
Kirschen 331
Kleven, Elisa 119, 120, 290, 291
Knowlton, Ken 283
Krone, Beatrice 261
Kwapil, Marie Jo 20

Lado, María Dolores 233
Landeen, Sharon 231
Lasker, Joe 384, 385
Laurence 232
Lavallee, Barbara 275
Lea, Aurora Lucero White 183
Leard, Skeeter 297
Lechón, Daniel 272, 273
Lecuona, Consuelo Alvarez *see* Alvarez Lecuona, Consuelo
Leder, Dora 383
Lee, Alfonso Silva *see* Silva Lee, Alfonso
Lee, Arthur 79
Lemieux, Margo 36
Lewis, Wendy 89
Lisker, Emily 76
Littleboy, John 237
Liu, Lesley 78
Livingston, Myra Cohn 211
Lizardi-Rivera, Carmen 245
Loarca, Carlos 351
Lomas Garza, Carmen 238, 239, 240
Lopez, Graciela Carrillo de *see* Carrillo de Lopez, Graciela
Lopez, Loretta 129, 130
López de Mariscal, Blanca 242
Lorca, Federico García *see* García Lorca, Federico

Lowell, Jennifer Audrey 413
Lowery, Margaret A. 424
Lujan, Tonita 83
Lustig, Loretta 276
Luz, La 37

Macaluso Rodriguez, Gina 247
Madden, Peter 325, 327
Madrid Rivera, Susana *see* Rivera, Susana Madrid
Mae, Karen 155
Mahler, Michael 217
Maidoff, Jules 433
Mairena Guido, Toribia 316
Maldonado de Johnson, Carmen 212
Mandlin, Harvey 208
Ma-Pi-Wi *see* Herrera, Velino
Marcos, Subcomandante 248
Marín, Juan Francisco 413
Mariscal, Blanca López de *see* López de Mariscal, Blanca
Marsh, Gwen 217
Martín, Rosa 277
Martínez, Alba Nora 271
Martinez, Alejandro Cruz *see* Cruz Martinez, Alejandro
Martinez, Elizabeth 256
Martínez, Thelma R. 243
Martinez Vasquez, Ely Patricia 253
Marulanda, Sandra 30
Marulanda Dorros, Sandra *see* Dorros, Sandra Marulanda
Mascayano, Ismael 254
Matiella, Ana Consuelo 392
McCrady, Lady 257
McNaught, Harry 1
Memoirs of the American Folklore Society 135
Méndez, Consuelo 24
Mendez Castillo, Consuelo 338
Méndez Cruz, Marina 316
Mérida, Carlos 355
Mesa-Bains, Amalia 238
Mier, Colin 89
Miera, Virginia 252
Miles, Cyril 406
Miracle, Veronica Mary 166
Mistral, Gabriela 97, 267
Miyake, Yoshi 158
Mlawer, Teresa 214, 235, 258, 264
Moir, Valerie 381
Moliner, María Dolores García 89
Montañez, Marta 38
Montebello Gardens School 164, 165

Montez, Richard 347
Montoya, Malaquias 150
Mora, Francisco 93
Mora, Francisco X. 268, 269, 270, 271, 274
Mora, Pat 271
Morales, Rodolfo 51
Moreno, Elizabeth F. 334
Moreno, René King 168
Morrill, Leslie 17
Moya, René 381
Muñoz, Anna 256
Murray, Nancy 122
Murillo Peralta, Maria Ana 406

Nancarrow, Mary Ann 426
Nava, Julian 366
Negri, Rocco 399
Neuberger, Elsa 280
Ney, Stephanie Sove 110
Nicaraguan National Television 352
Nielson, Elizabeth Colwell 310
Nieto, Sonia 29
Nieves, Ernesto Ramos *see* Ramos Nieves,
   Ernesto
Noda, Phyllis 147
Novak, Matt 398

Oliden, Agustina 98
Olivas, Herlinda P. 293
Olivera, Fernando 96
Orellana, Ramón S. 281
Ormsby, Virginia 289
Orozco, José-Luis 290, 291
Osuna, Gloria 160
Osuna Perez, Gloria 183

Palacio Jaramillo, Nelly *see* Jaramillo, Nelly
   Palacio
Palacios, Argentina 357
Pardo DeLange, Alex *see* DeLange, Alex
   Pardo
Paschke, Barbara 52
Paterson, Diane 249
Payzant, Charles 379
Paz, Elena 105, 106
Paz, Octavio 282
Peña, Amado M. 13
Peña, Narciso 299, 300
Peña, Sylvia Cavazos 299, 300
Pepp, Margot 4
Peralta, Maria Ana Murillo *see* Murillo Per-
   alta, Maria Ana
Perez, Gloria Osuna *see* Osuna Perez, Gloria
Perez, Irene 339

Perez, Lucia Angela 183
Perez, Maria Consuelo 403
Perez Torres, Arturo 293
Pickens, Marjorie 46, 47
Pinkney, Jerry 250
Po, Lee 123
Prince, Amy 128, 428
Provensen, Martin 312
Puig Zaldívar, Raquel 313

Quinson, Mary Ann 230
Quintanilla, Guadalupe C. 420

Rabinowitz, Sandy 136
Rahman, Brunilda 46, 47
Ramírez Berg, Charles *see* Berg, Charles
   Ramírez
Ramos Nieves, Ernesto 43
Rea, Jesús Guerrero *see* Guerrero Rea, Jesús
Reed, Ronald E. 424
Reisberg, Mira 92, 264
Reisberg, Veg 352
Reposo, Mario 220
Retana, Guillermo 319
Retta, Luis 98
Revah, Patricia 52
Reyes, Roger I. 151, 345, 350
Ribes Tovar, Federico 322
Rice, James 323
Rios, Evelyn D. 328
Ríos, Ivannia Zambrana *see* Zambrana Ríos,
   Ivannia
Rios, Mike 347
Rios, Ray 340
Ríos Duarte, Luz 316
Rivas, Yolanda 321
Rivera, Carlos 124, 167, 292, 378
Rivera, Susana Madrid 329
Rivera Ruíz, Esmeralda 316
Roach, Jean 157
Robledo, Honorio 182
Rockwell, Anne 332, 333
Rodríguez, Doris 335
Rodriguez, Gina Macaluso *see* Macaluso
   Rodriguez, Gina
Rodríguez, Jesús M. 334
Rodríguez, Lisa 334
Rodriguez, Patricia 346
Rodriguez Gaspar, Tomás *see* Gaspar,
   Tomás Rodríguez
Rodriguez, William 38
Roeder, Virginia Marsh 419, 420
Rohmer, Harriet 96, 238, 239, 240
Rosado, Ana-María 105, 106

Rosenberg, Joe 354
Ross, Stacey 27
Rossi, Joyce 356
Rotsaert, William 135
Rowe, Barry 200
Ruben, Patricia 357
Rubiera, Saundra Smith *see* Smith Rubiera, Saundra
Rubio, Martin 38
Rueda, Marco Vinicio 418
Ruiz, Ana 162
Ruiz, Denise 77
Ruíz, Esmeralda Rivera *see* Rivera Ruíz, Esmeralda
Ruiz, Lidia Avila *see* Avila Ruiz, Lidia

Sabino de Benedetto, Armando *see* Benedetto, Armando Sabino de
Salas, Viria 316
Salgado, María A. 36
Salinas, Bobbi 363
Sam, Joe 342
Sanarabia, Ana Lorena 253
Sánchez, Enrique O. 225
Sanchez, Porfirio 155
Sandy, Percy Tsisete 84
Santos, Cynthia Ann 367, 369
Santos del Favero, Agustina *see* Favero, Agustina Santos del
Sattley, Helen R. 298
Savadier, Elivia *see* Elivia
Saxton, Dean 365
Schatschneider, Lori Ann 416
Schecter, David 96, 239, 240
Scherbatskoy, Mary 408
Schneider, Jorge 74
Sears, Nancy 40
Segarra de Diaz, Mary 409
Seiden, Art 42, 395
Serfozo, John 377
Shapiro, Jane 408
Sheheen, Dennis 380
Shekerjian, Haig 310
Shekerjian, Regina 310
Shepard, Gary 247
Sierra, F. John 213
Silva, Simón 3
Silva Lee, Alfonso 382
Simmons, Elly 27, 196
Smith, Ana 323
Smith, Lee 307, 309, 311
Smith Rubiera, Saundra 313
Soto, Armando 38
Soto, Gary 77

Speidel, Sandy 256
Star Light 229
Stark, William 101
Stearns, Virginia 348
Stevens, Cat 390
Stinson, Adele 237
Storni, Alfonsina 77
Strick, David 366
Strick, Juanita C. 328
Strumpen-Darrie, Robert 395
Swanson, María Medina 401, 402
Swift, Virginia 408
Symank, Yvonne 109
Syverson-Stork, Jill 171

Tablada, José Juan 282
Tabor, Nancy María Grande 397
Tallon, Robert 400
Tang, You-shan 258
Tardy, Gene 403
Tarrango, Leticia 386
Tartarotti, Stefano 172
Tasca, William 426
Taylor, José 358
Tholander, Earl 221
Thompson, Kathleen 158
Toledo, C. A. 99
Torres, Arturo Perez *see* Perez Torres, Arturo
Tovar, Federico Ribes *see* Ribes Tovar, Federico
Tracy, Libba 63
Travesi, Carlos García *see* Garcia Travesi, Carlos
Treviño, Elizabeth Borton de 406
Trez, Alain 407
Trujillo, Tom 115
Tufiño de Breitman, Nitza 409
Turkle, Brinton 7

UNICEF 262, 262, 298
Urquidi, Maria 421

Valcárcel, Emilio Diaz *see* Diaz Valcárcel, Emilio
Valenzuela, Liliana 82
Valerio, Felipe 252
VanStone, Mary R. 412
Vasiliu, Mircea 206
Vasquez, Ely Patricia Martinez *see* Martinez Vasquez, Ely Patricia
Vega, Anne 80
Vega, Tomás 113
Vidaure, Morris 342

Vigil, Angel  413
Vigna, Judith  414
Villa Fernandez, Pedro  321
Villavicencio, José  116
Viramontes, Xavier  343
Volkmer, Jane Anne  416
Von Mason, Stephen  111

Waddell, Margaret  8
Wang, Eva  174, 175
Warren, Harry  148
Weaver, Marian  319, 320
Weisgard, Leonard  215
Whipple, Rick  86
Wilde, Oscar  174
Williams, Herb  425, 426
Wilson, Dornmather  348
Wilson, Tona  62
Winant, Phyllis R.  408

Wintemute, Grace Catalina  418
Winter, Jeanette  428
Wood, Jakki  277
Worcester, Donald  234
Work Projects Administration  429
Woyde, Horst  94

Ybáñez, Terry  2, 82
Yeung, Ellen Lai-shan  258

Zacklin, Lyda Aponte de  76
Zaldívar, Raquel Puig  see  Puig Zaldívar,
  Raquel
Zambrana Ríos, Ivannia  316
Zamora, Deborah Ann  367, 369
Zeller, Beatriz  78, 79, 172, 173, 174, 175, 405
Zubizarreta, Rosa  3, 5, 6
Zubizarreta, Rosalma  96, 238, 342, 344

# Index of Titles, Series and Awards

# Índice de títulos, series y premios

*References are to entry numbers.*

*Los números se refieren a los números de cada entrada.*

A divertirnos con el fútbol 201
A es para amigo 237
A Is for Amigo 237
ABCDEFGHIJKLMNOPQRSTUVWXYZ in English and Spanish 400
ABC's in English and Spanish 400
Abecedario 328
Abecedario bilingüe en verso 241
Abuela 119
La Abuelita Fina y sus sombrillas maravillosas 360
Adiós Anna 156
Adivinanzas, fábulas y refranes populares 283
Los adultos también lloran 192
Adventures for Kids 284
The Adventures of Connie and Diego 150
Los aguinaldos del infante 53
Ah Ucu and Itzo 307
Ah Ucu e Itzo 307
Ahi, donde bailan las luciérnagas 92
La alacena 64
Albertina anda arriba 397
Albertina Goes Up 397
Alberto and His Missing Sock 147
Alberto y el calcetín perdido 147
El alfabeto 18
Una alfombra de flores 406
Alphabet 328

Alphabet Times Four 60
Américas Awards 3, 5, 6, 9, 10, 12, 25, 43, 75, 107, 109, 120, 121, 127, 146, 162, 196, 210, 211, 213, 220, 235, 239, 240, 245, 246, 282, 290, 291, 301, 336, 389, 393, 411, 427
America's Own Holidays 17
El amigo 65
Amigo Means Friend 136
Amigos del otro lado 24
Anaya Bilingual Classics 138, 139, 140
Los ángeles andan en bicicleta, y otros poemas de otoño 9
Angel's Kite 51
Angels Ride Bikes and Other Fall Poems 9
El anillo turquesa 112
El año nuevo 4
El apache 410
¡Aplauso! Hispanic Children's Theater 354
El árbol de Navidad 2
Are You My Mother? 124
El arroja ojos 112
Arroz con leche 105, 171, 333
Arroz con leche Awards 152, 247
Ashes for Sale 112
Ashkii and His Grandfather 148
Ashkii y el abuelo 148
At Home 179
Atariba & Niguayona 338
La aventura de Yolanda 155

Las aventuras de Connie y Diego 150
Aventuras infantiles 284

Babar's Spanish Lessons 61
The Baby 66
The Baby Chicks Sing 171
Baby Coyote and the Old Woman 398
La bailarina 71
¡Bailen, ratones, bailen! 172
Bajen la piñata 171
Bastante grande 225
El bebé 66
El bebe de los osos Berenstain 41
Bedtime Stories in Spanish 37, 404
Beginner Books 124, 167, 292, 378
The Beginner's English/Spanish Dictionary
    40
Belling the Cat 104, 283
Benito's Bizcochitos 31
The Berenstain Bears' New Baby 41
Berlitz Spanish Alphabet and Numbers for
    Children 42
Berlitz Spanish Zoo Animals for Children
    395
The Best Way to Carry Water 43
Best Wishes, Amen 276
Bestiario 280
Bestiary 280
¡Bienvenido, Roberto! 377
Big Dog, Little Dog 125
Big Enough 225
Bilingual ABC in Verse 241
Bilingual/Bicultural Foreign Language Series
    423
Bilingual Children's Literature 251
Bilingual Fantasy 287
A Birthday Surprise 14
Los bizcochitos de Benito 31
The Blanket 67
La Boda 411
A Book of Seasons 312
Bopo Joins the Circus 334
Bopo se une al circo 334
Borinquen, and Then Columbus 113
Borinquen Before Columbus 409
Borinquen, y después Colón 113
Born into the Pack 319
The Bossy Gallito 161
Bowmar Early Childhood Series 208
A Boy Named Paco 293
The Boy Who Cried Wolf 103, 283
The Boy Who Killed the Giant 413
A Brief Natural History of the Galapagos
    Islands for Young People 99

Brother Anansi and the Cattle Ranch 111
La buena suerte 77
Buenas noches a todos 277
Buenas noches mis pollitos 141
The Burro and the Wise Man 297
The Busy Day 14

El caballito de siete colores 345
Un caballo para alquilar 112
Caballos y ponies 72
The Cactus Wren and the Cholla 152
Caldecott Awards 163, 304, 305
Caldo, caldo, caldo 45
Calling the Doves 196
Calor 13
Caminando 134
El camino verdadero a la felicidad 413
Canción de los Cunas 339
Canciones de mi isla 38
Canciones de nuestra cabaña 430
Canciones y juegos de Nuevo México 159,
    429
El canto de las palomas 196
El canto de roble 354
Cantos de México 261
Caperucita roja 56, 255
Carlos and the Carnival 391
Carlos and the Cornfield 392
Carlos and the Skunk 393
Carlos and the Squash Plant 394
Carlos y el zorrillo 393
Carlos y la feria 391
Carlos y la milpa de maíz 392
Carlos y la planta de calabaza 394
A Carpet of Flowers 406
Carrousel 386
Carrusel 396
El castillo de Chuchurumbel 422
The Castle of Chuchurumbel 422
The Cat in the Hat 378
The Cat in the Hat Beginner Book Dictio-
    nary in Spanish 279
The Cat Who Had No Friends 354
The Cat With Boots 37
El cazadorcito de Picuris 85
Los cazadores invisibles 342
Cenicienta 255
Cenizas a la venta 112
El cerdo que no es cerdo 320
El chaparrón torrencial 356
Chato's Kitchen 389
Chave's Memories 109
A Chicano Christmas Story 95
Chicano Chronicle and Cosmology 238

Chicos en la cocina 116
A Child's Gifts 53
A Child's Picture Dictionary 380
Chiquita and Pepita 48
Chiquita y Pepita 48
Chocolate 171
Christmas Fantasy 77
The Christmas Gift 210
The Christmas Tree 2
Cielito lindo 333
Cinco cuentos escrito en español y inglés 20
Cinco huevos 112
Cincuenta en la cebra 397
Cinderella 37, 255
La cobija 67
Colección mini-libros 145
Colección pre-escolar bilingüe 64, 65, 66, 67, 68, 69, 70
Come to the Pond 115
Comepasteles 258
Como el sol nació 122
Como en mi tierra 264
Cómo vinimos al quinto mundo 341
Con mi hermano 337
A Concept Book 383
El conejo 68
El conejo y el coyote 413
Cool Salsa 75
Coplas 399
Coquí & His Friends 382
Coquí y sus amigos 382
The Corn Woman 413
Council on Interracial Books for Children Awards 250
Cowboy Small 234
El coyote loco 413
El coyotito y la viejita 398
The Cricket Sings 153
Crickets and Frogs 267
The Crocodile Man 112
The Cú Bird 194
Cuadros de familia 238
¡Cuando estás muy enojado! 231
Cuando me enojo 383
Cuando vamos a la escuela 327
Cuando vamos al mercado 326
La cucarachita 243
Cuckoo 127
The Cuckoo's Reward 221
Cucú 127
¡El cucuy! 182
Cuéntame un story 188
Un cuento navideño chicano 95
Cuentos bilingües para niños 251

Cuentos de cuanto hay 135
Cuentos de los niños chicanos 297
Cuentos de nuestros niños 297
Cuentos del quinto mundo: cuentos de los muchos pueblos de América para todos los niños 150, 151
Cuentos del quinto mundo: leyendas en español e inglés para todos los niños de Norteamérica 338, 339, 340, 343, 345, 346, 347, 350, 351
Cuentos favoritos 285
Cuentos matemáticos 286
¡Cuidado con las mujeres astutas! 190
Cuna Song 339
The Cupboard 64
Curious George 321

La dama y Juan Diego 417
Dance, Mice, Dance! 172
The Dancer 71
The Daughter of the Sun 254
The Day It Snowed Tortillas 190
De colores 171
De colores and Other Latin-American Folk Songs for Children 290
¡De ninguna manera, José! 187, 188
¿De quién es esta casa? 154
De tal palo, tal astilla 413
Decimos feliz cumpleaños 324
Del ombligo de la luna y otros poemas de verano 10
Delicious Hullabaloo 271
Demasiado listo 112
The Desert Is My Mother 272
The Desert Mermaid 52
El desierto es mi madre 272
El día atareado 14
El diablo de polvo 413
Diarios de vacaciones 367
Días de fiesta de los Estados Unidos 17
Diccionario bilingüe ilustrado 114
Diccionario español/inglés para principiantes 40
Diccionario Oxford en imágenes 200
Diccionario pictórico para ayudar el conocimiento 424
Diego 428
Diego quiere ser 335
Diego Rivera 158
Diego Wants To Be 335
Diez deditos 291
A Dime a Jug 43
Dinero bien gastado 265
El Dios poderoso Viracocha 347

Do Not Sneeze, Do Not Scratch—Do Not Eat! 43
The Dog 70
Don Leonardo's Horseshoe 286
Don Radio 121
Doña Blanca and Other Hispanic Nursery Rhymes and Games 372
Donde hay ganas, hay mañas 191
Donde soplan los vientos de canela 361
Los dos Jorges 166
A Doubleday Book for Young Readers 6
A Dream in the Road 77
The Dust Devil 413

Elacio Was Elacio 410
El elefante y su secreto 97
The Elephant and His Secret 97
The Emerald Lizard 112
El emperador y el ruiseñor 173
The Emperor and the Nightingale 173
En mi familia 239
English for Children 388
¿Eres tú mi mamá? 124
Erste Worte 81
La escuela 69
El espíritu de tío Fernando 235
Los espíritus de mi tía Otilia 151
Esta casa está hecha de lodo 63
Esta cosa se ve así 421
Esto goza chupando un caramelo 357
Estos zapatos míos 77
La estrella de Angel 51
Estrellita de oro 183
Everybody Has Feelings 30
Un examen sobre la experiencia de los mexicoamericanos 212
The Eyes of the Tiger 284

Fables are Forever 370
Fables in Spanish and English 48, 49, 50, 102, 103, 104, 193, 194, 195
Fábulas bilingües 48, 49, 50, 102, 103, 104, 193, 194, 195
Fábulas para siempre 370
A Faithful Friend 297
Familia 44
Family 44
Family Pictures 238
Fantasía bilingüe 287
Fantasía de Navidad 77
Favorite Spanish Folksongs 295
Favorite Tales 285
Feliz Navidad 126
Fernando's Gift 220

¡Fiesta! 168
A Fiesta of Folk Songs from Spain and Latin America 433
Fifth World Tales: Legends in Spanish and English for All the Children of North America 338, 339, 340, 343, 345, 346, 347, 350, 351
Fifth World Tales: Stories for All Children from the Many Peoples of America 150, 151
Fifty on the Zebra 397
First Day of School 14
First Words 81
A Fish Out of Water 292
The Fisherman and His Wife, 284
Fishing with Peter 178
Five Eggs 112
500 palabras nuevas para tí 1
500 Words to Grow On 1
Five Stories Written in Spanish & English 20
La flautista 137
The Flood 112
The Flute Player 137
Folk Songs of Mexico 261
Folktale Series 254
The Foolish Coyote 413
Football for Fun 201
The Fried Buns of Euphemia 297
The Fried Eggs 286
The Friend 65
Friends from the Other Side 24
Frijoles calientes 229
From Albatross to Zoo 57
From the Bellybutton of the Moon and Other Summer Poems 10
From the Jungles of Chiapas to American Bookstores 248
Fun with Spanish 90
Fútbol soccer 403

Gabriel, el fantasmita simpático, en el Caribe 375
Gabriel, el fantasmita simpático, en España 374
Gabriel, el fantasmita simpático, en México 373
Gabriel, el fantasmita simpático, en Pamplona 374
Gabriel, el fantasmita simpático, en Puerto Rico 375
Gabriel, the Happy Ghost in Mexico 373
Gabriel, the Happy Ghost in Pamplona 374
Gabriel, the Happy Ghost, in Puerto Rico 375
Gabriel, the Happy Ghost, in Spain 374

Gabriel, the Happy Ghost, in the Caribbean 375
El gallo de bodas 161
El gallo sabio 311
Games, Games, Games 366
Gathering the Sun 3
El gato ensombrerado 378
El gato sin amigos 354
El gato travieso 407
Gatos y gatitos 72
The Giant and the Spring 174
A Gift for Abuelita Celebrating the Day of the Dead 246
A Gift from Papá Diego 359
The Gift of the Poinsettia 273
The Gifts of the Holy Family 413
El gigante y el niño primavera 174
The Girl Who Waters Basil and the Very Inquisitive Prince 77
Goldilocks and the Three Bears 37, 56, 255
Good Night My Little Chicks 141
Good Times with Football 202
Goodnight Everyone 277
The Goose with the Golden Eggs 283
Gracias, Rosa 249
El gran César 358
La gran fiesta 268
The Grandfather 297
Grandma Fina and Her Wonderful Umbrellas 360
Grandmother's Adobe Dollhouse 387
Grandmother's Nursery Rhymes 207
Grasshopper Grump and Other Poems of Wonder 376
Green Corn Tamales 247
Gregorio y sus puntos 414
Grillos y ranas 267
Grownups Cry Too 192
Guarda di nuovo, parla di nuovo 142
Guarda e parla 143
The Gullywasher 356
El gusto del mercado mexicano 397

Hairs 82
Half-chicken 6
Hansel and Gretel 37
The Hare and the Tortoise & The Tortoise and the Hare 123
The Harvest Birds 242
Have You Seen a Comet? 298
Hay un toro en mi balcón 216
He Went for Nails 410
The Headless Pirate 340
Herman the Helper 222

Hermanas 294
El hermano Anansi y el rancho de ganado 111
La heroína Hua Mulan 209
La hija del sol 254
Hispanic Folk Songs of the Southwest 423
La historia de Ana 253
La historia de los colores 248
Historia natural de las islas Galápagos, breve relato para jóvenes 99
Ho, Ho, Benjamin, Feliz Navidad 156
¡Hola, amigos! 401, 402
El hombre caimán 112
Horses & Ponies 72
Hot Boiled Beans 229
The House of Joe Frog Maracas 286
The House on Mango Street 82
How Sweet You Are 21
How the Sun Was Born 122
How the Toad Got His Spots 193
How We Came to the Fifth World 341
Humpty Dumpty and Friends in the Southwest 229
The Hungry Moon 355

I Am Here 55
I Can Read Spanish 89, 277
I Didn't Say a Word 46
I, Juan de Pareja 406
I Like Birds 28
I Like You to Make Jokes with Me, But I Don't Want You to Touch Me 36
I Love the World and Other Voices from the Chorus 4
I Speak Your Name with Respect 298
I Was So Mad 383
I Wish I Lived at the Playground 281
IBBY Congress Awards 381
Icy Watermelon 146
Idalia's Project ABC 353
Iguanas en la nieve and Other Winter Poems 11
Iguanas in the Snow y otros poemas de invierno 11
I'm Going to California 419
I'm Going to Texas 420
In My Family 239
In School 180
In the Days of King Adobe 190
In the Park 181
Incompatible Roommates 284
International Year of the Child Publication 251
La inundación 112

Isla 120
The Invisible Hunters 342
It Doesn't Have to Be This Way 336
It Looks Like This 421

Jack and the Beanstalk 37, 56, 255
El jinete orgulloso 112
Jitomates risueños y otros poemas de primavera 12
Jo, Flo and Yolanda 110
Joanna Cotler Books 197
Johnny Lost 308
Jorge el curioso 321
Una jornada de esperanza 176
La jornada del sol 84
José el gran ayudante 222
Josefina 427
José's Christmas Secret 236
A Journey of Hope 176
Juan Bobo 43, 112
Juan Diego and the Lady 417
Juan Tuza and the Magic Pouch 269
Juan y los frijoles mágicos 56, 255
Juanita 304
Juanito perdido 308
Juegos, juegos, juegos 366
Jump In 77
Just Like Home 264
Just Say Baaaa 190

La Kasa KK 410
Kids Are Authors Awards 122
Kids in the Kitchen 116
Kikirikí 299
The King, the Mice, and the Cheese 167
A Kite for Carlos 309
Kittens & Cats 72
A Knowledge Aid Picture Dictionary 424

La lagartija esmeralda 112
La lagartija y el sol 5
El lago mágico 112
La laguna de la luna 112
The Lake of the Moon 112
Land of the Icy Death 343
Language Learning Story Books 277
Larousse Word and Picture Book 230
The Last Will 286
Latin American Christmas 418
Latin American Game Songs 100
Latino Read-Aloud Stories 397
Laughing Out Loud, I Fly 197
Laughing Tomatoes and Other Spring Poems 12

Un lazo a la luna 128
A Learn-a-Language Book in English and Spanish 324, 325, 326, 327
Las lecciones españoles de Babar 61
La lechera y su cubeta 102
The Legend of Food Mountain 344
The Legend of Mu Lan 209
The Legend of the Bellringer of San Agustín 251
The Legend of the Two Moons 270
Leo el capullo tardío 223
Leo, the Late Bloomer 223
Leonard the Lion and Raymond the Mouse 49
Leonardo el leon y Ramón el ratón 49
Let's Go 131
Let's Play Games in Spanish 205
La leyenda del campanero de San Agustín 251
El libro de las estaciones 312
El libro grande de las palabras de Spot 199
La liebre y la tortuga & La tortuga y la liebre 123
Like Cat and Dog 284
Like Father, Like Son 413
Listen to the Desert 274
Little Boy with Three Names 83
Little Frog Finds the Rainbow 139
Little Frog in the City 138
The Little Frog Leaves Her Pond 140
Little Gold Star 183
The Little Horse of Seven Colors 345
The Little Mouse 362
The Little Red Hen 425
Little Red Riding Hood 37, 56, 255
The Little Seven-Colored Horse 364
The Lizard and the Sun 5
Lizzi 266
La Llorona 184, 371, 413
Luck 77
Una luminaria para mis palomitas 252
Lunes, martes, miércoles, ¡O! 186, 188

Magda's Tortillas 80
The Magic Boys 346
Magic Dogs of the Volcanoes 27
The Magic Drum 284
The Magic Lake 112
Magic Moments 245
The Magic Thread 286
Magic Windows 240
Making Magic Windows 240
Las manchas del sapo 193
Mano fashico 410

Margaret and Margarita 315
A Margaret K. McElderry Book 97, 267
Margarita y Margaret 315
María 401
María Teresa 29
Mariposa, mariposa 185, 188
Masquerader 107
Math Tales 286
Me gusta que bromees conmigo, pero no
 quiero que me toques 36
Mediopollito 6
Melody's Mystery 177
Merry-go-round of Games in Spanish 415
Mexican Folklore 16
Mexican Proverbs 32
Mexican Tongue Twisters 169
México mío 213
Mi abuela fumaba puros y otros cuentos de
 tierra amarilla 410
Mi canción es un pedazo de jade 101
Mi casa 133
Mi día 132
Mi libro de valores 39
Mi mamá la cartera 257
Mi mamá y yo nos hacemos fuertes 256
Mi primer diccionario 98
Mi primer diccionario ilustrado 259
Mi primer diccionario ilustrado de inglés 117
Mi primer libro de dichos 162
Mi primer vocabulario de inglés 260
Mi propio cuartito 301
The Mighty God Viracocha 347
The Milkmaid 37
The Milkmaid and Her Pail 102
Milton el madrugador 224
Milton the Early Riser 224
Mira de nuevo, habla de nuevo 142
Mira y habla 143
Mis colores 134
Mis formas 134
Mis números 134
Mis opuestos 134
The Mischievous Cat 407
Missy and the Duke 94
Missy y el duque 94
Mr. Sugar Came to Town 349
El misterio de Melodía 177
Mochito 74
Momentos divertidos con el fútbol 202
Momentos mágicos 245
Mon livre de mots de tour les jours 217
Monday, Tuesday, Wednesday, Oh! 186,
 188
Money Well Spent 265

La montaña del alimento 344
Moon Rope 128
Mother Goose on the Río Grande 15, 16
Mother Scorpion Country 348
The Mouse Bride 78
A Movie in My Pillow 26
El muchachito con tres nombres 83
El muchacho que gritó ¡el lobo! 103
El muchacho que mató al gigante 413
Muchas palabras sobre animales 58
Muchas palabras sobre mi casa 59
La mujer del maíz 413
La mujer del mundo-cielo 350
La mujer que brillaba aún más que el sol 96
La música de la chirimia 416
The Musical Palm Tree 34
My Aunt Olilia's Spirits 151
My Book of Values 39
My Colors 134
My Day 132
My Dog Is Lost 218
My Everyday Spanish Word Book 217
My First Book of Proverbs 162
My First Dictionary 98
My First Picture Dictionary 259
My First Spanish & English Dictionary 278
My Grandma Smoked Cigars and Other
 Stories of Tierra Amarilla 410
My House 133
My Mexico 213
My Mother 298
My Mother and I Are Growing Strong 256
My Mother the Mail Carrier 257
My Numbers 134
My Opposites 134
My Shapes 134
My Song Is a Piece of Jade 101
My Uncle Cirilo 410
My Very Own Room 301

Nacer en la manada 319
Las nanas de abuelita 207
Navidad latinoamericana 418
Las Navidades 106
El negro aguilar 410
The New Year 4
Newbery Awards 406
La nieve y el sol 144
La niña que riega la albahaca y el príncipe
 preguntón 77
El niño de cabeza 198
Un niño llamado Paco 293
Los niños mágicos 346
The Nit and the Louse 329

No Company Was Coming to Samuel's House 91
No dije una palabra 46
No llegaban invitados a la casa de Samuel 91
No tiene que ser así 336
No Way, José! 187, 188
Un nombre chistoso 160
La novia ratón 78
Nuestra Señora de Guadalupe 413
Nuestro libro 365
Los números con los ositos 149

Oferta de una familia 118
One for You, One for Me 413
100 Words about Animals 58
100 Words about My House 59
One, Two, Three 275
Orgullo 4
Our Book 365
Our Friends in Spain 331
Our Lady of Guadalupe 413
Oxford Children's Picture Dictionary 200
Oye al desierto 274

Pablo and Pimienta 93
Pablo Remembers 22
Pablo y Pimienta 93
Pachanga deliciosa 271
El pajaro Cú 194
Los pájaros de la cosecha 242
Papa Pequeño 233
Papa Small 233
Un papalote para Carlos 309
The Paraguayan Bell Bird 284
Patient Pepita 297
Pedacito de mi corazón 238
Pedro, His Perro and the Alphabet Sombrero 314
Pedro Pelícano 330
Una película en mi almohada 26
Pelitos 82
The Penitentes 410
Pepita habla dos veces 227
Pepita, siempre tarde 226
Pepita Takes Time 226
Pepita Talks Twice 227
Pepita Thinks Pink 228
Pepita y el color rosado 228,
La pequeña gallina roja 425
Pérez and Martina 195
Pérez y Martina 195
El perro 70
Perro grande, perro pequeño 125
El perro guardian 164

El Perro Guardian, the Watchdog 164
Los perros mágicos de los volcanes 27
Perros y perritos 72
Pescando con Pedro 178
Peter Pelican 330
Un pez fuera del agua 292
The Pharmacist's Accounting 286
A "Picture-Practice Book" for Learning to Speak Spanish with Our Friends in Spain 331
Pie-Biter 258
A Piece of My heart 238
The Pied Piper of Hamlin 37, 172
A Pig in Sunday Clothes 43
The Pig That Is Not a Pig 320
The Piñata 297
The Piñata Maker 23
Piñatas and Paper Flowers 302
Piñatas y flores de papel 302
El piñatero 23
El piojo y la liendre 329
El pirata sin cabeza 340
Platero and I 211
Platero y yo 211
Play It in Spanish 310
Poemas pe-que pe-que pe-que-ñitos 145
Los pollitos dicen 171
Poniendo la campana al gato 104
Porqué es hermoso el escarabajo 112
Las Posadas 296
Premiers mots 81
El premio del cuco 221
Pride 4
Prietita and the Ghost Woman 25
Prietita y la Llorona 25
Prime parole 81
El primer día de escuela 14
Primeras palabras 81
A Prism Press Book 74, 91, 147, 166, 219
A Probe into Mexican American Experience 212
The Proud Horseman 112
Proyecto ABC 353
Puerto Rico en mi corazón 322
Puerto Rico in My Heart 322
Puppies & Dogs 72
Pura Belpré Awards 3, 10, 12, 22, 161, 197, 238, 239, 240, 389

¿Qué será? 206
Queen Isabella I 86
¿Quién eres tú? 47

The Rabbit 68
The Rabbit and the Coyote 413

Radio Man 121
Ramón and the Pirate Gull 35
El rancho grande 333
La ranita en la ciudad 138
La ranita encuentra el arco iris 139
La ranita sale de su charco 140
El ratoncito pequeño 362
Reading Adventures in Spanish and English
    33
Los recuerdos de Chave 109
El regalo de Fernando 220
El regalo de la flor de nochebuena 273
El regalo de Navidad 210
Un regalo de Papá Diego 359
Un regalo para abuelita en celebración del
    Día de los Muertos 246
Los regalos de La Sagrada Familia 413
Regarde de nouveau, parle de nouveau 142
Regarde et parle 143
Remembranzas tropicales 77
Renting a Horse 112
El rey, los ratones, y el queso 167
El reyezuelo y la cholla 152
A Richard Jackson Book 137
Ricitos de oro y los tres osos 56, 255
Robert and the Statue of Liberty 232
Robert Goes Fishing 313
Roberto va de pesca 313
Rockabye Baby 262
The Rooster and the Fox 37
Rosie, the Oldest Horse in St. Augustine
    157

Sadness in the Rain 298
Salsa 88
Sancho, Pronto, and the Engineer 219
Sancho, Pronto, y el ingeniero 219
Sandía fría 146
Say Hola, Sarah 156
Say Hola to Spanish 129
Say Hola to Spanish at the Circus 130
Say Hola to Spanish, Otra Vez (Again!) 130
The School 69
Sé quién soy 108
Searchbooks in the Social Sciences 212
See Again, Say Again 142
See and Say 143
Selections from Spanish Poetry 317
The Selfish Giant 174
Señor Baby Elephant the Pirate 215
The Señorita and the Puma 112
La señorita y la puma 112
The Seven Kids 37
Seven Magic Brothers 175

The Shirt of the Happy Man 284
Siete hermanos mágicos 175
Simon and His Boxes 405
Simón y las cajas 405
Sing, Children, Sing 263
Sip, Slurp, Soup, Soup 45
La sirena del desierto 52
Sisters 294
"Skram" corre, patea y tira 203
"Skram" Runs, Kicks, and Throws 203
Skyworld Woman 350
Sleep Rhymes Around the World 431
The Snow and the Sun 144
Soccer 403
Sol a sol 76
El sombrero del tío Nacho 352
Somos un arco iris 397
Song of the Chirimia 416
The Song of the Oak 354
Song of the Swallows 305
Songs and Games of New Mexico 159, 429
Songs from My Island 38
Songs of My Island 38
Sopena inglés de los niños 388
Una sorpresa de cumpleaños 14
Spanish-American Poetry 318
The Spanish-American Song and Game
    Book 429
Spanish Folk Songs of the Southwest 412
Spanish Folk-Tales from New Mexico 135
The Spanish for Young Americans Library
    Series 15, 37
Spanish Nuggets 204
Special International Year of the Child Pub-
    lication 251
The Spirit of Tío Fernando 235
Spot's Big Book of Words 199
The Squirrels 284
Stories of the Spanish Southwest 297
Stories That Must Not Die 371
The Story of Ana 253
The Story of Colors 248
Story of the Chinese Zodiac 79
Street Rhymes Around the World 432
Un sueño en el camino 77
Sun Journey 84

"T" es por "terrifico" 170
"T" Is for "Terrific" 170
T Is for Tortilla 19
The Tailor from Salta 286
Taking a Walk 134
Tales from Spanish New Mexico 135
Tamales de elote 247

The Tamarindo Puppy 306
Tan sencillas como tu 21
A Taste of the Mexican Market 397
Teaser and the Firecat 390
The Teddy Bear Number Book 149
Tejanitos 368
Tell Me a Cuento 188
Tell Me Please! What's That? 208
Ten Little Fingers 291
Teresa 402
El terrible tragadabas 188, 189
The Terrible Tragadabas 188, 189
El tesoro de Guatavita 351
Tesoro de refranes populares 288
That Will Teach You 190
There Is a Bull on My Balcony 216
These Shoes of Mine 77
This Can Lick a Lollipop 357
This House Is Made of Mud 63
The Three Branches 413
Three Friends 62
The Three Little Javelinas 244
The Three Little Pigs 37
The Three Pieces of Good Advice 413
The Three Pigs 363
Three Questions 284
The Three Simpletons 413
La tierra de la madre escorpión 348
Tierra de la muerte glacial 343
The Tiger! 426
¡El tigre! 426
Tina la tortuga y Carlos el conejo 50
Tina the Turtle and Carlos the Rabbit 50
Todos tenemos sentimientos 30
Tomasa the Cow 303
Too Clever 112
T-O'ohana 365
El toro pinto and Other Songs in Spanish
    332, 333
Tortillas and Lullabies 316
Las tortillas de Magda 80
Tortillas y cancioncitas 316
Tortillitas 171
Tortillitas para mamá 163
The Tortoise and the Hare 123
La tortuga y el conejo juegan una carrera 8
La tortuga y la liebre 123
Tossing Eyes 112
Trabalenguas mexicanos 169
El trayecto 214
The Treasure of Guatavita 351
A Treasure of Popular Proverbs 288
Treasures for Tomás 7
The Tree Is Older Than You Are 282

Treehouse Paperbacks 425
The Trek 214
Tres amigos 62
Los tres buenos consejos 413
Los tres cerdos 363
Los tres pequeños jabalíes 244
Los tres ramas 413
Los tres simplones 413
Triccionario, español-chino-inglés 408
Trictionary, English-Chinese-Spanish 408
A Trip to Mexico 379
Trip to the Pyramids 369
Tropical Memories 77
The True Path to Happiness 413
Tun-ta-ca-tun 300
The Turquoise Ring 112
The Turtle and the Rabbit Run a Race 8
The Two Georges 166
The Two Hunchbacks 284

Una para tú, una para mí 413
Uncle Nacho's Hat 352
Uno, dos, tres 275
The Upside Down Boy 198

La vaca Tomasa 303
Vacation Diaries 367
Vamos 131
Vamos a pasear el sábado 325
Vaquero Pequeño 234
Vaqueros 323
Vejigante 107
Ven a saltar 77
Vengan al estanque 115
Ventanas mágicas 240
Versos and Verses 381
Very Very Short Nature Poems 145
Viaje a las pirámides mexicanas 396
Un viaje a México 379
Vilma Martinez 87
La visita del Sr. Azúcar 349

Watch Out! 190
Watch Out for Clever Women! 190
The Water Sprite and the Woodcutter 37
We Are a Rainbow 397
We Say Happy Birthday 324
We Take a Saturday Walk 325
The Weeping Woman 184, 413
Welcome, Roberto! 377
What Can It Be? 206
What Do I Do? 384
What Do I Say? 385
What's Wrong with Julio? 289

When We Go to Market 326
When We Go to School 327
When You Get Really Mad! 231
Where Fireflies Dance 92
Where the Cinnamon Winds Blow
   361
Where There's a Will, There's a Way
   191
Who Are You? 47
Whose House Is This? 154
Why Beetle Is Beautiful 112
The Wise Rooster 311
Witcheries or Tomfooleries? 410
With My Brother 337
The Woman Who Outshone the Sun
   96
World Folklore Series 413

Yagua Days 250
A Yearling Book 156
Yo estoy aquí 55
Yo lo puedo leer solo 124, 167, 292, 378
Yo quisiera vivir en un parque de juegos
   281
Yo voy a California 419
Yo voy a Tejas 420
Yolanda's Hike 155
Young Hunter of Picuris 85
You're On! Seven Plays in English and
   Spanish 77

Zenaida 73
El zodíaco chino 79
El zorrito 165
El Zorrito, the Little Fox 165

# Index of Subjects

*(and see Índice de temas, following)*

*(y véase Índice de temas, siguiente)*

*References are to entry numbers.*

Aguilar, Josefina 427
Alebrijes 275
Alphabet books 3, 18, 19, 42, 57, 60, 166, 170, 237, 241, 260, 328, 353, 397, 400
Alvarez, Luís W. 87
Anger 231, 383
Animals 58, 208, 214, 259, 277, 311, 395
Art 240, 298, 427
Aunts 44, 108, 151, 361
Autograph albums 276
Aztecs 5, 341

Babies *see* Infants
Baby sitters 249
Ballet dancers 71
Bears 41, 224
Belize 178
Bestiaries 280
Bilingual children 227
Birds 152, 194, 252, 304, 305
Birthdays 14, 275, 324, 359
Bizcochitos 31
Blankets 67
Body language 46, 357
Bolívar, Simón 158
Boxes 405
Boys 335, 385, 414
Brothers 175, 337
Bullfights 293
Butterflies 177, 185, 188, 386

California 196, 419
Carnivals 391
Cats 72, 94, 104, 378, 390, 407
Chickens 6, 141, 161, 187, 188, 425
Children's art 164, 165, 170, 298

Children's writings 298
Chile—Poetry 267, 381
Chinese in the United States 258
Christmas 302
Christmas songs 106, 126, 418
Christmas stories 2, 95, 156, 210, 236, 268, 273, 296, 311
Churches 51, 406
Cinderella 183, 255
Circus 130, 334
Cockroaches 243
Colors 134, 228, 248
Columbus Day 302
Cookery 31
Corn 344, 392
Costa Rica 220
Counting books 28, 42, 62, 149, 275, 397
Cowboys 234, 323, 356
Cows 303
Cruz, Juana Inés de la 158
Cuba 2
Cumulative tales 144, 161, 187, 188, 422
Cupboards 64
Cut-paper art 240

Dampier, William 340
The Day of the Dead 22, 235, 246
Death 361
Deserts 272, 274
de Soto, Hernando *see* Soto, Hernando de
Dinosaurs 122, 266
Dogs 70, 72, 74, 125, 164, 199, 218, 314
Doll houses 387
Drama—Collected works 77, 354

Ecology 398
El Salvador 26, 27
Elephants 97, 215
Emotions 30, 36, 192
Emperors 173
Epiphany 53, 54, 302

Fables 97, 102, 103, 104, 193, 195, 267, 283,
    287, 370, 371
Fall—Poetry 9
Family life 7, 44, 108, 233, 238, 239
Farming 196, 242
Finlay, Carlos 87
Fireflies 92
Fishes 292
Fishing 178, 313
Flutists 137
Folk songs, Latin American 290, 295, 433
Folk songs, Mexican 261
Folk songs—Southwest 412, 423
Folk songs, Spanish 295, 310, 433
Folk tales see Legends
Food 349, 389
Football 201, 202, 203
Foxes 165
Friends 24, 65, 136, 155, 166
Frogs 138, 139, 140

Galapagos Islands 99
Galvez, Bernardo de 86
Games 100, 159, 205, 263, 310, 366, 372,
    415, 429
Gangs 336
Ghosts 373, 374, 375
Giants 174
Girls 73, 110, 315, 384, 401, 402
Goldilocks 56, 255
Grandfathers 148, 309, 356, 359
Grandmothers 119, 120, 246, 360
Grandparents 109, 146, 247
Guadalupe, Our Lady of 406, 417
Gulls 35

Hair 82
Halloween 302, 373
Hats 314, 352
Hidalgo y Costilla, Miguel 158
Holidays 17, 302
Horses 72, 157
Houses 59, 63, 154
Hunting 85, 342

Immigrants 92, 93, 196, 253, 258, 264, 308,
    397

Immigrants, Illegal 24
Infants 66
Isabella I, Queen of Spain 86

Jack and the Beanstalk 56, 255
Javelinas 244, 320
Juarez, Benito 158

Kingsville, Texas 238, 239
Kites 51, 309

Lanterns see Luminarias
Latin American poetry 318
Latin American songs 105, 290, 291
Latin American stories 112, 245, 396
Legends—Bolivia 347
Legends—Chiapas 248
Legends—Chile 343
Legends—China 78, 209
Legends—Costa Rica 340
Legends—Colombia 351
Legends—Cuba 161
Legends—Guatemala 346, 416
Legends—Latin America 112, 364, 413
Legends—Mayans 127, 248, 307
Legends—Mexico 25, 96, 127, 164, 165, 184,
    190, 194, 221, 307, 341, 344
Legends—New Mexico 135
Legends—Nicaragua 111, 342, 345, 348, 352
Legends—Panama 339
Legends—Peru 128, 254, 347
Legends—Philippines 350
Legends—Puerto Rico 43
Legends—San Agustín, Tucson 251
Legends—San Juan Capistrano 305
Legends—Taino Indians 338
Lions 49
Little Red Riding Hood 56, 255
Lizards 271
Los Angeles 245, 253, 304, 389
Lullabies 163, 207, 262, 316
Luminarias 252

Mardi Gras 302
Markets 168, 275, 326, 397
Martí, José 158
Martinez, Vilma 87
Masquerades 107
Mathematics 286
Mayans 127, 248, 307
Menendez de Aviles, Pedro 86
Mermaids 52
Mexican Americans 24, 29, 245, 358
Mexican Americans—History 212

Mexican poetry 101, 355
Mexico 160, 216, 219, 242, 282, 369, 379, 401, 402
Mexico—Poetry 109, 213, 282
Mice 48, 49, 78, 104, 167, 172, 362
Migrant workers 121, 210
Miskito Indians 342
Monarch butterflies 177
Money 265
Mongooses 14
Monkeys 321
Monsters 182, 188, 189
Moon 270
Mothers 256, 257
Multilingual books 57, 60, 81, 142, 143, 179, 180, 181, 230, 258, 365, 408
Muñoz Marín, Luís 158
Music 88

Nahuatl poetry 101
Names, Personal 160
Nature in poetry 145
Navajos 148
New Mexico 191, 367
New Year's Day 302
New York City 232
Numbers 134
Nursery rhymes 15, 16, 163, 207, 229, 355, 372, 431, 432

Oaxaca, Mexico 219, 275, 411
Octopus 222
Opposites 125, 134
Our Lady of Guadalupe *see* Guadalupe, Our Lady of

Pamplona, Spain 374
Pandas 224
Papago Indians *see* T-O'ohana Indians,
Parks 181, 281
Pelicans 178, 330
Personal names *see* Names, Personal
Pigs 363
Piñatas 23
Pirates 215, 340
Poetry 4, 15, 16, 75, 76, 145, 197, 282, 299, 300, 306, 318, 329, 376, 399
Poinsettias 273
Points of view 421
Ponds 115
Ponies 72
Las Posadas 273, 296
Privacy 301
Proverbs 32, 39, 162, 204, 283, 288

Pueblo Indians 85
Puerto Rico 34, 35, 107, 113, 151, 250, 322, 338, 375, 382, 409
Puppets and puppet plays 29
Pyramids 369

Rabbits 8, 50, 68, 123
Radio 121
Railroads 258
Rain forests 220
Recipes 116
Restaurants 225
Riddles 206, 207, 283, 357
Rivera, Diego 428

Salsa music 88
School stories 14, 29, 47, 55, 69, 147, 180, 198, 289, 327, 377
Seasons 312
Seasons—Poetry 9, 10, 11, 12
Sebastian, Juan 92
Serra, Junipero 158
Servants 191
Shapes *see* Size and shape
Sheep 103, 148
Short stories 20, 37, 188, 282, 284, 285, 286, 287, 297, 299, 300, 316, 368, 396, 404, 410
Sisters 294
Size and shape 134
Skunks 393
Soccer 403
Songs 21, 38, 100, 105, 106, 118, 126, 159, 171, 261, 263, 290, 291, 295, 310, 332, 333, 399, 412, 423, 429, 430
Soto, Hernando de 86
Soup 45
Spain 211, 374
Spanish language—Dictionaries 1, 40, 98, 114, 117, 200, 259, 278, 279, 380, 388, 408, 424
Spanish language—Readers 61, 89, 90, 129, 130, 131, 132, 133, 134, 217, 331
Spanish poetry 153, 317
Spring—Poetry 12
Squash 394
St. Augustine, Florida 157
Statue of Liberty 232
Sugar 349
Summer—Poetry 10
Sun 5

Tamales 247
Taos Indians 83

Teddybears 149
Teenagers 75, 294
Texas 367, 420
Thanksgiving Day 91
Tigers 223, 426
Time 226
Toads 193
Tongue twisters 169, 207
T-O'ohana Indians 365
Tortillas 80, 316
Triplets 110
Turtles 8, 50, 123, 176
Twins 150

Umbrellas 360

Vacations 367, 369
Viewpoints *see* Points of view

Walking 325
Warmth 13
Watermelons 146
Weather vanes 6
Weddings 411
Windows 240
Winter—Poetry 11
Wolves 319
Women 186, 188

Zapata, Emiliano 92
Zenteno, Lucía 96
Zodiac 79
Zoological gardens 57, 208, 321, 325, 395
Zuni Indians 84

# Índice de temas

*Los números se refieren a los números de cada entrada.*

Abecedarios *véase* Alfabeto
Abuelas 119, 120, 246, 360
Abuelos 109, 146, 148, 247, 309, 356, 359
Acertijos 206, 207, 283, 357
Adivinanzas *véase* Acertijos
Adolescentes *véase* Muchachas adolescentes,
   Muchachos adolescentes
Agricultura 196, 242
Aguilar, Josefina 427
Alacenas 64
Alebrijes 275
Alfabeto 3, 18, 19, 42, 57, 60, 166, 170, 237,
   241, 260, 328, 353, 397, 400
Alimentos 349, 389
Alvarez, Luís W. 87
Amistad 24, 65, 136, 155, 166
Animales 58, 208, 214, 259, 277, 311,
   395
Arte 240, 298, 427
Autógrafos—Colecciones 276
Aves 152, 194, 252, 304, 305
Aztecas 5, 341
Azúcar 349

Bailarinas 71
Bebés 66
Belice 178
Bestiarios 280
Bizcochitos 31
Bodas 411
Bolívar, Simón 158
Bosques 220

Caballos 72, 157
Cabello 82
Cajas 405
Calabazas 394
California 196, 419
Calor 13
Canciones 21, 38, 100, 105, 106, 118, 126,
   159, 171, 261, 263, 290, 291, 295, 310, 332,
   333, 399, 412, 423, 429, 430
Canciones de cuna 15, 16,163, 207, 229, 262,
   316, 355, 372, 431, 432
Canciones folklóricas españoles 295, 310,
   433
Canciones folklóricas latinoamericanas 105,
   290, 291, 295, 433
Canciones folklóricas mexicanas 261
Canciones folklóricas—Sudoeste 412, 423
Caperucita Roja 56, 255
Carnaval 391
Casas 59, 63, 154
Casas de muñecas 387
Caza 85, 342
La Cenicienta 183, 255
Cerditos *véase* Colchinitos
Chile—Poesía 267, 381
Chinos en los Estados Unidos 258
Circos 130, 334
Cobijas *véase* Mantas
Cocina 31, 116
Colchinitos 363
Colores 134, 228, 248
Cometas 51, 309
Conejos 8, 50, 68, 123
Corridas de toros 293
Costa Rica 220
Criados *véase* Servicio doméstico
Cruz, Juana Inés de la *véase* Juana Inés, de
   la Cruz, Sor
Cuba 2
Cucarachas 243
Cuentos 20, 37, 188, 282, 284, 285, 286, 287,
   297, 299, 300, 316, 368, 396, 404, 410
Cuentos de fantasmas 373, 374, 375
Cuentos escolares 14, 29, 47, 55, 69, 147,
   180, 198, 289, 327, 377
Cuentos latinoamericanos 112, 245, 396
Cumpleaños 14, 275, 324, 359

Dampier, William 340
Desiertos 272, 274
de Soto, Hernando *véase* Soto, Hernando de,
Día de acción de gracias 91
Día de año nuevo 302
Día de Colón *véase* Día de la Raza
Día de la Raza 302
Día de los muertos 22, 235, 246
Días festivos 17, 302
Dinero *véase* Moneda
Dinosaurios 122, 266
Dormitorios 301
Drama—Colecciones 77, 354

Ecología 398
El Salvador 26, 27
Elefantes 97, 215
Emigración e inmigración 92, 93, 121, 196, 210, 253, 258, 264, 308, 397
Emociones 30, 36, 192
Emperadores 173
Enojo 231, 383
Epifanía 53, 54, 302
España 211, 374
Español—Diccionarios 1, 40, 98, 114, 117, 200, 259, 278, 279, 380, 388, 408, 424
Estaciones del año 31
Estaciones del año—Poesía 9, 10, 11, 12
Estanques 115
Estatua de la Libertad 232

Fábulas 97, 102, 103, 193, 195, 267, 283, 287, 370, 371
Familia 7, 44, 108, 233, 238, 239
Fantasmas *véase* Cuentos de fantasmas
Ferrocarriles 258
Finlay, Carlos 87
Flautistas 137
La Flor de nochebuena 273
Formas *véase* Tamaño y forma
Fútbol 403
Fútbol, Americano 201, 202, 203

Gallinas 6, 141, 161, 187, 188, 425
Galvez, Bernardo de 86
Gatos 72, 94, 104, 378, 390, 407
Gaviotas 35
Gemelos *véase* Mellizos,
Gigantes 174
Guadalupe, Nuestra Señora de 406, 417

Halloween *véase* Víspera del Día de Todos los Santos

Hermanas 294
Hermanos 175, 337
Hidalgo y Costilla, Miguel 158

Iglesias 51, 406
Inmigrantes indocumentados 24
Invierno—Poesía 11
Isabella I, Reina de España 86
Islas Galápagos 99

Jabalíes 244, 320
Juan y los frijoles mágicos 56, 255
Juana Inés, de la Cruz, Sor 158
Juarez, Benito 158
Juegos 100, 159, 205, 263, 310, 366, 372, 415, 429

Kingsville, Tejas 238, 239

Lagartos 271
Lenguaje del cuerpo 46, 357
Leones 49
Leyendas—Bolivia 347
Leyendas—Chiapas 248
Leyendas—Chile 343
Leyendas—China 78, 209
Leyendas—Costa Rica 340
Leyendas—Colombia 351
Leyendas—Cuba 161
Leyendas—Filipinas 350
Leyendas—Guatemala 346, 416
Leyendas—Latinoamérica 112, 364, 413
Leyendas—Maya 127, 248, 307
Leyendas—México 25, 96, 127, 164, 165, 184, 190, 194, 221, 307, 341, 344
Leyendas—Nuevo Mexico 135
Leyendas—Nicaragua 111, 342, 345, 348, 352
Leyendas—Panamá 339
Leyendas—Perú 128, 254, 347
Leyendas—Puerto Rico 43
Leyendas—San Agustín, Tucson 251
Leyendas—San Juan Capistrano 305
Leyendas—Tainos 338
Libros de contar 28, 42, 62, 149, 275, 397
Libros de lectura 61, 89, 90, 129, 130, 131, 132, 133, 134, 217, 331
Libros multilingües 57, 60, 81, 142, 143, 179, 180, 181, 230, 258, 365, 408
Lobos 319
Los Angeles 245, 253, 304, 389
Luciérnagas 92
Luminarias 252
Luna 270

Madres 256, 257
Maíz 344, 392
Mangostas 14
Mantas 67
Mariposas 177, 185, 188, 386
Martes de carnaval 302
Martí, José 158
Martinez, Vilma 87
Mascaradas 107
Matemáticas recreativas 286
Mayas 127, 248, 307
Mellizos 150
Menendez de Aviles, Pedro 86
Mercados 168, 275, 326, 397
Mexicano-americanos 24, 29, 245, 358
Mexicano-americanos—Historia 212
México 160, 216, 219, 242, 282, 369, 379, 401, 402
México—Poesía 109, 213, 282
Miskitos (Indios) 342
Moneda 265
Monos 321
Monstruos 182, 188, 189
Muchachas 73, 110, 315, 384, 401, 402
Muchachas adolescentes 294
Muchachos 335, 385, 414
Muchachos adolescentes, 75
Muerte 361
Mujeres 186, 188
Muñoz Marín, Luís 158
Música 88

Naturaleza en la poesía 145
Navajos 148
Navidad 302
Navidad—Canciones véase Villancicos
Navidad—Cuentos y leyendas 2, 95, 156, 210, 236, 268, 273, 296, 311
Niñeras 249
Niños artistas 164, 165, 170, 298
Niños autores 298
Niños bilingües 227
Nombres personales 160
Nuestra Señora de Guadalupe véase Guadalupe, Nuestra Señora de
Nuevo Mexico 191, 367
Nueva York 232
Números 134

Oaxaca, México 219, 275, 411
Opuestos 125, 134
Ositos de peluche 149
Osos 41, 224

Otoño—Poesía 9
Ovejas 103, 148

Pájaros véase Aves
Pamplona, España 374
Pandas 224
Pandillas 336
Papagos (Indios) véase T-O'ohana Indios
Papel picado 240
Paraguas 360
Parques 181, 281
Parques zoológicos 57, 208, 321, 325, 395
Paseos 325
Peces 292
Pelícanos 178, 330
Pelo véase Cabello
Perros 70, 72, 74, 125, 164, 199, 218, 314
Pesca 178, 313
Piñatas 23
Pirámides 369
Piratas 215, 340
Poesía 4, 15, 16, 75, 76, 145, 197, 282, 299, 300, 306, 318, 329, 376, 399
Poesía española 153, 317
Poesía latinoamericana 318
Poesía mexicana 101, 355
Poesía nahuatl 101,
Las Posadas 273, 296
Primavera—Poesía 12
Proverbios 32, 39, 162, 204, 283, 288
Pueblos (Indios) 85
Puerto Rico 34, 35, 107, 113, 151, 250, 322, 338, 375, 382, 409
Pulpos 222
Puntos de vista 421

Radio 121
Ranas 138, 139, 140
Ratones 48, 49, 78, 104, 167, 172, 362
Recetas de cocina véase Cocina
Refranes véase Proverbios
Restaurantes, cafeterías, etc. 225
Ricitos de oro 56, 255
Rivera, Diego 428
Rimas acumuladas 144, 161, 187, 188, 422

Salsa música 88
Salvador, El véase El Salvador
San Agustín, Florida 157
Sandías 146
Sapos 193
Sebastian, Juan 92
Selvas de lluvia véase Bosques
Serra, Junipero 158

Servicio doméstico 191
Sirenas 52
Soccer *véase* Fútbol
Sol 5
Sombreros 314, 352
Sopas 45
Soto, Hernando de 86

Tainos 338
Tamales 247
Tamaño y forma 134
Taos (Indios) 83
Tejas 367, 420
Tias 44, 108, 151, 361
Tiempo 226
Tigres 223, 426
Títeres 29
T-O'ohana Indios 365
Tortillas 80, 316
Tortugas 8, 50, 123, 176

Trabalenguas 169, 207
Trillizos 110

Vacaciones 367, 369
Vacas 303
Vaqueros 234, 323, 356
Veletas 6
Ventanas 240
Verano—Poesía 10
Villancicos 106, 126, 418
Víspera del Día de Todos los Santos 302,
373

Zapata, Emiliano 92
Zenteno, Lucía 96
Zodíaco 79
Zorrillos 393
Zorros 165
Zuñis 84